Leisure Studies in a Global Era

Series Editors
Karl Spracklen
Leeds Beckett University
Leeds, UK

Karen Fox
University of Alberta
Edmonton, AB, Canada

In this book series, we defend leisure as a meaningful, theoretical, framing concept; and critical studies of leisure as a worthwhile intellectual and pedagogical activity. This is what makes this book series distinctive: we want to enhance the discipline of leisure studies and open it up to a richer range of ideas; and, conversely, we want sociology, cultural geographies and other social sciences and humanities to open up to engaging with critical and rigorous arguments from leisure studies. Getting beyond concerns about the grand project of leisure, we will use the series to demonstrate that leisure theory is central to understanding wider debates about identity, postmodernity and globalisation in contemporary societies across the world. The series combines the search for local, qualitatively rich accounts of everyday leisure with the international reach of debates in politics, leisure and social and cultural theory. In doing this, we will show that critical studies of leisure can and should continue to play a central role in understanding society. The scope will be global, striving to be truly international and truly diverse in the range of authors and topics. Editorial Board: John Connell, Professor of Geography, University of Sydney, USA; Yoshitaka Mori, Associate Professor, Tokyo University of the Arts, Japan; Smitha Radhakrishnan, Assistant Professor, Wellesley College, USA; Diane M. Samdahl, Professor of Recreation and Leisure Studies, University of Georgia, USA; Chiung-Tzu Lucetta Tsai, Associate Professor, National Taipei University, Taiwan; Walter van Beek, Professor of Anthropology and Religion, Tilburg University, The Netherlands; Sharon D. Welch, Professor of Religion and Society, Meadville Theological School, Chicago, USA; Leslie Witz, Professor of History, University of the Western Cape, South Africa.

More information about this series at
http://www.palgrave.com/gp/series/14823

Tenley Martin

Transnational Flamenco

Exchange and the Individual in British and Spanish Flamenco Culture

Tenley Martin
School of Film, Music and Performing Art
Leeds Beckett University
Leeds, UK

Leisure Studies in a Global Era
ISBN 978-3-030-37201-9   ISBN 978-3-030-37199-9   (eBook)
https://doi.org/10.1007/978-3-030-37199-9

This Palgrave Macmillan imprint is published by the registered company Springer Nature Switzerland AG.
The registered company address is: Gewerbestrasse 11, 6330 Cham, Switzerland

To the memory of my father, John Randolph Martin, and grandfather, Charles 'Duck' Bradley, who were there when I began my flamenco journey. To Trish Anderton, a lovely bailora who exemplified and inspired many of my theories.

Preface

Flamenco, an art complex with its roots situated in Andalucía, is often assumed by outsiders to be a representative of a coherent national identity. This is a false assumption, both with regards to the realities of the art form and in terms of Spanish identity. My research suggests flamenco is a subculture appreciated by a minority of Andalucía-centric Spanish aficionados. Most outside of the scene reject it for reasons including identifying with another region, preferring popular music, or negatively associating flamenco with Franco and *Gitanos*. Significantly, as early as the nineteenth century, it developed a considerable following outside of Spain's borders amongst non-Spanish aficionados. Utilising information acquired from ethnomusicological fieldwork in Sevilla, Madrid, and the UK, the book examines the relationship between local (Spanish) and foreign flamenco culture. The aim is to provide insight into how flamenco travels, manifestations in its new locale, and possible effects on the Sevilla scene. Preliminary UK investigations revealed sub-scenes revolving around the efforts of singular cultural brokers who developed connections with flamenco in Spain and transported the information to the UK forming a glocal cultural model. This foreign interest has resulted in a commercial flamenco industry in Sevilla, as well as a vibrant associated ex-pat community there. These realisations inspired a methodological approach involving the individual experience and its importance in music migration. Further research revealed that flamenco is transmitted outside of Spain primarily by foreign individuals (cosmopolitan hubs) who possess transcultural capital from the Andalucían flamenco community, as well as from their home country. This transcultural capital is utilised to create economic capital in the UK. Overall this research suggests a postnational approach and explores the role of cosmopolitan hubs in cultural transmission, thus suggesting an alternative approach to music migration and glocalisation in a world increasingly less focused on ethnicity or nationality for individual identity formation.

Leeds, UK   Tenley Martin

Contents

List of Figures

1

Introduction

1.1 A Distinctly British Flamenco Evening

Alicia's long bata de cola[1] swung in a wide arc, narrowly missing both the audience and the rest of her cuadro—a tocaor, Adrian, and cantaor, Edu. She was dancing a spirited alegrías choreographed specifically to accentuate the movement of the long train of her bata dress.[2] The trio performed with a style that somehow appeared both practiced and improvised. This exemplifies the essence of flamenco—an art complex that relies on a knowledge of the compás specific to the palo being performed, with the performers improvising around that style.[3] Alicia's trio demonstrated this characteristic, seamlessly moving through temporal and stylistic changes without verbal communication. The small audience, who were seated on metal folding chairs, sat enraptured throughout the performance, only clapping at the end of each

---

[1] A type of flamenco dress with a long, weighted train used as a rhythmic tool in the dance. All unfamiliar terms are explained in the glossary in Appendix A.

[2] A *cuadro* refers to a flamenco performing group; a *tocaor/a* is a flamenco guitarist; *alegrías* is a style of flamenco.

[3] *Compás* refers to a flamenco's rhythmic backbone; *palo* is the name to refer to one of the many styles that form flamenco as a genre.

© The Author(s) 2020
T. Martin, *Transnational Flamenco*, Leisure Studies in a Global Era,
https://doi.org/10.1007/978-3-030-37199-9_1

Fig. 1.1 Bata de Cola in Sevilla

'piece'—apart from my friend Nancy and I who quietly clapped compás along with Adrian's guitar accompaniment (Fig. 1.1).

Alicia performed several dances throughout the hour-long espectáculo,[4] interspersed with solo guitar and cante to allow time for the bailora's[5] costume changes. Alicia finished the performance to a standing ovation from the tightly packed audience. Turning to Nancy (a local flamenco teacher), Alicia beckoned her onto the stage for the fin de fiesta. This began with the tocaor playing a few compás of bulerías[6] and a short solo followed by an improvised letra from Edu. Then it was Nancy's turn. She danced several improvised pataitas[7] of bulerías while Alicia clapped palmas. She had not, of course, come prepared with a routine and was wearing trainers instead of proper flamenco shoes, but that is the intrigue of fin de fiesta—spontaneity. After Nancy finished dancing, Alicia moved to centre stage and 'announced' her intent to begin with a series of frenzied but metrical zapateado.[8] She danced several

---

[4] 'Spectacle', a performance.

[5] Dancer.

[6] A flamenco *palo*.

[7] Short improvised dance segments.

[8] Flamenco footwork.

pataitas to the enthusiastic, but unmetered clapping of the audience. Alicia finished with another complex, rhythmical llamada⁹ which announced the cierre¹⁰ to the rest of the cuadro, who continued playing as she danced out of the room.

The raucous cheers of the small audience echoed off the walls of the cramped attic room, which was located not in a cosy tavern in flamenco's perceived ancestral homeland of sunny Andalucía, but in the tiny Derbyshire town of Wirksworth on a rainy October night. This was the first time I witnessed a fin de fiesta in the UK. The improvised ending to a flamenco show, so archetypal in local Andalucían espectáculos, is usually overlooked in UK performances. The erosion of the organised line between structured performance and polite audience into a spontaneous display of unified flamenco is typically outside of the British comfort zone.

Alicia and I had been corresponding via *email for several months and she had invited me to the Coach House Studios that evening while she was on tour in the UK, visiting from Sevilla. She is, however, not Spanish, but British, from London. Alicia moved to Sevilla at the age of 20 to study flamenco and had never looked back. We had arranged to meet at a nearby pub after the show so she could tell me a bit about life as a foreign flamenco dancer in Sevilla. Over the course of our conversation, I learned that Alicia made her home in Sevilla as a student and aspiring flamenco professional. She has remained primarily because of the belief that the most complete way to understand the dance was to immerse herself in all its aspects: song (cante), dance (baile), guitar (toque), rhythm (compás), and the audience participation (palmas and jaleo). While it is possible to learn these elements outside of Andalucía, Alicia surmises that there is something about being in Sevilla that makes sense of flamenco. Everything you do, wherever you play flamenco, it is totally in context with everything around you; the climate, the smell, the mentality, the dialect, and the people. This is known as the aire and does not exist outside of Andalucía—a feeling that is corroborated by other informants for this study. In towns in Andalucía, such as the flamenco hotspot of Sevilla, all four flamenco elements, as well as aire, are of equal importance and a necessary part of the whole. These elements, in the minds of aficionados, are*

---

⁹ 'A call', cues that the dancer gives the *cuadro*.

¹⁰ 'Closing'—the end of a piece.

Fig. 1.2 A fin de fiesta with ex-pats at Sala Garufa (Sevilla)

intrinsic to the development and execution of the dance. However, these are factors often overlooked when the music culture is transported abroad and thus when it travels it becomes an interpretation or adaptation of the original. Foreign aficionados, like Alicia, move to Spain for this level of understanding.

Over the years, Alicia has journeyed from the status of student to aspiring professional. The difficulties associated with this process, specifically within Sevilla, will be discussed at length later in this book. Alicia now visits the UK several times a year as a performer and workshop technician, often in collaboration with a flamenco cuadro formed of two other British-turned-Spanish dancers, a Franco-Anglo tocaor, and Sevillana cantaora[11] (Fig. 1.2).

Alicia described the ex-pat flamencos of Sevilla as a large, loosely associated community existing alongside the Sevilla scene having, like her, moved to the city to immerse themselves in the flamenco lifestyle and take classes. They often had issues being taken seriously and gaining acceptance within the native flamenco scene, especially on a professional level. Although gradually a few foreigners were making a name for themselves, which was helping the overall status of the foreign flamenco community. She offered to tell me their stories

---

[11] Singer.

and introduce me to the community's subculture should I wish to visit her in Sevilla. I was intrigued, as previous field research in Sevilla had not uncovered an ex-pat flamenco scene below the predominant tourist façade. My conversation with Alicia that evening not only introduced an intriguing layer to the Sevillano flamenco community but also inspired thoughts regarding identity and conflicts that occur between ex-pat and local performers.

The experience described above exemplifies how flamenco has travelled and been reinterpreted in the UK, which is one of many international manifestations of this art form. Throughout my research and participation in flamenco culture (since 2010), friends, acquaintances, and academics alike would often incredulously query the existence of a flamenco scene in the UK and, following on from an affirmative, how it is manifested here. While perhaps the persistence of a locally specific music culture outside of its imagined homeland is surprising to some, it is hardly unheard of. In the case of flamenco, not only does it have a following in many countries, its globality is a feature that keeps the scene alive in Spain. In this book, I explore how a global flamenco culture has been formed and what that might tell us about how a music culture propagates in the increasingly interconnected reality of the twenty-first century. In doing so, I will explore theories surrounding globalisation, transnationalism, cultural migration, and the importance of the individual in cultural transmission. Flamenco makes for a unique example of local-gone-global concept because of its development abroad in emulation of the original scene and its rejection as a national identity at home. However, once abroad, it has also had to adapt to the new locality. This is described by sociologist Roland Robertson as the concept of glocalisation. It is a term adapted from the Japanese business notion of dochakuka which involves the 'tailoring and advertising of goods and services on a global basis [...] to increasingly differentiated local and particular markets' (Robertson 1995, p. 28). In flamenco, this glocalisation represents a certain erosion of national and regional boundaries to create an intertwining, global identity, instead of national and regional cohesion. These glocalised scenes are created and maintained primarily through individual cultural brokers. This book describes, broadly, the story about how flamenco impacts the lives of these cosmopolitan hubs —non-native culture brokers who are the centre of local scenes—and how they influence its development and maintenance both at home and in Spain. Through an examination of flamenco's global pathways, this book provides insight into the individual's role in the appropriation and transmission of music cultures and the impact this method of cultural migration has on the perception of rhythmically and socially complex musical cultures outside of their places of origin.

1.2   What Is Flamenco?

Most people, when they consider flamenco, would envision a dark-haired, mysterious dancer wearing a polka-dot dress stamping about with castanets. It is an image that has been fed to the general public by Hollywood, tourism campaigns, and the nationalist regime of Franco, among others. While a more detailed explanation of the art complex and its history is explored in subsequent chapters, in brief, 'flamenco' describes a music, a dance, a singing style, a variety of song styles called palos, and a surrounding culture. A typical performance in Andalucía will consist of a singer (*cantaor/a*), guitarist (*tocaor/a*), and dance (*bailor/a*). Oftentimes the ensemble (*cuadro*) includes a percussive element such as clapping (*palmas*) or the cajón (a wooden box drum).

Flamenco originated primarily in Andalucía (with influences from other parts of Southern Spain) around the eighteenth century, coagulating local folk styles such as fandangos and siguiriyas. While popularly assumed to be Gitano music, it is a melding of many cultures that passed through Southern Spain, including Gitanos, Spanish, Jewish, Moors, nineteenth-century Romantic composers, and Latin American. In this way, flamenco developed from a series of transcultural interactions. Due to internal migration and tourist interest, the art complex now is practiced, at the very least in a touristic capacity, throughout Spain.

Outside of Spain, flamenco manifests in a variety of different ways, primarily focused around the guitarist and dancer. In the UK, there exist small pockets of flamenco aficionados consisting of British enthusiasts with a smattering of relocated Spanish performers, most of whom are impermanent fixtures. These groups, operating mostly independently of one another in a growing number of locales across the country, represent a faction devoted to the practice and preservation of a passionate and emotionally intense art complex persisting independently of its Andalucían homeland.

Despite their autonomous existences, these groups share several common characteristics. Firstly, they are predominantly focused around a dance class, which is their main source of interactions with flamenco. Secondly, these classes are mainly composed of non-Spanish participants who approach the complex art form as an exotic hobby to be engaged with on a superficial, one-a-week level. Finally, in each locale there are individuals who have become infatuated with flamenco, to the extent that they have made it a way of life, often quitting jobs for periods of time because they have recognised that the best way to understand the art form is to spend time studying it in Andalucía. These individuals become revered as local experts and become the drivers of specific flamenco scenes, which would often cease to exist without them. I refer to these individuals as 'cosmopolitan hubs'.

1.3 Making Sense of the Flamenco Journey

The bio-ethnographic vignette about British flamenco dancer Alicia contextualises how individual cosmopolitan hubs, through their travels and transnational interactions, contribute to the creation of a glocal music culture, both within the music's area of origin (Andalucía) and in the 'receiving' country (in this case, the UK). Kiwan and Meinhof, in their book *Cultural Globalization and Music*, define four types of hubs according to the way they support transnational flows: Human, Spatial, Institutional, and Accidental (Kiwan and Meinhof 2011b, p. 3). Human hubs are primary agents who are the focus for everyone in the local network—they know and are known by everyone. Their social networks cross and link diverse geographic spaces and through their activities some translocal and transnational networks not only remain rooted in origin cities but also create an exchange between origin and receiving locales (Kiwan and Meinhof 2011a, p. 6). My research indicates that this is especially true in the creation and maintenance of flamenco cultures both at home in Andalucía and abroad. Significantly, in the case of flamenco, these human hubs who transmit the art complex to new scenes are quite often foreign aficionados who through one avenue or another have developed a passion strong enough to lead them to Spain to learn more about the tradition. Therefore, equally important to specific locales in which flamenco exists are the scenes in between. It is these in-between spaces that occur in the course of the journey down the corridor by individuals who link specific places via flamenco, which shape and create these glocal scenes.

Although Kiwan and Meinhof's 'human hubs' framework does, to some extent, encapsulate how a postnational glocal flamenco scene is created, it falls short of a perfect match. This is because their theory is based on the premise that these culture brokers are from the same country as the music culture they are transporting. However, the fact that British flamenco culture brokers and scene creators are not typically Spanish demonstrate this theory is inadequate to characterise the UK flamenco scene.

Therefore, I propose a new model for cultural migration—cosmopolitan hubs—building on the solid foundation of Kiwan/Meinhof's 'hub' theory. This model focuses on individual human hubs that move cultural information between the sending country and receiving country (in this case, Spain and the UK). The new type of human hub is not ethnically connected with the cultural capital they convey and are characterised by having gained an interest in the art form in their home country. This 'hub' designation incorporates the globalisation of 'cosmopolitanism', which refers to 'an intellectual and aesthetic stance of openness towards divergent cultural experiences' (Hannerz 1990, p. 239). My new model marks a significant departure from Kiwan/Meinhof's theory in that the primary actors that are transmitting culture are foreigners transmitting cultural information from its homeland to theirs. In this case, cosmopolitan hubs from the UK study flamenco in their home country, travel to Andalucía to gain social and cultural capital, and then return to the UK to act as a cosmopolitan hub for the glocal flamenco community there.

Within this model, the individual maintains contact with the sending country, through transnational interactions such as visits or relationships with artists who they bring to the UK for flamenco performances or workshops. The British cosmopolitan hub, that has transcultural knowledge of both the sending and receiving culture, must make decisions that balance economic and cultural capital. These decisions are aimed at attracting British leisure and entertainment consumers to the art form. In doing this, these cosmopolitan hubs utilise their transcultural capital to create a glocal version of flamenco culture. This benefits the art form by creating significant economic benefits in Spain, which manifests in the form of a cultural industry.

Despite the best intentions of these human hubs, they are limited by the typical British approach to leisure—something to be cherry-picked and consumed before moving on to another exciting activity. Many of the flamenco cosmopolitan hubs I interviewed reported that their students usually begin classes without previous flamenco knowledge other than castanets and polka dots. Unless they become one of the few that embraces the art complex, they are generally disinterested in the broader cultural landscape, including how the routines they learn fit into it. Cosmopolitan hubs and teachers must present flamenco in a manner that keeps students' interest—a routine they can see through to completion, with only brief flirtations with technique, palos, and the surrounding culture. Thus, cosmopolitan hubs create the perception of what flamenco is and is not for the students. This is a complex question to answer even in Spain. Suffice it to say, this designation is much contested and combines several historically complex identities and opinions. Nonetheless, cosmopolitan hubs enact variations which comply with UK cultural norms, expanding the ability for them to create economic capital and ensure the continuance of Flamenca Britannica in their localities.

These 'cosmopolitan hubs' are influential in the grand scheme of flamenco because of its status within the broader Spanish cultural landscape. While foreigners journey to Spain with the expectation that flamenco dancing is an integral part of the culture (a perception that has been encouraged and perpetuated by numerous national and regional governments and institutions), it is really an art complex which only a comparative handful of Spanish (primarily Andalucíans) claim as an identity. Early flamencologist, Antonio Machado y Álvarez (or 'Demófilo' as he referred to himself), noted that flamenco was a peculiar genre of music, which fell into neither folkloric nor popular styles, because it was not the property of the people as a whole but an isolated group of *cantaores* and aficionados of the *cante* (Ingelmo and Smith 2012, p. 8). In modern times, this 'isolated group' now includes individuals in foreign countries. Due to both the voracity of the institutional insistence on flamenco as a national identity and its somewhat false association with Gitano culture, the vast majority of Spanish nationals (including many Andalucíans) view flamenco with emotions ranging from indifference to resentment to outright hatred. This was exemplified by many Sevillanos I encountered, including Maria, mentioned in the above ethnography.

Because of this animosity and lack of identity towards flamenco within Spain, these transient foreign cosmopolitan hubs are crucial to the creation of global flamenco cultures abroad, as well as nurturing the scene in Andalucía through the maintenance of it as an economic industry as well as contributing to cultural performances. This interest from foreigners (ex-pats and tourists included) has, through fear of dilution, led some Andalucían enthusiasts to view flamenco, for better or worse, as something to be safeguarded, as evidenced by the successful 2010 bid for UNESCO protection and unwillingness amongst some to accept foreigners as legitimate performers. The idea of 'protection' from dilution has resulted in the emergence of an off-shoot ex-pat flamenco culture in Sevilla which, as a site of pilgrimage for foreign flamenco aficionados, is the scene that many of our cosmopolitan hubs travel to and from.

Varying 'Roles' of Human Hubs

The ethnographic excerpts featuring Alicia aids us in understanding how flamenco cosmopolitan hubs radiate and influence culture in Spain, at home in the UK, and in the transient space between the two. Notably, she has different 'roles' in each locale. In the UK, we observe Alicia as a cultural broker, performing flamenco for an audience unfamiliar with the art complex and largely from the UK. Here, she is a teacher, a revered professional, demonstrating flamenco and creating a perception of what it is for the audience. Alicia's identity as a flamenco dancer is not called into question, nor is she perceived as a foreigner. Many of the concepts she presents to the audience are foreign, though. This includes not only the exotic-seeming dance itself, and the idea of audience participation during the performance (through *palmas* and *jaleo*), but most notably the idea of improvised audience dancing (through the *fin de fiesta*) at the end.[12]

Within the Sevilla scene, by contrast, Alicia's role is that of student and aspiring professional. In the realm of the *peña*, she is perceived as a foreigner, albeit one that is in the know in terms of cultural conventions regarding flamenco dancing. In some circles, she might have her ability as a flamenco called into question or viewed with scepticism because of her ethnicity and associated ideas of cultural ownership. Despite this, she is an active participant in the scene, interacting with locals on a flamenco level and participating in the *juergas* and *fin de fiestas* which are typical at the end of local performances.

Because of differing roles in each location, cosmopolitan hubs, such as Alicia, navigate each flamenco scene in different ways, creating a glocal culture within and as a response to the greater [non-flamenco] cultural landscape. For example, in the UK, conventions in flamenco performance differ from those in Sevilla. Alicia was not thrown by the lack of interaction during the performance (in the form of *palmas* and *jaleo*), which would be normal in Andalucían flamenco performances. She also specifically invites someone on stage to perform a fin de fiesta, as spontaneous performance by audience members is not the norm. Furthermore, even if another British flamenco dancer had been present, it is unlikely they would have volunteered to dance spontaneously. Despite this, Alicia creates an idea of what constitutes 'flamenco' through the act of performing in this way and introducing these ideas of spontaneity in flamenco performance to a UK audience, which will influence how the culture continues to develop.

In the Sevilla flamenco scenes, ex-pat cosmopolitan hubs, such as Alicia, respond to the existing culture, with its conflicting ideas of cultural ownership and rejection of flamenco as its identity, in several different ways. Firstly, they engage in transnational interactions (such as Alicia hiring Sevillano musicians and acquiring a Gitana mentor) to improve

---

[12] '*Palmas*' are rhythmic hand claps; '*jaleo*' translate to 'hellraising' and refers to audience interactions with flamenco performers.

her skills, to acquire knowledge of the historical context in which flamenco was created, and to absorb the cultural behaviours that accompany its performance. Secondly, due to their attempt at finding a place within Sevilla flamenco, foreign aficionados have inadvertently created an ex-pat subculture. This is not only a response to the transience of these flamenco ex-pats—members of the subculture are forever coming and going—but also a reaction to their foreignness to the local culture and the resistance that is sometimes directed towards their professionalisation within the flamenco scene from natives. The scene in Madrid, on the other hand, is almost exclusively commercial and more accepting of foreign flamenco performers and fusions. At the same time, the professional focus of the scene creates a high level of competition, sometimes bordering on animosity, which creates less cohesion and camaraderie amongst foreign flamenco aficionados.

Flamenco in the Global Flow

In a broader sense, Alicia's bio-ethnography demonstrates how flamenco is glocalised in the UK, how the transmission abroad influences the scene in Sevilla (through an influx of foreigners), and how cultural identity is formed and maintained outside of an all-encompassing national or regional identity. Many UK informants, including Alicia, cite the overall lack of understanding of flamenco amongst British audiences and casual dance students (those who just approach it as a leisure activity). Other than individual aficionados, such as Nancy, who serve as cosmopolitan hubs for the art form in their local area, flamenco is something that is enjoyed superficially by leisure seekers who want to engage with singular aspects (usually dance or guitar) on an occasional basis, with no inclination towards grasping its full impact. Despite this, foreign aficionados refer to a mystical *aire* in Sevilla that makes sense of flamenco. This encourages them to keep reaching towards Andalucían flamenco hotspots for inspiration. It demonstrates the importance of place for the art complex, which exists irrespective of the lack of mass Spanish identification with it. It also indicates that even glocalised versions of the art complex are not assuming flamenco as their own or striving to dilute it.

Conflicts in Cultural Identity and Cultural Ownership

Also exhibited in the opening ethnography is the lack of identification with flamenco that some Spanish and Andalucíans have, such as Louis' girlfriend, Maria. While flamenco is considered by many outside of Spain to be one of the primary symbols of national identity, with the accompanying assumption that everyone appreciates it, this is mostly false. It is a concept largely created by various nationalist (through the Franco regime) and regionalist (through the recent Andalucían autonomy movement) campaigns, which attempted to create unity through cohesiveness, as well as attract the tourist eye away from Fascist dictatorships and bullfighting, and towards the lady in the red polka-dot dress.[13] However, within Spain, flamenco is an art complex that is appreciated only by a small handful of individuals. This creates an interesting similarity with the scene in the UK (and other international flamenco communities) in that flamenco is but a small subculture (or series of subcultures) which represents the identity of a relative few dedicated individuals.

Uniquely, the individuals who are transmitting the flamenco culture to the UK are largely British nationals who have, like Alicia, assumed flamenco as an identity. Due to access to a multitude of global cultures (perpetuated by transient cosmopolitan hubs), there are those that are attracted to a culture different from their own and choose to assume it as a new identity—in this case flamenco. Because of reciprocal access to other music cultures within the sending locale (in this case, Sevilla), oftentimes these foreign aficionados appreciate it more than locals that grew up with the culture. This problematises ideas of cultural ownership regarding flamenco. While dilution of the art form as a result of globalisation is not desired, foreign interest, specifically amongst tourists and flamenco ex-pats, is important to the continuance of the culture. Industrial economist Yuko Aoyama (2009) supports this notion in her article 'Artists, Tourists, and the State: Cultural Tourism and the Flamenco Industry in Andalusia, Spain'. She maintains that cultural industries like flamenco, while relying on a unique place-specific heritage, are sustained

---

[13] For more information on the Franco regime, see Stanley G. Payne, *The Franco Regime*, 1936–1975 (London: Phoenix 2000).

by global demand, occupying a specific economic space within Andalucía (Aoyama 2009, p. 81). Thus foreign involvement is important for flamenco's continuance in a globalised era, specifically via tourists and cosmopolitan hubs. This book explores the phenomenon of a reliance on the individual for cultural development and transmission. It sets the scene for a transnational study of cosmopolitan hubs, examining the transience that accompanies the formation of culture in the era of globalisation; specifically, a study that examines how these individuals create and transmit culture through a series of transnational interactions and transience between the existing scenes.

1.4   Approach

The material in this book draws upon research gained during my Master's and Doctoral study into flamenco groups in the UK and their modes and processes of cultural exchange with Spanish and international practitioners in Spain (specifically Sevilla and Madrid). I utilised participant observation, both as an audience member and as a flamenco percussionist, as well as over 40 interviews with individuals in Spain and the UK. The interviewees came from a wide range of socio-economic backgrounds and several different countries with varying levels of engagement with the flamenco art complex (including a few with an active hatred of it). All informants granted permission for interviews, but for the purposes of this book, most have been given pseudonyms, with the exception of Merche Esmeralda, Ron Hitchens, Bandolero, and Juan Verguillos—all so prominent on the global flamenco scene that their description would give away their identity. A cast of characters is in Appendix B, which provides a brief description of each informant's role within the flamenco world. When researching the UK groups, particular attention was dedicated to group composition, dynamics, individual motivations for participation, performance trends, level of involvement, pedagogy, and professional presence. The focus of my investigations in Spain included not only an examination into the structure and mechanics of the local scene itself, but more significantly the transnational interactions, globalisation, and concepts of identity and belonging that exist within the flamenco scene there.

Most importantly, I explored what I came to refer to as the 'flamenco ex-pat community'—a loosely interconnected group of foreign flamenco students and aspiring professionals (such as Alicia) who travel to (and often live for many years in) various flamenco hubs in Spain (such as Sevilla and Madrid) to immerse themselves in the flamenco art complex—broad a term referring to all aspects of flamenco performance, culture, and industry. The Sevilla and Madrid flamenco communities, although localised in its interactions, is heavily influenced by foreign tourists, flamenco ex-pats, and non-Andalucían aficionados. External flamenco scenes, such as that in the UK, are reciprocally affected by inputs from Spain—primarily arriving in the form of visiting or returning artists, mass media (such as the films of Carlos Saura), and Spanish governmental and tourist institutions (who sometimes sponsor artist tours and international flamenco festivals), which in one way or another traverse borders. A traditional ethnographic approach to flamenco might examine the broader local scenes over time, exploring behaviours and interactions within those specific social situations, as well as participants' understanding of the observed behaviours. This ultimately results in an understanding of the group culture. Chapters 3 and 4—case studies about Sevilla and Madrid—do just this, creating an illustration of the Sevilla flamenco scene and its intricacies. This demonstrates what cosmopolitan hubs and other transnational flamenco actors encounter when they experience local flamenco in Spain—what actually IS the culture that foreign and 'native' flamenco practitioners alike immerse themselves in? Through initial examinations of Sevilla, Madrid, and British flamenco scenes, however, it became apparent that this holistic group viewpoint provided by traditional ethnography would not be enough to understand trends in flamenco's globalisation. Perhaps more poignant than the stationary scenes themselves were the transnational journey the art form takes via various cosmopolitan hubs and culture brokers, necessitating the use of individual ethnography.

The Art Complex in Transit

The transient nature of many of my research subjects, as well as its focus on music cultures in flamenco's cross-border transmission and re-creation, presented initially a methodological conundrum. The examination of multi-site, dual-national scenes shaped by globalising forces, transnational interactions and the people who transmit flamenco knowledge between the two locales, presents some difficulties when identifying the location of 'the field' of study. This is especially difficult when examining globalised music cultures through the lens of the actors that travel between the music's 'home' and 'receiving' locales. My investigations involved an exploration of transitory cultural brokers in moments of both travel and stasis necessitated the usage of mobile ethnography, as advocated by O'Reilly (2009). This is a method that enables ethnographical inquiry which 'invokes a sense of voyage where the ethnographer traces clues by travelling along pathways, spatially, temporally, virtually, or bodily' (O'Reilly 2009, p. 146). The researcher is looking for relationships and connections that explain cultural formations beyond borders (O'Reilly 2009, p. 145). Mobile ethnography pertains well to my study, as neither locale in and of itself holds the key to understanding the transactions and transmissions that occur between the UK and Spanish scenes via these cosmopolitan hubs; nor do they independently present a picture of how flamenco has responded to globalisation, varying conflicting cultural identities, and foreign interest. Thus, my approach involved moving between the two locales, much like the human hubs I write about, experiencing flamenco as an ex-pat, and viewing it in states of transience.

This method of inquiry is particularly appropriate because the art complex itself is one that historically evolved as a result of global forces (such as immigration, colonialism, tourism, and commercialisation). Second, in the present day, flamenco exists, to a large degree, as an industry almost entirely reliant on foreign audiences and students, thus necessitating an understanding of global interconnections in order to grasp the broader structures and influences of flamenco in the global flow. A multi-sited approach is, thus required to grasp how the art complex is interpreted in varying locales and the means in which it travels. Furthermore, mobile ethnography proved a useful methodological tool because the 'action', as it were, occurred not so much in Sevilla or in the UK, but in the interactions and travels between the two locales. Finally, I chose mobile ethnography as a methodological tool because my initial inquiries revealed that flamenco globalises, in part, due to the efforts of transient culture brokers and cosmopolitan hubs who carry and shape its manifestation in new locales. Studying cross-border macroconcepts such as globalisation and transcultural interconnections negates the complete efficacy of static traditional ethnography. To gain an understanding of this, I travelled the pathways of these individuals between the UK and Spain as neither locale in its own right could reveal how flamenco has travelled and responded to forces of globalisation and cross-cultural transactions.

The Transcultural Individual in Cultural Creation and Maintenance

Perhaps one might think that the experiences of individual flamenco aficionados are not relevant. What difference, after all, does a single individual make? However, the example of Alicia within the UK flamenco scene alludes to the importance of the individual in cultural transmission. Flamenco is, despite its Andalucían roots, a cross-border art form, practiced in numerous locations around the globe. Because of the postnational location of flamenco scenes, as well as evidence that those communities outside of Andalucía are primarily maintained by cosmopolitan hubs, it is appropriate to have the individual culture broker as the ethnographic voice behind this study. As this book will demonstrate, individuals are the primary catalysts for global flamenco transmission, facilitating interconnections between Spain and various international flamenco localities. However, this suggests 'individual ethnography' as an appropriate method for researching and communicating my investigation. Utilising a variation of individual ethnography proved a useful tool for describing the complex identities and aesthetic shifts that occur when a local art form goes global, particularly when facilitated by individual actors.

As globalisation and political instability have led to deterritorialisation (as described in Appadurai 1990), ethnomusicologists have looked to individual musical actors who are, themselves, 'trying to make sense of collapsing worlds, create new individual identities, and [merge into] newly encountered social formations' (Rice and Ruskin 2012, p. 299).

Stock (2001), in his article 'Toward an Ethnomusicology of the Individual', suggests that whilst a culture itself is viewed holistically, individuals are the catalysts, and thus have great agency over how it progresses. He surmises that 'the personal, the idiosyncratic, and the exceptional turn out to be the building blocks of the collective, the typical, and the ordinary' (Stock 2001, p. 15). Accordingly, the ex-pat flamenco experience has significant bearing on the rendition that individuals transport back to their home countries (in this case, the UK). Reciprocally, the scene that ex-pats create abroad forges expectations foreigners have of the booming flamenco tourist industry when they visit Spain. Alicia's brief vignette hints at the role an individual can play in flamenco's transnational cultural transmission because of the transience between original and receiving locales. It also demonstrates the place of individualism in flamenco through the depiction of an ensemble that had never performed or really rehearsed together before executing a professional performance. Flamenco is an art form that consists of independent elements (*cante, toque, baile, percusión*) making up a whole, united by a mutual understanding of the culture and the compás. If an aficionado has a grasp of these elements, they can communicate with other flamencos, even if they have never met nor have other cultural or linguistic commonalities; and yet it is an art form which communicates deep individual emotions, as opposed to cultural symbolisms. Stock (2001) cites three motivations for an increase in ethnographical writing on individuals:

1. A recognition that certain societies give exceptional attention to exceptional individuals
2. A reappraisal of representational stances in ethnographic writing—the 'voice of God' problem
3. A reconceptualization of 'culture' as a mosaic of individual decisions, evaluations, actions and interactions; consequently, a desire to draw attention to individual cultural agency. (Stock 2001, p. 10)

The third point epitomises how flamenco travels and evolves on a global level. During the course of my research, I perceived flamenco's globalisation as a recontextualisation of a product of individual actors' transmissions and artistic decisions, as well as their transcultural interactions with aspects of the Spanish flamenco community. For this reason, parts of this book will take the form of individual ethnographies demonstrating specific aspects of flamenco from differing viewpoints in each locale.

Rice and Ruskin (2012), in their article 'The Individual in Musical Ethnography', present a survey of ethnomusicological studies that incorporate the individual. Their aim was to develop an understanding of how the ethnomusicologist copes with 'competing poles of the social and the individual in their musical ethnographic work' and field work (Rice and Ruskin 2012, p. 300). In doing this, they exhibit the relevance and usefulness of individual focus in ethnography. Rice outlines several categories which provide insight into the sorts of studies in which individual ethnography is used. Most notably are his first two categories: studies based on the concept of cultures as consisting of shared ideas and studies focused on difference. The former category revolves around the theory of shared culture and uses individuals as 'specific examples to illustrate and give a human face to the social and cultural principles at stake in the book' (Rice and Ruskin 2012, p. 307). The latter category sees individuals as 'agents who operationalize, put into motion, give meaning to, and change social, cultural, and musical systems' (Rice and Ruskin 2012, p. 308). My approach to flamenco's transient individuals is a combination of these two categories. On the one hand, I promote flamenco as a shared experience and use individual actors to demonstrate how global structure and movements are formed and re-formed, as well as how it travels. On the other hand, I portray individuals as culture brokers who enact changes in flamenco, especially as it travels and adjusts to new locales.

Peter Adler, in his seminal paper 'Beyond Cultural Identity', examines the rise of the in-between subject, identifying it as a new personality type that has evolved, particularly in First World countries. He defines this actor as one who is fluid, is mobile, and can exist at societal boundaries by transcending cultural constraints (Adler 1977, p. 26). Building on this, Marotta (2014) describes transcultural subjects as 'cultural hybrids' that connect and integrate two or more cultural forms. They exist between the local and the global and have access to a 'total perspective' which is unavailable to those that exist on either side of border, immersed in the local (Marotta 2014). These individuals are not free from embedded prejudices, as they are susceptible to pre-existing cultural meanings from their home country. However, these transcultural subjects occupy a lofty post which allows them to transcend ideologies of cultural essentialism and ethnocentrism (Marotta 2014).

My ethnographic approach is a hybrid between traditional, individual, and mobile ethnography because the individuals in question are transcultural subjects. They were chosen specifically because of not only their roles within their own local flamenco scenes but also their position in developing the global version of this art complex. Their role as transcultural subjects quite often involves interactions with flamenco scenes both in Spain and in the UK. If the actor is foreign (to Spain), they usually travel there to more completely engage with the culture, take lessons, attend performances, and go to juergas. Their role in the UK is generally that of a cultural broker, performer, and teacher. If the actor is Spanish, they are usually performers or teachers in Spain who travel to the UK under these same roles and are considered experts by British participants. They rarely set up their own scenes in the UK and, if permanent residents, usually have a permanent profession other than flamenco. However, we cannot understand how flamenco globalises by looking at individual cosmopolitan hubs alone. It is also crucial to understand the scenes in which they operate and gain a zoomed-out view of the local Spanish culture that transcultural actors and foreign flamenco aficionados encounter and both shape and are shaped by. In Chap. 3's examination of Sevilla's flamenco scenes and sub-scenes in particular, I utilise traditional ethnography to highlight the surrounds in which these actors operate.

Case Studies

In this book I illuminate first how both the British and Spanish flamenco scenes structure themselves; second how British and Spanish flamenco aficionados interact with each other within the local environments; and third how flamenco travels between these locales. As the art form was originally a specifically local tradition (to Andalucía) that has become globalised, it is important to consider whether the UK groups are striving to keep the Andalucían format or if flamenco is tailored to fit within a local cultural comfort zone. Within the Sevilla flamenco scenes, it is crucial to understand how foreign cultures interact with the local in the realm of flamenco, how Spanish institutions (governmental and tourist) encourage these connections, and the perceived positive and negative effects of the transcultural links. With regards to the Madrid scene, it is crucial to understand how commercialism affects the art complex, broadens its possibilities, and encourages international engagement. These factors are important because they have bearing on how and what aspects of the culture travel. Through case studies of Sevilla, Madrid, and the UK, I highlight how transcultural interactions, identity, and aesthetics both inside flamenco scenes in Spain and internationally, contribute to a global flamenco culture that is transnational in its very essence.

Sevilla

Sevilla, the site of Case Study 1, is considered one of the *cuñas* (cradles) of flamenco and is perhaps the most historically and economically important epicentres of the art complex, with the possible exception of Madrid. The purpose of this case study is to demonstrate how the local scene is structured and how its interactions with foreignness have affected not only this structure but also what aspects are transferred abroad by cosmopolitan hubs. Flamenco occurs in many different situations and is practised by a diverse variety of people with often conflicting motivations and perceptions regarding these practices, usages, tradition, and authenticity. The research purpose of this case study was to gain an understanding of the multi-layered and oftentimes paradoxical flamenco scene in Sevilla, with specific attention paid to the interactions between foreigners, ex-pats, and locals in a flamenco context.

Here, I used interviews and participant observation to gain differing perspectives on the nature of the flamenco scene. To investigate the structure, interactions, and issues surrounding the various players in the Sevillano flamenco scene, I attended *peñas*, theatrical performances, tablaos, dance classes (for both locals and foreigners), and fiesta days. I interviewed several foreigners residing in Sevilla—often for years at a time—to ascertain reasons why an enthusiast would give up their life in another country to learn and perform flamenco there. I also endeavoured to understand the structure of the ex-pat flamenco community, such as where they learn and perform, their reception amongst Sevillanos, and the difficulties they face in integrating with the native population. I also interviewed a cross-section of native Sevillanos, with a focus on flamenco performers, but also including a handful of informants who, while from the region, did not consider flamenco an aspect of their identity. With these interviews, I ascertained the politics of flamenco in Sevilla, through an understanding of the local institutions and foreign interactions that affect the average local flamenco performer and aficionado.

Madrid

The second case study, Madrid, is not widely considered an important location for flamenco by aficionados (especially those from abroad); however, it has played a crucial role in the art complex's development. Here, I explore a history of the art complex in the capital city to gain an understanding of how it came to be such an influential place for development. I also examine how the scene is primarily a commercial concoction, and indeed developed as such. The commercial nature of the Madrid scene marks it as a significant place for transcultural interactions, as well as projection onto the international flamenco scene. Madrid, historically and currently, has more performance opportunities than any other city in Spain. These include tablaos, small performance venues, dance companies, and theatres, among other places. As a result, many of the top flamenco artists from all over Spain migrate the Madrid to increase their employment opportunities. Furthermore, Madrid is a more open-minded city than Sevilla, thus fusions and variations are more common in performance realms. As flamenco exists primarily in the public sphere, this case study presents a different angle on the scene that foreign cosmopolitan hubs that come to Madrid encounter. This commercial interpretation, aimed primarily at non-aficionado audiences, therefore is another manifestation that hubs bring home with them when they re-interpret flamenco upon return to their home countries.

UK

The final case study that I utilise to demonstrate transcultural aspects of flamenco occurs in the various pockets of flamenco that dot the UK. Its purpose is to present a picture of the structure and cultural norms of the UK flamenco scene, develop an understanding of the transcultural interactions that shape it, and demonstrate how individual cosmopolitan hubs, the transient flamenco aficionados, are instrumental in the creation of local flamenco groups in the UK. In this chapter, firstly I develop a concept of the demographics and structure of the British flamenco scene, thus creating a model of not only how the UK understands a perceived musical 'other' but also how this art complex is re-created and localised outside of its homeland. Secondly, the purpose is to demonstrate how transnational interactions occur in an example of a flamenco scene exterior to Spain, specifically with regards to how the British understand and interpret Andalucían culture and how the Spanish participants fit into and make sense of the UK scene.

There is significant focus on flamenco's adaptation to fit in with British cultural sensibilities as well as how locally re-created music and dance enable non-Spanish participants to connect with what they claim as the original Andalucían meaning behind the artform. Furthermore, I explore what the significance of this connection with Spain is when considering the development of UK flamenco. Evidence suggests factors such as Andalucían immigration, 1960s tourism (Benidorm and Beneficio), visiting Spanish artists, internationally released albums and Hollywood have all contributed to the establishment of UK flamenco and intercultural connections with Spain. In this case study, interviews helped gain insight into local perceptions of the flamenco complex, as well as structure, and transnational interactions with flamenco. My interviews with Spanish flamencos working in the UK were focused on their perceptions of and roles within the local scene, as well as their reasons for migrating and their thoughts on how flamenco is received outside of Spain. I utilised participant observation in the context of dance classes, workshops, and performances that I either contributed to or observed. I employed these methods in several capacities: as a dancer, as a cajón player, and as a participating audience member.

1.5   Chapter Summary

This book is divided into three sections. First, I set out the theoretical and historical parameters that contextualise and advise my research findings. Second, I utilise traditional, mobile, and individual ethnography to demonstrate how flamenco plays out in Sevilla, Madrid, and the UK, specifically examining structures, demographics, locations, and transnational interactions and how various cultural identities are manifested. Furthermore, I explore how individual foreign aficionados interact with each scene and the difficulties they encounter. Third, I examine the process by which these transnational interactions occur between Spain and the UK and analyse how cosmopolitan hubs transport information between them. This further influences how flamenco is glocalised and interpreted in each place.

In Chap. 2, I provide a broad overview of flamenco itself, including a description of its components, performance practices, stylistic norms, and geographical nuances. I also construct a reading of the contested history of the art complex, with a focus on the globalising forces that influenced its development. This incorporates a contextualisation within more recent periods of Spanish History (namely the Civil War, Franco Regime, and post-democratisation) which have influenced flamenco's development, foreign interactions, and concepts of Spanish/Andalucían cultural identity, cohesiveness, and ownership. I will also explore the development of flamenco performance and participation abroad, which began as early as the mid-nineteenth century.

In Chap. 3, I provide a detailed traditional ethnography of the Sevilla flamenco scene, significant because it is considered one of the birthplaces of the art complex and a locale where it is still practiced 'authentically', outside of the tourist gaze. I discuss the structure, cultural aspects, and competing identities that characterise flamenco's manifestation in this locale, which often differ drastically from outside perceptions. I also examine the ex-pat subculture that exists alongside the more broadly entrenched flamenco tradition there. Through this, I will demonstrate how various foreign interactions contribute to the transcultural social space, thus affecting the scene which is transported abroad by cosmopolitan hubs (Roudometoff 2005, p. 119).

Chapter 4 is a case study exploring the flamenco scene in Madrid. While not considered a flamenco birthplace, it is, in many ways, the place of flamenco's commercial inception and where many of the influential artists live due to its international airport and recording studios. Because it evolved primarily as a commercial endeavour in the capital, flamenco's history is much more conclusively documented and therefore easier to understand its development in the city. Similar to the previous chapter, I examine the transnational interactions of foreigners within the Madrid scene, but these differ from Sevilla due to the more cosmopolitan nature of the city.

In Chap. 5, I develop an understanding of the UK flamenco scene through an ethnography encompassing various loosely connected groups across the country. Through this, I discuss the structure, demographics, and cultural norms that shape its appropriation. Most notably, I examine the cosmopolitan hubs that are crucial to the maintenance of local British flamenco scenes. I provide insight into how the British approach leisure and multiculturalism, which often has bearing on how foreign music cultures are interpreted. Furthermore, I demonstrate how cosmopolitan hubs and transient ex-pat flamenco aficionados are instrumental in the creation of local flamenco groups in the UK. I also examine the forces within British culture that inspire these British aficionados to assume flamenco as a cultural identity to the extent that they are led to become these transient cosmopolitan hubs. However, similar to Graham St. John's discussion of the Global-Local Psytrance culture which takes its inspiration from Goa, these flamenco hubs (and through them, local British collectives) are constantly reaching outwards towards Andalucían scenes for inspiration instead of inwards towards UK culture (St. John 2010, p. 3). Nonetheless, UK cultural influences result in the creation of a glocal flamenco identity, in the image of Andalucía but informed by regional variations.

In Chap. 6, I analyse how the individual cosmopolitan hubs, through transnational interactions and transience between both locales, are influential in the development and maintenance of flamenco culture. I also discuss the conflicts surrounding cultural ownership in flamenco. I maintain that, rather than there existing a broad embrace of flamenco across Spain (or even Andalucía), the art complex is one assumed as identity by small enclaves around the world, creating a loosely integrated glocal culture that reaches towards the original for inspiration (Robertson 1997, p. 221).

Ultimately, this book offers a distinctly musical reading on how transcultural interactions shape local cultures. Most importantly, it provides an original approach not only to Kiwan/Meinhof's transnational hubs theory to incorporate the foreign aficionado as culture bearer, but also to flamenco academic scholarship. Previously, the latter has neglected discussions of the individual's role in cultural transmission, with very little written about its globalisation. Notably, this research will shed light on foreign cosmopolitan hubs, brokering culture, as an important aspect This is a crucial distinction because, as cultures become increasingly interconnected and individual access to 'the music of the other' becomes quicker, nationalist-centric concepts of identity erode, leaving in their place widespread individual cultural identities.

References

Adler, P. (1977). Beyond Cultural Identity: Reflections on Cultural and Multicultural Man. In R. W. Brislni (Ed.), *Culture Learning: Concepts, Applications and Research* (pp. 24–41). Hawaii: East-West Center Press.

Aoyama, Y. (2009). Artists, Tourists, and the State: Cultural Tourism and the Flamenco Industry in Andalusia, Spain. *International Journal of Urban and Regional Research, 33*(1), 80–104.

Appadurai, A. (1990). Disjuncture and Difference in the Global Cultural Economy. *Theory, Culture and Society, 7*, 295–310.

Hannerz, U. (1990). Cosmopolitans and Locals in World Culture. *Theory, Culture and Society, 7*, 237–251.

Ingelmo, L., & Smith, M. (2012). *Cantes Flamencos: The Deep Songs of Spain*. Bristol: Shearsman Books.

Kiwan, N., & Meinhof, U. (2011a). Music and Migration: A Transnational Approach. *Music and Arts in Action, 3*(3), 3–20.

Kiwan, N., & Meinhof, U. (2011b). *Cultural Globalization and Music: African Musicians in Transnational Networks*. Basingstoke: Palgrave Macmillan.

Marotta, V. (2014). The Multicultural, Intercultural and the Transcultural Subject. In F. Mansouri & B. E. de B'béri (Eds.), *Global Perspectives on the*

Politics of Multiculturalism in the 21st Century: A Case Study Analysis (pp. 90–102). London: Routledge.

O'Reilly, K. (2009). *Key Concepts in Ethnography*. London: Sage Publications.

Rice, T., & Ruskin, J. D. (2012). The Individual in Musical Ethnography. *Ethnomusicology, 56*(2), 299–327.

Robertson, R. (1995). Glocalization: Time-Space, and Homogeneity-Heterogeneity. In M. Featherstone, S. Lash, & R. Robertson (Eds.), *Global Modernities* (pp. 24–44). London: Sage Publications Ltd.

Robertson, R. (1997). Comments on the 'Global Triad' and 'Glocalization'. In N. Inoe (Ed.), *Globalization and Indigenous Culture* (pp. 217–225). Tokyo: Institute for Japanese Culture and Classics.

Roudometoff, V. (2005). Transnationalism, Cosmopolitanism and Glocalization. *Current Sociology, 53*(1), 113–135.

St. John, G. (2010). *Local Scenes and Global Culture of Psytrance*. London: Routledge.

Stock, J. P. (2001). Toward an Ethnomusicology of the Individual or Biographical writing in Ethnomusicology. *The World of Music, 43*(1), 5–19.

2

An Introduction to Flamenco and Globalisation

There is a general assumption by the broader public (at least in the UK and the US) that they understand what flamenco is—an image that usually involves a tall, thin, dark-haired woman in a polka-dot dress, stamping about with castanets. This is evidenced both by my personal experiences (being told 'oh that's the dance with the red dress and castanets, right?') and by the depiction of flamenco in performance posters, programmes, and media. Throughout the course of my research, I began to understand that these outsider assumptions about flamenco, and even those presented in academic books, are vastly different to the complex and multi-dimensional reality that is flamenco. These differences are extensive, including where it takes place, who does it, what 'authenticity' is, and what the art complex entails. Flamenco is a tradition composed of a wide variety of genres, styles, conventions, creative aesthetics, identities, and performance contexts. The first part of this chapter provides an overview of flamenco with regards to its components, terminologies, styles, common misconceptions, and what I mean when I refer to flamenco and its 'original culture'. This will clarify references in latter sections of this book. In the second part, I examine the locations of flamenco, describing its original geographies, as well as typical performance locations. In the

© The Author(s) 2020
T. Martin, *Transnational Flamenco*, Leisure Studies in a Global Era,
https://doi.org/10.1007/978-3-030-37199-9_2

third section, I discuss who does flamenco, ascertaining the ethnicities and identities that are formed. Finally, I provide an overview of the art complex's historical timeline to situate its trajectory from a local, minority subculture to one practised by countless individuals around the world. This chapter contextualises flamenco culture and its path towards globalisation to provide a backdrop for the modes of cultural migration, such as network migration theory and cosmopolitan hubs, which I reference throughout this book.

2.1   What Is Flamenco? A Clarification of Components and Materials

The populist view of flamenco, especially outside of Andalucía, is that it is a dance. The term conjures up images of a woman stamping about in a long frilly dress with castanets, while a guitar provides the necessary melodic element in the background. This image has been perpetuated by promoters, tourist organisations, media outlets, and various regional and national movements within Spain in an effort to centralise identity. This is possibly because it is the easiest aspect to grasp for the non-flamenco enthusiast. Within Spain, the association also involves drugs, crime, and *gitanos*. The guitar is complicated and often seems arrhythmical. The singing often includes Andalucían dialect and utilises many non-Western vocal techniques, such as *melismas* and usage of micro-tones. Thus, the dancing becomes the focal point (Pohren 1962, p. 26). In reality, flamenco consists of four main performance components: song (*cante*), guitar (*toque*), dancing (*baile*), and percussion (usually *palmas* or cajón). Integral to the art form as well is the *jaleo* (audience participation) (Fig. 2.1).

To complete this list of elements is the *aire* (literally 'air') which is a common flamenco term with dual meanings: in the first, referring to a performer's unique qualities of animation, expression, and rhythm. More importantly *aire* references the atmosphere at a flamenco event, the sounds, the smells, the people, and, above all, historical allusions to 'place' and 'origin'. Because of these diverse components, I refer to flamenco as an 'art complex'—a term advocated by economic geographer and flamen-

Fig. 2.1 Leeds-based cuadro with the author playing cajón

cologist Yuko Aoyama (2007, p. 104). It is important to note here that flamenco is not, strictly speaking, a folk music, as it does not consist of known songs, only styles which are re-created by each performer. Many are simply referred to as *por bulerías* or *por soléa*, which means 'in the style of' *bulerías* or *soléa*—both common flamenco *palos*, or song styles. Flamenco is not a popular music either, as it has never held widespread cultural appeal in Spain. It is something that falls outside of the normal designations of music cultures. It does, however, hold significant commercial value, as discussed throughout the following chapters.

Details surrounding the origins of flamenco's components are vague. Until the mid-twentieth century, flamenco has primarily subsisted as an oral tradition and is to this day mostly taught by ear in Spain. As will be discussed later in this section, flamenco started first with the *cante*, as it evolved from various song styles (*palos*) pre-dating the art complex itself. It is the most important aspect for most Andalucían enthusiasts. The *cante* is often the focal point of non-tourist flamenco performances. Its magnitude rests not only on what is sung but also in *how* it is sung.

Ricardo Molina (1967) in *Misterios del Arte Flamenco* describes what is sung as:

> a deeply human factor, as an artistic expression of a collective, *el cante fla-menco* [...] is a wail of complaint from a people who had been repressed for centuries. Flamenco is the primal scream in its primitive form, from a people sunk in poverty and ignorance. Only their utter need and their instinctive emotions exist [... the] songs are desperation, dejection, lamentation, distrust, superstition, curses, magic, wounded spirit, a gloomy confession from a suffering and abandoned race. (as quoted in Thiel-Cramér 1991, p. 34)

This quote exemplifies typical song lyrics, which are often of unrequited love, persecution, death, loss, political dissent, and (occasionally) happiness. *Cante* is song with deep emotion, often seeming to be rhythmically free. *Cantaores* (flamenco singers) perform a variety of *palos* which are formed of *coplas* (verses). Lyrics—or *letra*—traditionally have come from a variety of sources such as orally (through families, performances, recordings, etc.), poetry, or self-written (Manuel 2006, p. 99). Allegedly, the first mention of flamenco *cante* dates to the late eighteenth century, in José Cadalso's novel *Cartas Marruecas* (Heffner Hayes 2009, p. 31) (Fig. 2.2).

Fig. 2.2 *Cantaor* Capullo de Jerez performing in Jerez de la Frontera

Originally unaccompanied, most contemporary *palos* utilise some sort of guitar accompaniment. There are records indicating the presence of guitar in Andalucían folk music starting from the late 1700s; however, most scholars attribute its usage in a flamenco context starting more towards the middle of the nineteenth century; a delayed entry which is perhaps explained by there not being enough guitarists familiar with the style (Thiel-Cramér 1991, p. 69). It was solidified as part of the culture in conjunction with flamenco's emergence into the realm of public entertainment in the mid-nineteenth century. It existed primarily as an accompaniment for the *cantaor* until the turn of the twentieth century, when it began to evolve as a solo instrument (Manuel 2006, p. 99). Flamenco guitar gained significance as an international art form since, unlike the singing, it was free from cultural conflicts such as language barriers. These days, flamenco-style guitar is used in solo performances or in group contexts with *toque* at the forefront (such as Paco Peña's world-renowned performing group). Several techniques are unique to this style, such as *falsetas*[1] and *rasgueados*.[2] In an ensemble, the role of the guitar is often still as an accompaniment for the *cantaor/a* and timekeeper for the dancer.

Baile (the dance) is undoubtedly the best-known and internationally recognised component of flamenco. Outside of Andalucía it is rare to see a performance without a dancer, unless it is of a particularly prominent singer or guitarist. *Baile* was the last of the elements to come under the auspice of 'flamenco', although similar to *cante*, it was most likely influenced by centuries of folk and popular dance forms that came into to contact with Andalucía. It emerged around the end of the nineteenth century, possibly also as a reaction to commercialisation (Heffner Hayes 2009, p. 31). The *bailor/a* is a prominent feature in flamenco group performances. The dance is typified by a paradoxical choreography of gentle, expressive arm and body movement and choreography, interspersed with periods of rapid spins and footwork. Contrary to popular belief, castanets are not traditionally a feature of *baile*—they hail from Spanish classical dance and are periodically incorporated into *siguiriyas* (a sombre fla-

---

[1] Short complex melodies which act as introductions or interludes in a piece.
[2] Scratching or plucking the strings of the guitar in a flicking motion with four or five fingers consecutively.

menco *palo* with energetic bursts) (Thiel-Cramér 1991, p. 61). The main percussive element on the part of the dancer is in their feet. Flamenco shoes (or *tacones*) have strong, thick leather soles, wooden heels, and clusters of small nails in the heel and toe. The *bailor/a* leads the ensemble by providing cues to signify the beginning and end of song sections, tempo changes, and alterations to the 'feel' of the piece. These signals usually take the form of *llamadas*, which are energetic series of percussive *zapateado* (footwork) to bring the ensemble together. This level of collaboration is vital to the flamenco group performance and requires each performer to have detailed knowledge of the particular *palo*. It is important to note that flamenco is mainly an individual dance; use of a troupe, while done in some *palo* variations or stage shows, is not traditional. It is meant to be introspective and is supposed to reflect the interpreter's emotion, both in movement and in facial expression (Thiel-Cramér 1991, p. 65).

The *percusión* element of flamenco has most likely existed since flamenco's birth as a music culture. The form these percussive contributions take has evolved since the late eighteenth century, however. Older *palos*, such as those from the *tonás* family, were allegedly accompanied by singular hits on an anvil, a reference to one of the historical *Gitano* occupations of blacksmithing. *Palmas*, or rhythmic hand claps, are one of the older percussive features of flamenco. While they may sound simplistic, *palmas* involve rhythmically specific patterns, different timbres of clapping (*sordas* and *fuertes*), and often clapping *contratiempo* (cross-rhythms) with other participants. A more recent development in flamenco percussion is the use of the cajón, which is essentially a wooden box hit with the hands. The cajón is a testament to flamenco's history of globalisation. The cajón is one of the best-known Peruvian percussion instruments. Somewhat ironically, it originated with African slaves working in Peru's coastal towns under Spanish rule. Fearing a revolt, Spanish overlords ordered the slaves' drums to be confiscated. Drumming is an integral part of many African religions, so the slaves compensated by reconstructing drums out of the fish crates from the harbours where they toiled. Thus, the cajón was born. In the 1970s, renowned flamenco guitarist Paco de Lucía visited Peru on a tour and was gifted one by composer and Afro-Peruano cajón master, Caitro Soto. De Lucía liked the instrument's sound

Fig. 2.3 *Bulerías compás*

so much he bought another cajón to bring back to Spain ("Paco de Lucía", 2011). He began to integrate it into his performances and it gradually became part of flamenco culture. It is now taught at many of the Andalucían flamenco schools and the top troupes utilise them as part of the ensemble.

The primary purpose of *percusión* in whatever instrumental format is to keep the *compás*. This is the rhythmic backbone of flamenco. The *compás* provides a thread that links the entire ensemble together. It is a marker of expertise for an individual or an ensemble to correctly maintain *compás*, which is more than just maintaining a beat. It involves intricate accents which define each style. For example, a *bulerías compás* is a twelve-beat cycle with counting (somewhat confusingly) beginning on '12' (see Fig. 2.3). Other percussion innovations include Middle Eastern instruments and the marimba.

The term '*Compás*' describes the basic rhythmic and accent structure which is unique to each type of *palo*. It is something that is felt by all performers, even if no one is directly playing it. The modern flamenco group is referred to as a *cuadro* and on average is composed of a *cantaor/a*, *tocaor/a*, *bailor/a*, and *percusión*. Variations regarding instruments which comprise the flamenco ensemble have emerged as flamenco has globalised, such as flute, saxophone, and marimba.

Jaleo, derived from the verb *jalear* (Eng: to stimulate or encourage) is audience participation. It includes words of encouragement (such as '*olé*', '*toma!*', or '*huasa!*') shouted to the performers and *palmas* clapped by the audience members (versus a member of the ensemble). Both types of *jaleo* must be done in the correct place in the piece. *Jaleo* is vital not only for the performers, but for establishing an *aire*, as it is generally only present amongst flamenco-educated audiences. Onlookers who are in-the-know will often clap *palmas* more intricately than the performers themselves.

During my research I attended several performances put on by Peña Juan Bravo (in Malaga) where seemingly most of the thirty-person audience were clapping *contratiempo*.[3] Another aspect which blurs the line between audience and performer is the *fin de fiesta*, which was described in the previous chapter. This occurs at the end of a performance, usually in more intimate settings (such as bars and *peñas*), when members of the audience (usually limited to dancers or singers) are invited on stage to perform a few improvised *pataitos*.[4] The ability to participate in this aspect of *jaleo* is the mark of an extremely confident performer, and often provides an outlet for one to demonstrate skills to an audience with the hope of being hired for future performances.

Palos

Flamenco repertoire comprises around about a dozen song styles known as *palos*, which have several dozen subtle variants. The *palos* differ from one another in terms of singing and playing styles, lyrical form, distinct *toque* and *cante* melodies, *compás*, song structure, and modality (Manuel 2006, p. 95). They can be categorised along many different lines such as the type of music they originated from, *compás*, character, and geographical place of origin. Due to flamenco's status as a primarily oral tradition, a proper classification tool is widely debated. Suggesting a fool-proof method of classification is outside of the scope of this book.[5] For the purposes of my research surrounding flamenco globalisation, I find it useful to consider *palos* in terms of their purpose or the ethnic groups they originated with; primarily because in this way, *palos* represent a trajectory of flamenco's globalisation.

Flamenco *palos* emerged from several ethnic groups: Sephardi Jews, Arabic, *Gitano*, Indian, Celtic, Andalucían, and Latin American. Some styles also have specific performance contexts, used only in specific circumstances or reflect a particular scenario. For example, *saetas* are unac-

---

[3] On the off-beats.
[4] Footwork sections which fit within the confines of a few *coplas*.
[5] For a detailed analysis of this topic, see William Washabaugh's *Flamenco Music and National Identity in Spain* (Surrey: Ashgate Publishing, 2010).

companied chants sung only during Semana Santa (Holy Week processions) and take their roots from Sephardic religious song. *Alboreas* are wedding songs of *Gitano* origin. *Tanguillos* are songs originally used during Cádiz's carnival celebrations. *Carceleras* are songs whose lyrics refer to the singer being in prison and emanate from historic *Gitano* persecution and incarcerations.

Flamenco *palos* have been broken up into several main categories, based on the seriousness of the emotional range being conveyed. These designations are *cante jondo, cante intermedio*, and *cante chico. Cante jondo*, also known as 'deep song', is widely believed to be the 'original expression of flamenco', the oldest types of *palos*, and derived from religious songs (Manuel 2006, p. 48). It is considered to include the most difficult *palos* to interpret, due to the effort required to sing with the amount of voice control required for these powerful laments, as well as the emotional effort needed to express the seriousness of the content. The vocal style required is known as '*afillá*', which describes a rough quality that can crack or split at will (Manuel 2006, p. 48). They include *palos* such as *siguiriyas, carceleras*, and *tonás. Cante jondo* evolved in private or semi-private settings, as opposed to in the commercial realm.

Cantes intermedios are less intense than *jondo*, although still difficult and profound. They are distinctive because of their strange dissonances and Eastern-sounding melodies. They evolved from *fandangos*, which pre-date flamenco as song styles. Many of the *cante intermedio palos* derived from songs of miners, farmers, and fisherman. They include *palos* such as *tarantas, cartageneras*, and *mineras* (Manuel 2006, p. 48).

Cantes chicos are technically and emotionally simpler than the former two categories. They are generally more obviously rhythmic than the other forms and are often more upbeat. Pohren describes *chico palos* as characterised by 'the ability to restimulate one's faith in mankind, life, and faith itself' (Manuel 2006, p. 48). Essentially, these are the party *palos* and include song styles such as *bulerías, tangos*, and *alegrías. Cantes chicos* are more festive than the other two categories and evolved in public contexts such as *ferias* and commercial venues.

Most *palos* (across all three categories) and their accompaniments were solidified with the era of commercialisation by the end of the nineteenth century (Manuel 2006, p. 96) These categories are significant designations because *cantes chicos* are the *palos* most often displayed to tourists, because of their accessibility, whilst the other two categories tend to remain in the domain of aficionados.

2.2   Where Is Flamenco? Geography and Performance Situations

Flamenco's geographical and performance locations are crucial considerations when investigating issues of globalisation and identity. The actual place of origin is unknown, and a source of great debate in the flamenco world, especially in recent years as it has been appropriated as a source of identity for use as a political tool. The general opinion is that flamenco emerged in Andalucía in a region known as *triangúlo de oro* (the Golden Triangle) which encompasses the area between Cadíz, Sevilla, and Ronda (including Jerez de la Frontera). Others place this triangle between Ronda, Córdoba, and Linares; and still others between Ronda, Granada, and Malaga. These are all areas which are associated with landing points for *Gitanos*, Sephardic Jews, and Moors during the Spanish inquisition (Thiel-Cramér 1991, p. 35).

Although many generalise flamenco as an Andalucían art complex (including UNESCO, as discussed later), there are several *palos* that claim Extremadura and Murcia as their source of origin.[6] The latter even boasts one of the most prestigious flamenco *cante* and *baile* competitions—*Concurso de las Minas*. These *concursos* occur in cities in towns across the South of Spain with varying degrees of prestige. They are generally not tourist attractions and are attended primarily by aficionados. *Concursos* serve as a way would-be flamenco professional (both Spanish and foreign) can gain distinction, thus providing an easier pathway to paid performances.

With this in mind, it is reasonable to generalise that flamenco emerged from the *palos* of Southern Spain. However, it is also accurate to say that it did not remain there. Flamenco quickly moved into Spain's metropolitan centres, namely Madrid, with the advent of commercialisation (as

---

[6] Such *palos* include tangos de Extremadura and la minera from Murcia.

will be discussed later in this chapter). As early as 1840 there are records of commercial flamenco in Madrid, in what is referred to as part of the 'Andalucización de Madrid' movement (Blas Vega 2006, p. 93). Flamenco's development in Madrid will be discussed in more detail in Chap. 4. These locations, as well as Barcelona, are the primary locations for flamenco performance in Spain, although nowadays there are many more locations that boast flamenco as a tourist attraction.

Performance Locations and Instances

Significant to note are the venues, performance locations, and forms which are typical of flamenco. These instances include private family or friend gatherings, festivals (*ferias*), impromptu *juergas, peñas,* theatre shows, and tablaos. Flamenco occurs privately, not so much as performances, but as a party activity, at family or friend gatherings. This is most common if flamenco is something that 'runs in the family', as is the case especially with some *Gitano* dynasties, such as the Sorderas or Farrucos. Local festivals or *ferias,* held across Andalucía during the spring and summer months, are street festivals (usually celebrating the town's patron saint or of some other religious origin) and residents turn up in their finest to eat, drink, and dance sometimes for days at a time. They often feature spontaneous outbreaks of the more upbeat *palos,* such as *bulerías* and *tangos* in to street musicians, piped music, or simply to *palmas.* Often local *peñas* set up marquis and hold free flamenco performances featuring local artists during the afternoon (Fig. 2.4).

Different from these Andalucían town *ferias* are the flamenco-specific festivals. The first one of these was the famous *Concurso de 1922* (also the first official *concurso*[7]), organised by Manuel de Falla, Federico García Lorca, and Andrés Segovia, among others. The *Concurso's* purpose was to showcase *cante jondo* and differentiate it from the less pure forms of flamenco, namely *flamenquismo* and *ópera flamenco* (Washabaugh 1996, p. 45). This significant event in flamenco history is described in more detail in Chap. 4. There are now big flamenco festivals across Southern

---

[7] A flamenco competition.

Fig. 2.4   Feria de Malaga: Dancing *bulerías* in the street

Spain, as well as in Madrid and Barcelona. The most prominent of these are Festival de Jerez and the Bienales de Sevilla and Malaga. They tend to feature popular flamenco artists whose fame is on an international level, as the shows presented are also often taken to significant flamenco festivals abroad (such as in London, Nimes, and Moscow). Many of the larger festivals are primarily marketed to foreign audiences, which are reflected in the price. The implications of expensive travelling shows marketed to foreigners will be discussed later. Oftentimes, as in Jerez, there are festival fringe events in smaller local venues that showcase locally famous artists and up-and-comers.

The flamenco danced in the street at *ferias* is not limited to aficionados; many Andalucíans are familiar with the basic *bulerías* rhythm and style but do not claim flamenco as an identity. *Juergas*, or flamenco jam sessions, on the other hand, are a common space for flamenco experimentation and improvisation by aficionados. A *juerga*, similar to that described in the introduction, can be a planned event, where a group decides to get together and practice or a *peña* is held specifically for that purpose. It can also be a spontaneous occurrence, where a few people are sitting in a bar, one starts singing, another starts tapping *compás* on a table, and eventually someone gets a guitar. I have mainly experienced *juergas* in small bars and *peñas* in Andalucía and Madrid, although a few flamenco groups put them on in the UK periodically. While *juergas* are common amongst Andalucían aficionados, serious flamenco students, such as those in the Sevilla ex-pat scene, also schedule them for practice. The term '*juerga*', however, at times in Spain's (and especially Madrid's) history has also referred to notorious, debaucherous private parties hosted by wealthy *señoritos* which also included hired flamenco performers. These will be discussed in more detail in Chap. 4.

'*Peña*' is a term already referred to multiple times in this book. To clarify, it is a simply a flamenco club for aficionados. In Andalucía, many of them take place in spaces that the club owns or rents. *Peñas* are usually run by committee and hold events on a semi-regular basis which can be attended by members and guests (who must usually pay a nominal fee to attend). The typical *peña* event that I experienced involved a performance by local artists followed by a *juerga*. *Peñas* in Andalucía often sponsor *concursos*, which are flamenco competitions usually specific to a particular element (*baile*, *cante*, or *toque*) or *palo* (such as *Concurso de Taranta* in Linares.) The phrase 'to have a *peña*' (which I have only heard outside of Spain) refers to holding an event similar to those that *peña* clubs typically put on.

The final two performance locations, theatres and tablaos, veer towards the more commercial side of flamenco. Flamenco performances that occur in theatres generally take two formats: concerts by prominent *cantaores/tocaores* or more elaborate, more artistically daring events often conveying some sort of theme or message (such as political activism, saving the environment, or a *homenaje* to a specific artist). The latter type of show usually features a singer or dancer (or collaboration) and involves increasingly elaborate costumes and special effects (such as LED-infused *tacones*). These theatre shows are often created by artists for the purpose of presenting them in different flamenco festivals, both inside and outside of Spain.

Tablaos are flamenco-specific performance venues aimed at tourists. They feature spectacular, highly choreographed shows which heavily feature the dancer. Tablao shows generally include the more upbeat and flashier *cantes chicos palos* and play to audience stereotypes, especially with regards to mode of dress. The price tag for entrance is often upwards of €60, which may include a drink and *tapas*. These commercial performance locations differ from the previously mentioned flamenco occurrences because they lack *jaleo*, an omission which detracts from the *aire* of the experience. This is because foreign audiences, overall, are usually unfamiliar with the performance conventions of the art complex. They attend to experience the exotic novelty of flamenco. Tablaos came into prominence in the late 1950s and 1960s as part of Franco's tourism campaign, which will be discussed in more detail in Chap. 4.

2.3 Who Does Flamenco?

There are several sweeping popular assumptions regarding who practises flamenco. The first of these is that flamenco is appreciated by all Spaniards and is an important source of national identity. The second is that flamenco is only a *Gitano* music culture. Neither of these statements is true. Most Spaniards do not consider flamenco a form of identity; this was a construct of the Franco regime in an effort to create a unified national culture. The assumption that flamenco is a *Gitano* construct casts a negative light on the art complex as Spain, as a whole, has never learnt to embrace the 650,000 *Gitanos* who live there (Tremlett 2012, p. 160). While many *Gitanos* do consider flamenco *their* music, not all of them practice flamenco (Tremlett 2012, p. 163). It is an art form which, from its origins, has developed in conjunction with Andalucían historical and cultural developments. However, even amongst the Spanish and *Gitano* populations in Andalucía, flamenco exists as a minority music culture, appreciated only by a small percentage of the population. I refer to these people as 'aficionados', which is a term in flamenco lingo for someone who is a fan of the art complex. I utilise the term 'aficionado' to refer to anyone who is a dedicated fan, practitioner, or performer.

As noted earlier, there is significant foreign interest in flamenco. While foreign aficionados do not come from a location associated with flamenco, they nonetheless embrace it and take it back to their home countries. It is imperative to note that no singular ethnic group claims flamenco holistically as part of its identity, even though both the Spanish national and Andalucían regional governments have attempted to encourage this. Instead, flamenco exists across ethnic lines, which sets the scene for designating it as a postnational art complex. I elaborate on flamenco and postnationalism in Chap. 6.

2.4 Flamenco and Globalisation

Many Andalucían and *Gitano* aficionados ascribe to the idea of flamenco as an art form which is purely a product of their cultures and, thus, must be protected from global contamination. They view it as an art complex which communicates 'heritage' and transmits the sentiment of suffering and common history which must be protected from foreign adulteration (Malefyt 1998, p. 67). Even some flamencologists, such as Cristina Cruces Roldán, argue for flamenco being an art complex which emerged as a response to nineteenth century socio-cultural stresses which involved *Gitanos* coming into contact with lower-class Andalucíans in an urban environment; that it is a 'musical mixture that gradually became a cultural fixture' (Washabaugh 2012, p. 28). Roldán suggests that flamenco's hybridisation occurred during a fixed period of time, in the mid-1800s and after this was synonymous with Andalucían regional identity. Peter Manuel, in 'Flamenco in Focus', argues a similar line of thought—that flamenco is a crossroads, an 'eclectic entity, syncretizing the legacy of the Arabs, Berbers, Jews, Christians, and pagans who cohabitated for several centuries' (Manuel 2006, p. 92). This represents a line of rhetoric favouring flamenco cultural essentialism which demonises further global influences.

Other scholars, such as Gerhard Steingress argue that flamenco arose and developed as a response to commercialism and the role of the market. Steingress argues for the universal appeal of flamenco, as opposed to Roldán's cultural essentialism on the grounds that:

> While it seems evident that the majority of the population considers [flamenco] to be a consistent element of the Andalucían cultural system, this does not necessarily mean that they identify with it or consider it as a "marker" of their identity. (Steingress and Baltanás 2002, p. 57)

Having read several accounts by flamenco historical theorists, the main point to become clear is that no one really knows exactly how, when, and where flamenco materialised. It is an art form which has been orally transmitted until very recently. Its musical etymology is not a neat and tidy affair, but one that is a compilation of cultural interactions. Furthermore, since its pre-commercial origins existed amongst largely illiterate Andalucían lower classes and *Gitanos*, written accounts prior to 1900 are limited to when flamenco encountered other cultures (including upper-class Andalucíans and foreigners). Based on these accounts and various flamencology theories, my perception of flamenco's evolution is that it is an art form influenced by the foreign cultures which have musically contributed to it, the regional and national socio-political forces which have affected its practitioners, and the influence of commercialisation.

When examining the history of various *palos* that flamenco's origins reach further afield than Andalucía. For example, styles such as *rumba, colombianas*, and *guajira* were influenced by Latin American and African music styles coming into contact with Andalucía because of colonialism and the slave trade. The *palo, farruca*, originates with Galician miners' songs, brought by Northern Spanish sailors who sailed on colonial voyages from Cádiz. Furthermore, most flamenco *palos* are based on a modal harmony reliant on the Andalucían Phrygian mode, which takes its pitch resources from the Arabic *Bayati* and *Hijaz* maqams—a nod to Moorish influences (Manuel 2006, p. 96).

The pre-history of flamenco is a history of the peoples who have passed through Andalucía over the last millennia and, by proxy, created a musical footprint. Between the twelfth century B.C. and fifteenth century A.D., Andalucía became a melting pot for various nationalities to merge and interact. The first Sephardi Jewish settlements supposedly date to about 1000 B.C., although their age of greatest influence occurred between the eleventh and thirteenth centuries, when they were permitted to hold office and even intermarried with Christian families (Thiel-Cramér 1991, p. 19). The Moors ruled Spain from 711 A.D. to 1492. Under their rule there was a fair amount of tolerance for the other ethnicities who resided there, including Christians, Jews, and *Gitanos*.

The *Gitano* arrival in Spain, however, is considered the most important influence on flamenco development. It is rumoured that the *Gitanos* arrived in Spain towards the end of Moorish rule and then were relegated to rural enclaves with other non-Christians upon the onset of the Spanish Inquisition. The earliest references to flamenco began from the late 1700s in the form of literary allusions in Sevilla and Cádiz (Manuel 2006, p. 96).

While a full debate on the many theories of flamenco ownership is outside the scope of my research, I feel a brief overview of flamenco's evolution overview enables a greater understanding of the individuals and situations portrayed in my case studies and analysis. For the purposes of this book, the most important aspect shaping the current flamenco climate has been the Franco regime and, in particular, his tourism policies.

2.5   The Recording Industry

A significant development in flamenco's history, especially as it relates to transmission abroad is the advent of the recording industry. Flamenco recordings started to appear around the late nineteenth century—in the form of wax cylinders. This is remarkably early on in the history of commercially recorded music, as the first jazz record was not released until 1917 (Washabaugh 1996, p. 62). In 1901–1902, the first flamenco discs were released of prominent *cantaores* of the time El Canario Chico, El Mochuelo, La Rubia Nino del Cabra, Nino de la Hera, and Sabastian Scotta. The US company International Zonophone Company, seeing the commercial potential, dominated the flamenco recording industry from 1903 to 1912, succeeded by the French company, Du Gramophone La Voz de su Amo (Washabaugh 1996, p. 62). This indicates an early foreign interest in the art complex as leisure listening, something that was known overseas even at the turn of the twentieth century. The recordings were marketed as a cosmopolitan song style to both tourists and middle-class Spaniards, which helped promote the flamenco as an art music, as opposed to a folk music (Washabaugh 1996, p. 63). The recording process, as with other music style, transitioned flamenco from loosely improvised to a genre with canons dictating how it should be performed. Records also changed how flamenco was learned, making it possible for an aspiring performer to gain information from the recordings, as opposed to oral transmission. This extended its geographical reach. Furthermore, the advent of microphones and amplifiers in the recording process altered the roles of the singer and guitar in particular. The earlier days of the *tocaor* featured the instrument as a 'quiet and introspective instrument, generally incapable of projecting anything but vague percussive sounds over long distances' (Washabaugh 1996, p. 63). The *cantaor*, aesthetically, had a forceful, powerful voice, meant to project over the instrument and across large space. Amplification allowed the guitarist and singer both to employ more subtly in their performance. As these came across in recordings, public preference began to lean towards dynamic contrasts and intricacy. Recordings also put a time limit on song lengths, which had previously been long, and sometimes unstructured with lengthy improvisation sections. These alterations set expectations, in particular, for foreign consumers who may not have ever encountered flamenco inside of Spain.

2.6   Tourism

To understand the impact of globalisation on flamenco, it is crucial to contextualise its presence as an element of touristic interest since this has significant bearing on both its transmission abroad and as an identity signifier at home. While it has existed and been influenced by commercialism practically since it has been recognised as a genre, flamenco's status as a specific tourist attraction has only gained prominence since the middle of the twentieth century. This is, in part, because affordable, mass tourism really did not begin in earnest until 1938, when the UK established widespread paid vacation laws and air travel became more affordable (Pack 2006, p. 6).

In post-1945 Europe many politicians, intellectuals, and industries viewed mass tourism as a potential instrument of peace and an instigator of Federalism. This was based on the German concept of *Tormuswissenschaft*, which was the belief that tourism could broaden trade scope and improve international income distribution, also possibly contributing to intercultural understanding and removing age-old prejudices (Pack 2006, p. 5).

Daniel Boorstin, possibly the first social critic to recognise contemporary culture's usage of simulations and contrivances to transcend mundane everyday life, argued that the purpose of tourism was to 'satisfy a widespread craving for "pseudo-events"', which were often merely a popularised illusion of culture. Sociologist Joffre Dumadezier described this European trend towards leisure as a remedy for the numb routines of modern urban life and labour (Pack 2006, p. 7).

Since the eighteenth century, Spain's modernisation programmes have been closely tied to the concept of expanding 'social, cultural, and economic contact with Europe via travel' (Pack 2006, p. 10). This culminated with the creation of, most likely, the world's first state tourism commission, undertaken by King Alfonso XIII in 1905, which continued through Spain's Second Republic (1931–1936.) During the Spanish Civil War, Franco's Nationalist forces began to use tourism for propaganda purposes, offering battlefield tours in an attempt to influence public opinion. Post-1945, Franco became uneasy with the continued encouragement of foreign tourism because they could no longer restrict freedom of movement without allying themselves with Soviet policies (Pack 2006, p. 11). However, by the late 1940s, foreign and commercial policy figures began to envision tourists witnessing progress, order, and tranquillity of Franco's Spain. This also enabled them to extract wealth from European countries which were, at that time, benefitting from the Marshall Plan.

The years 1957–1969 marked a political era known as *desarrollista* (Eng: development-guided) in the Franco regime. During this time, the administration enacted policies which essentially created heritage tourism, focusing on print media, speeches, films, and tourism promotion (Afinoguénova 2010, p. 417). By the 1960s, Spain's coastal regions were Europe's most popular holiday destinations, surpassing all other countries in tourism per capita except the US and Italy by 1968. One social critic described Franco-era tourism as a propagandist function since 'the substantial presence of foreign tourists would demonstrate the acceptance of the regime abroad and reinforce the legitimacy of the Spanish economic model' (Pack 2006, p. 2). This shift came about in part because of a refocused advertising strategy. This approach, which began to be adopted in the 1950s, was meant to highlight Spain's difference from the rest of Europe, but at the same time its familiarity.

There was a public call for proposals by the Dirección General de Turismo (DGT)[8] in 1953, in search of focal points for the national advertising plan. One entry, from ten-year DGT veteran Carlos Gonzalez Cuesta stands out from the rest, stating that:

> Spain has no alternative but difference. [T]he tourist wants amenities and ease of travel, comfort in hotels, good food at the restaurant, better wine, and *Españoladas*: bulls, dance, flamenco, singing, Gypsies … Sevilla, Córdoba, Granada … we must resign ourselves, where tourism is concerned, to being a country of *panderata*,[9] or we will have lost 90% of our attractiveness for tourism. (as quoted in Pack 2006, p. 69)[10]

Following this line of reasoning, eighteen regional themes were selected, most significantly for this paper, Andalucía and Sevilla. This ultimately resulted in a DGT newsprint campaign with the slogan 'Spain is Different' ('España es Diferente'), erupting in the 1960s. The promotion emphasised specific local cultures that, to the Franco regime, defined national culture and placed it outside the European norm—such as religious festivals, bullfighting, and flamenco (Afinoguénova and Martí-Olivella 2008, p. 6). These advertisements, 72% of which were in English, highlighted for UK tourists images of 'beaches and bullfights, crumbling red castles, flamenco singers, and the ting-tong-tang of the guitar' for less than £1 a day (Pack 2006, p. 71).

These tourist campaigns were often distributed alongside tapes of Fiesta Flamenca (such as *sevillañas* and *rumbas*). They targeted audiences around Europe, but specifically the UK, France, Germany, and the US (because of their post-war presence on the continent). By the end of the 1960s, foreign tourism covered two-thirds of Spain's trade deficit and was its largest industry (Pack 2006, p. 2). Due to the poor socio-economic state of the country, localities were doing all they could to attract foreign interest. Across Spain, 'places with no tradition of flamenco or bullfighting hurried to build bullrings or Gitano caves to lure the American

---

[8] Government publicity agency.
[9] A small tambourine.
[10] AGA 3:49, 84/18520.

or European tourists for whom "Spain" was Andalucía' (Álvarez Junco 2000, p. 9). This is also demonstrated in popular culture of the time, for example the 1954 film, *Bienvenidos Mr. Marshall*, which farcically displays a Northern Spanish village donning flamenco gear and playing up Andalucían stereotypes when they hear that US Secretary of State Marshall might visit their village.

In this way, flamenco became part of a national tourism campaign with tablaos being opened not just in flamenco's native home in Southern Spain, or in Madrid (where there had been flamenco performance venues since the nineteenth century), but across the entire country, especially to the coastal regions that were developing reputations as coastal tourist destinations. In the process of developing this tourist campaign, a national identity and perception was also created—specifically to those outside looking in. Interestingly, through this process, Franco was also accomplishing his goal of formulating a cohesive national identity. This concept of national identity in Spain becomes important when assessing how foreigners fit into the broader scheme of Andalucían flamenco culture, as well as how flamenco is understood abroad. The following chapters will explore further this transnational movement of flamenco and how the experiences of foreign cosmopolitan hubs in Sevilla and Madrid dictate the scenes that are created in their home countries.

References

Afinoguénova, E. (2010). "Unity, Stability, Continuity": Heritage and the Renovation of Franco's Dictatorship in Spain 1957–1969. *International Journal of Heritage Studies, 16*(1), 417–433.

Afinoguénova, E., & Martí-Olivella, J. (2008). *Spain Is (Still) Different: Tourism and Discourse in Spanish Identity*. Plymouth: Lexington Books.

Álvarez Junco, J. (2000). *Spanish History Since 1808*. London: Bloomsbury.

Aoyama, Y. (2007). The Role of Consumption and Globalisation in a Cultural Industry. *Geoforum, 38*, 103–113.

Blas Vega, J. (2006). *Flamenco en Madrid*. Córdoba: Editorial Almuzara.

Heffner Hayes, M. (2009). *Flamenco: Conflicting Histories of the Dance*. Jefferson: McFarland & Company, Inc.

Malefyt, T. D. (1998). "Inside" and "Outside" Spanish Flamenco: Gender Constructions in Andalusian Concepts of Flamenco Tradition. *Anthropological Quarterly, 71*(2), 63–73.

Manuel, P. (2006). Flamenco in Focus. In M. Tenzer (Ed.), *Analytical Studies in World Music* (pp. 92–119). Oxford: Oxford University Press.

Molina, R. (1967). *Misterios del Arte Flamenco*. Barcelona: Sagitario.

Pack, S. (2006). *Tourism and Dictatorship: Europe's Peaceful Invasion of Franco's Spain*. London: Palgrave Macmillan.

Paco de Lucía. (2011). *All About Jazz*. Retrieved from http://www.allaboutjazz.com/php/musician.php?id=6218

Pohren, D. E. (1962). *The Art of Flamenco*. Jerez de la Frontera: Editorial Jerez Industrial.

Steingress, G., & Baltanás, E. (2002). El Flamenco como Patrimonio Cultural o una Construcción Artificial más de la Identidad Andaluza. *Revista Andaluza de Ciencias Sociale, 1*, 43–64.

Thiel-Cramér, B. (1991). *Flamenco: The Art of Flamenco, its History and Development Until Our Days*. Sweden: Lidingo.

Tremlett, G. (2012). *Ghosts of Spain: Travels Through a Country's Hidden Past*. London: Faber & Faber.

Washabaugh, W. (1996). *Flamenco: Passion, Politics and Popular Culture*. Oxford: BERG.

Washabaugh, W. (2012). *Flamenco Music and National Identity in Spain*. Surrey: Ashgate Publishing.

3

Sevilla: Local Scenes and Ex-Pat Communities

3.1 Introduction

Prior to my conversation with Alicia on that rainy night in Wirksworth (described in Chap. 1) I had never contemplated that there might be an ex-pat flamenco subculture in traditional flamenco locales, such as Sevilla, much less that these foreign practitioners might have significant impact on how flamenco manifests in their home countries. In January and February 2014, I accepted Alicia's offer to visit Sevilla (Fig. 3.1). Arriving on Día de los Reyes Magos (6 January), I weaved my way through the streets of central Sevilla crowded with processions of *hermanidades*[1] dressed like the three wise men, with their faces blacked and hurling sweets at the onlookers. After unloading my heavy pack at her flat, we headed out to a cosy bar on La Alameda. That evening, we met several of her ex-pat friends including aspiring Argentinian dancer, Jazmin, and Anglo-Franco guitarist, Louis, both of whom I would later interview. They all came to Sevilla with the specific purpose of learning flamenco, having developed an interest in their home countries. The only exception

---

[1] 'Brotherhoods'.

Fig. 3.1 Bailora practising/busking in front of Sevilla's famed Torre de Oro

amongst our party was Maria, Louis' girlfriend—a native Sevillana singer who hated flamenco. We spoke in Spanish and the three ex-pats told me a little about some of the difficulties they encountered in the Sevilla flamenco scene (Fig. 3.2).

Throughout my time in Sevilla, Alicia introduced me to the ex-pat flamenco scene, which exists as a subculture alongside both the tourist and local flamenco in Sevilla. It is connected to the local flamenco culture by a mutual appreciation for the art complex and a reliance upon it for cultural information. The ex-pat scene is, however, somewhat divided from the local flamenco community because of perceptions of cultural ownership amongst some locals and foreign tourist consumers. While I was in Sevilla, Alicia facilitated my introduction to a number of flamenco aficionados from around the world who were making their temporary home in Sevilla to experience the entirety of flamenco culture. She directed me to venues and schools frequented by ex-pat flamencos, which offer a level of flamenco generally not available in their home countries.

Unfortunately, Alicia was rarely able to join me on these adventures as she was occupied rehearsing for her flamenco lessons and an upcoming show. In addition to an intense practice schedule, she spent significant

Fig. 3.2 Juerga at Peña del Niño de Alfalfa

time and energy advertising for her performance, which would take place at a local bar on the north side of the city. She was, however, ever-present in my explorations, as seemingly all of the ex-pat flamencos I met knew her or had heard of her, regardless of how long they had been in the city—even though her role in the scene was not 'celebrated performer' (as it had been in the UK) but 'student' and 'aspiring *guiri*[2] performer'. Alicia spent a significant amount of time attending and performing in the fin de fiestas and juergas at local *peñas*.[3] She also often hired Sevillano cantaores or tocaores for her performances, which marks another point of convergence with the local culture. In the coming months, Alicia's contact with the local scene increased when she began to teach some of her mentor, Yoli's classes. Yoli is an internationally travelling Gitana flamenco *bailora*, who taught foreign and local students alike.

Alicia was making more significant in-roads into the Sevilla flamenco culture than many other ex-pat flamencos due to her connections with

---

[2] Andalucían slang for 'foreigner'.

[3] A *juerga* is a flamenco jam session. A *peña* (in this context) is a club devoted to the cultivation of flamenco, often hosting performances by local performers. While not specifically 'private' in most cases, *peñas* are not widely advertised and are intended primarily for 'insiders' in the flamenco world.

Yoli and prolonged presence on the scene. She was quick to point out other *guiri* who were having success. She also told many stories of the difficulties ex-pats had with acceptance into the often-closed local scene. Several other foreign flamencos I met indicated that this was due to a feeling that 'outsiders' could not understand the cultural context and therefore diluted the *aire* around the art complex. This meant that while they were welcome as paying students and audience members, often they were not accepted or respected as performers. Due to Andalucía's long-standing economic crisis, as well as the persistent perceptions of cultural ownership and identity, ex-pats finding professional success seems to be the exception rather than the rule.

On my final night in Sevilla, Alicia and I attended the weekly Thursday night performance at Peña Flamenca del 'Niño de Alfalfa'—a venue which will be discussed in more detail later in this chapter. This was a relatively new *peña* which, unlike many of the semi-private flamenco clubs of its kind, periodically would hire foreign performers. The attendees were a mix of local and ex-pat aficionados who lived in or around the old Gitano Barrio de la Macarena. We arrived towards the end of the performance, which was free to attend, and watched the *cuadro* perform their final piece—an *alegrías*. Similar to the performance in Wirksworth, after the *cuadro* took their bows, the *bailora* invited any audience members who wanted to come on stage and participate in the fin de fiesta. Alicia and four others got up on stage and each did an improvised *pataita* interspersed with the solo guitar and cante. After the lead dancer finished her improvisation, the *cuadro* and the invited *bailoras* danced off the stage.

Even as the performing *tocaor* was strumming his final notes, the performance began to seamlessly morph into a juerga, as several audience members picked up their guitars. The juerga involved improvised cante, toque, and baile executed in an informal manner by performers and audience, *guiri* and locals alike. It was a magical experience that involved guitarists playing various accompaniments in a *bulerías* compás together, while cantaores took turns singing a few of their own improvised *coplas*. Periodically a dancer stood up and danced a *pataita* as well. Alicia and I stood amongst the crowd, clapping palmas and shouting jaleo. Every once in a while, she would tap out some *zapateado* along with the song. As we watched and participated in the interplay and blurred lines between ex-pat and local aficionados, performers and onlookers engaging in the most raw and spontaneous form of the flamenco tradition, she turned to me and said 'Can't you see this is my culture, too? I live flamenco like the rest of these aficionados.' This phrase characterises foreign ex-pat interaction with the Sevilla flamenco scene as they struggle to find their place within it.

3.2   The Big Picture of a Local Scene

The last few chapters have created a picture of what flamenco consists of, how the art form itself is structured, and discussed how it is influenced by globalising forces. In order to understand the intricacies of flamenco globalisation, it is necessary to grasp the specifics of a local scene—in this case, Sevilla. This chapter will take a wide angle to create an understanding about the environment in which flamenco occurs, as well as the internal and external forces which affect its manifestation. This will demonstrate what the culture actually is, in execution, and how cosmopolitan hubs such as Alicia entangle themselves in the complex web of local flamenco scenes. I chose Sevilla as a case study because it is Andalucía's capital city and one of the *cuñas* of flamenco. While many of the Andalucían flamenco professionals have moved to Madrid for increased opportunity, Andalucía is still considered the 'art and soul' of the music culture (Aoyama 2007, p. 105). It boasts an *aire* and historical context that is essential to the art complex. Significantly, outsiders' perceptions (both within and without Spain) of Sevillano flamenco are often drastically different from the reality. Sevilla flamenco is more than the pretty dancer in the tablao which characterises the vision imagined by the foreign tourist. It is also distinct from its portrayal as the art form of *Gitanos*, as is envisaged by many non-flamenco Spaniards. Sevilla flamenco exists in a professional and amateur context. It is both revered as an integral component of identity and rejected for, among other reasons, its associations with *Gitanos* and Franco. Furthermore, Sevilla is a hotbed for tourists and foreign aficionados. Sevilla has the largest number of flamenco schools in Spain, generating close to €2 million in revenue per year (Aoyama 2009, p. 91). The Sevilla flamenco scene represents a complicated place of encounters between tourist and performer, ex-pat and local, formal and informal, and government and artist. These interfaces combine to create a culture that is formed by a series of transnational interactions stemming from a socio-political history characterised by nationalism, autonomy, persecution of minorities, and global encounters.

Flamenco in Sevilla is often simplified in the minds of those outside the scene (as well as some scholars and foreign aficionados) to be 'just' a *Gitano* art, or 'just' a tourist attraction, or 'just' something trivial to do at a *feria*. Many consider it an art form practised by a cohesive group of Andalucíans and *Gitanos*, with foreigner presence limited to casual students or uninitiated tablao audiences. The reality of the complex interactions between these groups is often trivialised. Also overlooked is substantial community of foreign flamenco students who come to Sevilla to live for various periods of time to absorb flamenco in what they perceive as its 'original setting'. The purpose of this case study is to explore the multifaceted and complex existence of flamenco in Sevilla, with specific focus on the interactions between the global and the local and how these coalesce. I explore the characteristics of the Sevilla flamenco scene, focusing on the internal and external socio-political and cultural factors that have influenced local flamenco.

I utilise the term 'local' flamenco to reference the art form that is performed by certain enclaves of native Andalucíans within, in this case, Sevilla. I pay particular attention to the transnational interactions that occur via flamenco and the existence of an ex-pat flamenco subculture. In doing this, I lay the groundwork for establishing how forces of globalisation have shaped a local scene, and, indeed, created a 'glocal' within the local. These transnational interactions also demonstrate the experience of the foreigner with flamenco in a local environ, setting the scene for what is transmitted abroad. This is significant because it is generally the ex-pats and visiting aficionados who function as the cultural brokers, the human hubs, who transport flamenco abroad, re-creating their perceptions of 'the real thing' in their home countries. Additionally, the experience of foreign tourists in tablaos colours their view of what constitutes 'good' flamenco, which serves to influence their expectations when viewing or learning flamenco back home.

This chapter is structured around the two primary categories of flamenco in Sevilla: local and foreign, similar to Malefyt's (1998) 'Inside and Outside' characterisation of the scene. In the former, I examine the local Sevillano flamenco culture. I assess the geography and location of the art complex, as well as its transmission amongst locals and the transnational interactions that occur in the process of developing flamenco as a profession. Drawing upon traditional ethnography, interviews, and participant observation, I will establish the structure of the Sevilla scene, socio-political factors that have affected it, flamenco's status as a marker of identity, and the subculture of ex-pat aficionados within the local scene. This stands in direct contrast to the simulacra presented to and envisioned by outsiders. Finally, I explore the impact of several socio-political developments that affect Sevilla flamenco; namely the perception of the art form within Spain, the Sevillano mind-set, tourism, and reactions to the 2007 Statute of Autonomy and 2010 UNESCO Intangible Heritage designation. These factors have informed both how flamenco is perceived as a marker of identity as well as the interactions locals have with foreign tourists and aficionados.

In the latter portion of the chapter, I will explore the development and characteristics of a distinct ex-pat flamenco culture. This has developed because of the existence of a strong local flamenco culture which reaches towards Sevilla for inspiration. However, due to issues of cultural ownership and idealism, the ex-pat community exists as a subsidiary of the native scene. I discuss ex-pat flamenco in Sevilla utilising ethnography based on participant observation. This is supplemented by numerous interviews which present the Sevilla flamenco scene through the eyes of the individuals who live it, as advocated by Rice (1994) in his study of Bulgarian musicians. Examining flamenco through the eyes of individual actors allows for an on-the-ground account of their expectations, goals, the cultural friction encountered, and the subculture that emerges as a result of these factors. The ex-pat subculture and the realities of the native culture which it is accompanying contributes to what these foreign aficionados will then transmit back to their countries of origin, in a circular migration pattern like that described by Kiwan and Meinhof in their discussion of human hubs.

Ultimately, this chapter endeavours to make sense of the complicated web of local and ex-pat identities which comprise the Sevilla flamenco community. I reveal the structure, performance instances, and cultural aspects that create the scene, as well as recent political exploitations which have affected it. I demonstrate the transnational interactions that occur between two loosely interconnected subcultures which have influence on flamenco's travels, what is transmitted by human hubs, and what is used as a pattern for glocal culture creation abroad. In the broader construct of this book, a case study on Sevilla exemplifies the effects of globalisation on a local scene and typifies the flamenco scene which is experienced by foreign human hubs who then carry it abroad.

3.3 Peña del Niño de Alfalfa: A Place for Transnational Exchange

A collective shout of '*huasa!*' arose from the crowd as the dancer began the final *bulerías* section of the *alegrías* she had been dancing. The *cuadro* was just finishing their final dance piece with the audience enthusiastically shouting *jaleo* to encourage the ensemble. The room was packed with people standing, seated in chairs, or crouched on the cement floor, with the focal point the area that the *cuadro* was performing in—which was not so much a stage but an area where the audience was NOT. The venue was a large, low-ceilinged room, dimly lit with incandescent light bulbs. It was off of a large patio surrounded by two floors of music rehearsal spaces and dance studios, which opened via a tall, wooden door out onto a quiet side street. Standing amongst the densely packed crowd, I joined in the *palmas*, cheers, and shouts of 'Olé!' that followed the *cuadro* as they danced and played their way off Peña de la Niña de Alfalfa's makeshift stage area. A group made up of a mixture of local and ex-pat performers, they had just completed an hour-long set in this *peña*, located in the heart of Sevilla's Barrio Macarena. The show was brilliant, and the crowd had participated for its entirety, which is typical of local Andalucían flamenco performances.

As the piece ended, the dancer walked off-stage to thunderous applause and foot-stomping, echoing off the cement floor and walls. The *bailora* came back 'on-stage' and invited any willing dancers in the audience to participate in the *fin de fiesta*. Literally translating to 'end of the party', the *fin de fiesta* is an invitation for further erosion of boundaries between audience and performers, and an opportunity for anyone to get up and improvise dance in front of an audience. The lead dancer was joined by three other young women, who would take turns dancing a few *pataitas* of *bulerías* interspersed with *cante* and *toque*. The *fin de fiesta* concluded with the original dancer performing a vigorous and complex series of footwork and then danced off-stage followed by the guest dancers and the rest of the ensemble. As the raucous applause and *jaleo* ended, the audience members gradually dispersed—some towards the small make-shift bar, others towards the large darkened, gated courtyard, which was surrounded by two stories of rehearsal rooms used for dance classes by the *peña* during the day (Fig. 3.3).

I had been brought to the *peña* on this occasion by a group of people whom I had met earlier that evening for the first time through a mutual friend—Paco. In typical flamenco-community fashion, a brief exchange of Facebook messages brought me to the door of a large flat on a dark Sevilla street, not far from Plaza de los Maldonados. I was welcomed in

Fig. 3.3 Performance at Peña del Niño de Alfalfa

like an old friend by 26-year-old Samuel. It is moments like this that have occurred on numerous occasions to me throughout the course of this research that have made me realise that, despite never-ending debates about origin, authenticity, and inclusion, flamenco is a unifying factor on a global scale. Proclaimed knowledge, respect, and love of it is enough of a cultural passport to gain entrance into many circles of like-minded people. What happens after that is up to you.

Samuel and I were joined at his parents' flat by his friends Pepa and Maru. It was Pepa with whom I shared a mutual friend—she and my friend Paco had met when they were both living in Newcastle. Samuel was just finishing a year of intense courses at Fundación Cristina Heeren, to which he had received a scholarship to study flamenco guitar—with the aim of becoming a professional *tocaor*. Pepa works in a manufacturing plant on the north side of Sevilla and plays flamenco cajón as a leisure activity at parties. Maru is among the many Sevillanos whom I met with no real involvement or interest in flamenco, besides dancing the odd *sevillañas*[4] at a fiesta or clapping palmas at a performance. For her, the involvement with flamenco did not go beyond ingrained cultural knowledge and bordered on indifference. Interestingly, oftentimes it is these indifferent Sevillanos that are the first to claim it as a symbol of cultural identity if a foreigner wants to perform it. After a few beers, some tapas, and an impromptu jam session—during which Samuel demonstrated an alternative way that I could play *alegrías* on the cajón—Pepa turned to me and said 'shall we go to the *peña*?' No one knew who the performers were that evening. The main purpose of the visit was the *juerga* afterwards.

Juerga: Crossing the Boundaries Between Performer and Audience

It did not take long after the *cuadro* had cleared the stage for someone to pick up a guitar and start plucking the beginning strains of a *bulerías*. My friends and I quickly bought our drinks at the makeshift bar and moved towards the small group of people now surrounding the table where the

---

[4] An Andalucían folk dance commonly danced in *ferias*.

guitarist sat. Soon a few people began clapping *palmas* as more people gathered around. Then an older gentleman stood up and, in a gravelly voice began to sing. He sang with such pain and passion, as if everything he said was of gravest importance. It felt as if he were singing directly to each individual in the room, and that all of his pain had been caused by them. He finished singing after a few *letra*, with a flourish of 'Olé's' and cheers from the onlookers. The first guitarist was joined in his playing by my new friend Samuel and after a few rounds of *compás*, another singer began to emote. This pattern continued—with singers taking turns to contribute their *letras* to the *juerga*, accompanied by various *tocaores*, *jaleo*, and *palmas* from the *peña* patrons.

This scene is not unusual and can, in fact, be experienced in many *peñas* and small taverns around the region for those who know how to access the pockets of this subculture. The uniqueness of my *peña* adventure lies in the demographics of the participants. As I looked around the room, I saw not only the faces of those who were obviously Sevillano, like the group I had arrived with, but at least half of the crowd and active *juerga* participants, I knew to be foreign. For Sevilla, with its world-famous reputation of flamenco identity, and its many dance schools (including the world-renowned Fundación Cristina Heeren), boasts a significant (and often little known) pocket of flamenco ex-pats. It is a sector of the Sevillano flamenco subculture largely unacknowledged outside (and sometimes inside) of the city limits but possesses its own pathways that often intersect with the local flamencos, while retaining its own unique, collective cultural identity born from foreignness and, often times, lack of acceptance inside of the largely close-minded Sevillano flamenco community. Peña del Niño de Alfalfa is one of those points of convergence between locals and foreigners. Among the reasons for this include its location in the heart of Barrio Macarena where many of the foreign students live, its acceptance and friendliness towards non-members and strangers who turn up, and, most importantly, that they are willing to book foreign performers. After about half an hour of *cantaores* and *tocaores* (both native and foreign) trading *letra*, a young Spanish woman stood up to sing. After she finished, she began to dance an energetic *bulerías*. Samuel stood up to play more vibrantly for her and he was soon joined by a male singer with light brown curly hair, who I knew to be French. The watching crowd heightened their *palmas* and *jaleo* as the three performers were joined by exuberant onlookers. Flamenco, in its most comfortable format, is unique amongst many other music cultures in the way in which the line between 'performer' and 'audience' is often blurred and transient. Pepa and Maru and I stood together, enthusiastically joining in the *palmas*, cheering Samuel on. Maru turned to me and, over the din, asked me, incredulously 'how is it at all possible that foreigners could ever really understand flamenco, it is En el Sangre?'

En el sangre or 'In the Blood', meaning something that an individual (in this case an Andalucían or *Gitano*) is born with. This is a statement I often hear not only from Sevillanos but also from other Andalucíans. It is uttered by flamenco aficionados as well as those like Maru who profess indifference. It is an attitude that reflects a feeling of exclusivity and ownership over a tradition which rejects the idea that someone can ever truly know flamenco if they do not have it in their heritage. Despite the acknowledgement by many that flamenco evolved as a result of globalising forces, it is viewed as something that must be protected and preserved. This insular view holds that foreigners (*guiri*) can only grasp the superficial elements of it. Of all the places I visited in the course of this fieldwork, Sevilla was the location where this attitude was the most evident. It is as a result of this exclusivity and insularity that the flamenco ex-pat community exists on the fringes of the broader flamenco subculture and has developed its own sense of identity and unity. My practiced answer to Maru on that occasion was to explain that while foreigners obviously did not grow up in the flamenco environment, I thought that the raw human emotions and individuality it expresses is something that can be accessed by anyone and if a foreigner practices, feels, and has a *corazón flamenco*, I believed they could understand and perform it as well as an Andalucían. Maru sceptically accepted this argument. The singing and dancing continued for a few minutes longer until word filtered through the crowd that one of the neighbours had called the police. We would all need to leave quickly. This is not an uncommon occurrence for flamenco venues. Even in the few weeks I was in Sevilla, I heard about two other venues—Peña Torre de Macarena and T de Triana—that were forced to temporarily close because of noise complaints. While this may seem normal, flamenco is not a particularly loud event and the audience (despite the *jaleo* and *palmas*) are not exceptionally rowdy. Peña del Niño de Alfalfa takes place within a room that is set off from the street in a gated courtyard, in a neighbourhood that is not really residential. My perception is that these complaints come from a lack of respect and tolerance for the art complex.

We all trickled out onto the dark and silent streets of La Macarena and I bid goodnight to my new friends and headed back towards my hostel, pondering the irony of locals criticising foreign abilities, whilst neighbours repeatedly called the police to shut down flamenco venues on dubious noise complaints. For me, this was a demonstration of how, while there is a mutual association of Sevilla with flamenco outside of the city, it is far from an art form appreciated on a mass scale.

The Sevilla Experience

The preceding ethnography is typical of the experience at a *peña* in Sevilla. There are several key observations to take from this encounter. Firstly, it is the atmosphere at the event itself. The attendees were all familiar with flamenco and had an understanding of the conventions required at a performance (as demonstrate by *jaleo* and the *fin de fiesta*). Secondly, it is the significance of a *juerga* which seamlessly evolved from the performance itself. Thirdly, it is important to note the presence of transcultural interactions: ex-pat flamencos and locals joined together to collaborate and trade *pataitas* and *letra* during the *fin de fiesta* and *juergas*. This marks a potential opportunity for education and cultural exchange. Fourthly, the preceding ethnography featured instances of the broader Sevillano lack of appreciation for flamenco. This can be seen in Maru's indifferent attitude towards flamenco and, somewhat paradoxically, her scepticism regarding foreign understanding of it. Additionally, it is demonstrated by the intolerance of the neighbours towards a flamenco session. Finally, the above ethnography depicts how foreign aficionados participate and experience flamenco while in Sevilla, at least those who chose to engage at a level outside of their classes. This indifference and intolerance towards flamenco amongst Andalucíans, combined with foreign enthusiasm foreshadows my later designations of the art complex as a postnational phenomenon.

3.4   The Andalucían Side of Flamenco

In order to understand the attitudes towards foreigners on the Sevilla flamenco scene, it is necessary to examine how the ex-pat subculture integrates with the broader Sevillano flamenco environments. Flamenco culture, even without the presence of foreigners, is a complex one which has, for centuries, been influenced by forces of globalisation, and is intrinsically linked with and influenced by politics, the economic situation, tourism, and conflicted concepts of national and local identity. In this section, the aim is to create a geographical and functional snapshot of flamenco's presence in the Sevilla cultural and economic environ and identify how economics, politics, and created concepts of cultural identity colour the interactions between foreign and native flamencos, as well as non-flamenco Sevillanos.

A populist reading of Flamenco's history situates Sevilla, including the suburb of Triana, as one of the primary epicentres of the art's evolution. While the nature of its local development is mythical at best (due to a lack of early written sources), mentions of it begin as early as the late eighteenth century and it is largely associated with a melding of *Gitano* and Andalucían local musics—with each side claiming their importance in its invention. The *Gitanos* have historically been an ostracised and isolated ethnicity in Spain—at least since the time of *Los Reyes Católicos*[5]— and it was not until the *Gitano* culture was romanticised by late eighteenth-century writers that it began to merge with *payo*. Despite this, while the two ethnicities do mix somewhat in the present day, especially in the field of professional flamenco, there is still often a fair amount of social division and mistrust between them. I have found, in various conversations with informants, that, while there is some degree of mutual respect between *Gitano* and *Payo* flamencos, there seems also an ethnic 'us versus them' mentality similar to that which exists towards foreigners.

---

[5] 'The Catholic Rulers' is how the Spanish refer to Ferdinand II and Isabella I, who defeated the Moors in Granada in 1492 to unite Spain under Catholic rule. They notoriously instigated the Spanish Inquisition which resulted in non-Catholics (i.e. the *Gitanos*, Sephardi Jews, and Moors already in residence) having to convert, leave the country, or be executed.

Local Flamenco Occasions and Norms: An Ethnography

Flamenco exists in several different Sevillano socio-economic constructs. The primary occasions are:

1. official advertised performances
2. tourist venues
3. pedagogical activities
4. unplanned cultural occurrences
5. fiestas and ferias

Some of these operate largely autonomously from foreign involvement, while others mark significant points of transnational convergence. The first three are discussed several times in this book. In brief, 'official advertised performances' refer to events organised for non-tourist venues such as *peñas*, bars, and theatres. 'Tourist Venues' refer to tablaos and dinner theatres catering directly to the foreign tourist industry. 'Pedagogical activities' references classes and workshops for any of the flamenco components for both foreign and local learners. The latter two occasions— 'unplanned cultural occurrences' and 'fiestas and ferias'—have not been discussed as much.

In terms of unplanned cultural instances, I am referring to the spontaneous outbreaks of flamenco that occur in family or neighbourhood gatherings, or perhaps in a bar in the format of an impromptu jam session, or maybe even on a quiet street or square after the clubs have let out. I have experienced many of these occurrences first hand. You are sitting around a bar, someone starts absentmindedly tapping a *compás* on a table or countertop, then someone else joins in with palmas, then before you know it the bar tender has produced an old guitar from behind the bar and a spur-of-the-moment juerga begins. One of the most memorable of these was walking home from a *peña*—with a Taiwanese flamenco traveller named Chia-Hao around 4:30 AM and we decided to go into a bakery, which we knew started making bread early and would sell it for €1. We walked into the bakery and told the workers we had been at a *peña* and would like some bread. Within seconds, the bakers started clapping *palmas* and them and Chia began an impromptu *juerga* around the building.

These spontaneous flamenco instances are a result of a certain ingrained cultural familiarity with the art complex. Unplanned cultural occurrences also spring up at the various ferias and festival days that occur through the year in Sevilla. During these occasions, it is not uncommon to see groups spontaneously combust into a joyous *bulerías* or *sevillañas* in the middle of the street. In addition to these unplanned outbursts, many of Sevilla's ferias and festivals have flamenco performances that play a vital part in the ritual of the event. An example of this occurs during Semana Santa. Semana Santa (or Holy week) is a grandiose and sombre affair featuring numerous processions of *hermanidades* (Sevilla has 32 of them) throughout the city on the week beginning with Palm Sunday (Domingo de Ramos) through Easter Monday (Lunes de Pascua). Each *hermanidad* has its own brass band, processors in hooded capes, and two elaborate gold-embossed floats adorned with hundreds of lit candles (called *pasos*)—one with an effigy of Jesus and one with the Virgin Mary. These weigh up to 7000 pounds and are carried on the shoulders of 15–30 men as it winds its way through the city. Whilst the occasion does not warrant much in the way of exuberant dancing, it does feature one of the older forms of *cante*: the *saeta*. In the course of the trek around the city, any time there is a palm frond above a door lintel, the procession stops and a *cantaor* comes outside and sings an *a capella* soulful lament to the Virgin—this is a *saeta*—rumoured to have its roots in Sephardi Jewish music. The *cantaor* does this for every procession that passes by. It is a particularly haunting experience because whilst one *hermanidad* has stopped for the *saeta*, it is against the backdrop of drums and brass from other *hermanidades* echoing across the city (Fig. 3.4).

Festivals and Ferias also sometimes feature planned flamenco performances in varying types of venues and presentation styles, including theatres, bars, outdoor stages, and street corners. An example of this in Sevilla is at the Feria de Abril, the city's biggest festival which typically begins two weeks after Semana Santa. It begins at midnight on Monday and finishes the following Sunday at midnight with a fireworks display. It occurs on the Reál de la Feria in Parque de María Luisa, just outside the city centre. Feria de Abril is a non-stop party with daily bullfights and

Fig. 3.4 Semana Santa *Paso* in Jerez de la Frontera

parades of men dressed in *trajés córtas* and women in *traje de flamenco*. A significant feature of the festival are the over 1000 temporary tents, called *casetas*, which are equipped with bars, kitchen, and large music systems. These *casetas* are where the majority of the parties occur and are usually owned by prominent *Sevillano* families and only accessible to invited guests. This phenomenon is metaphorical of the experiences had by foreigners in the flamenco scene—only being allowed in if you have certain connections.

Flamenco in the Feria primarily exists in the form of *flamenquito*—or light, more popularised version of the art which is also known as *fiesta flamenco*—such as rumbas, *sevillañas*, *fandangos locales*, and *bulerías* (L. Perez, personal communication, Aug. 1, 2015). These are not generally considered 'flamenco' by aficionados, although outsiders—both *Sevillano* and foreign—sometimes insist that because they like *sevillañas*, they like flamenco (J. Verguillos, personal communication, Feb. 11, 2014). *Sevillañas* is actually a music and dance with its roots in Castellano folk music that is considered a special genre in Sevilla and even has a place in mainstream radio. In the Feria, one can see these danced in the streets and the *casetas*, both to live musicians and music piped through sound systems. Other than this *fiesta flamenco*, the art is generally absent from this festival (L. Perez, personal communication, Aug. 1, 2015). The exception to these absences occurs if a *peña* is running a specific *caseta* or stage. It is important to note that while foreigners can appreciate the festival, they are not likely to be able to engage in much *flamenquito* unless they have become connected with one of these family owned *casetas*.

Performance Locations

Flamenco is most visible in Sevilla in the realm of its performance venues. They exist, depending on the context and type, both for foreign and Sevillano audiences. It is important to note that, with the exception of a few ex-pat dancers (described later) most of the performers are Spanish or *Gitano*. Additionally, with the exception of the later-described flamenco ex-pat aficionados, Sevillano and foreign punters do not often mix. The reasoning for this is unclear, but my observations throughout the course of fieldwork have suggested a few possible explanations. These include lack of Sevillano identity with flamenco, high entry prices, and negative associations with *Gitanos*.

When I visited Sevilla for the first time with the naïve intent of finding 'the real thing', I was armed with a few recommendations from UK friends and one contact (Catalina). I was confident that in a city renowned for its mythical levels of flamenco saturation and identity, I would be overrun with opportunities to witness the non-touristy side of flamenco. This was not the case. When I arrived, I discovered that the recommendations I was given were expensive tourist tablaos, except for La Carbonería, which was free and full of tourists. When I asked people at my accommodation and at the tourism offices, I was told that the only real flamenco to be seen nowadays in the city were these tablaos. I found no information on the *peña*s or the bars I would eventually discover. I got so frustrated that, after going out to my dance class with Catalina, I got on a train and headed to Jerez. It took meeting a few insiders—Alicia and Patricio—on my second trip to discover the breadth and depth of the Sevillano flamenco performance scene.

There are several primary types of performance locales in which flamenco exists in Sevilla: *peñas*, theatres, bars, and tablaos. *Peñas*, like the one described at the beginning of this chapter, are small flamenco-oriented social clubs normally run by aficionados with the aim of presenting 'good flamenco' to other aficionados, not leeching money from customers. The style presented is considerably more 'traditional' and focused more on *palos* that fall within the *cante jondo* category—generally considered the deeper, more emotive singing styles—than on the energetic, and easily accessible genres of the tablaos. According to La Federación Provincial de Sevilla de Entidades Flamencas, there are twelve registered *peñas* in the city of Sevilla, with an additional 80 listed in the rest of the province ('Actividades' n.d.). Although there is no ruling that a *peña* must be registered, membership in the Federación grants some level of prestige, although there is a membership fee. *Peña*s are a very social experience and the performances and *juergas* that frequently follow mark a liminal experience where the lines are blurred between performer and audience, and participation and interaction is part of the immersive culture (Malefyt 1998, p. 69). The artists who perform here are generally local stars and up-and-coming artists, and *peña* activities are largely unadvertised outside of local newsprint or posters (although a few now have Facebook pages). This makes them difficult to access for foreigners who are not 'in the know' and the attendees are usually Spanish aficionados, with a smattering of flamenco ex-pats if it is at a *peña* in the city centre. As mentioned earlier, *peñas* hold annual *concursos* in *cante* and *baile* to decide who will represent them in the city-wide competitions. The process involves a *peña*-specific competition, which qualifies for the city-wide and then larger provincial competitions. Non-flamenco foreign audiences are usually hard-pressed to find their way to one of these.

Another locale for flamenco performances are the numerous small bars with stages that present live music mentioned earlier in this chapter. There are countless of this type which will sometimes include flamenco shows. Some have a certain longevity to the point of nearly becoming an institution; like T de Triana, others have a short-lived flirtation with flamenco performances. Due to the extremely localised publicity—often just in the form of fliers and homemade posters—the clientele tends to be local—it will often include ex-pats if the performance is in the city centre. The tourist offices do not tend to advertise either these or the *peña* performances and rarely allow fliers to be left amongst their other leaflets, so as to direct tourists towards more expensive tablaos.

Tablaos and Cultural Controversy

While there are a few places around Sevilla that hold flamenco only occasionally, like theatres and organised street festivals, the majority of Sevilla's public-facing flamenco takes place in the form of the tablao. During my research, there were seven large tablaos—Tablao Arenal, Los Gallos, El Palacio Andaluz, El Patio Sevillano, El Museo de Baile Flamenco, Auditorio Álvarez Quintero, and Casa de la Memoria. A tablao is a performance venue specifically meant for tourists. They were developed during the Franco era as a throwback to the *cafés cantantes* of the late nineteenth century. They generally consist of an hour-long flamenco show preceded by dinner and drinks. They range in price from about €35–100. There are usually at least four performers in each troupe—a guitarist, singer, and two dancers—although often there are more and can include a percussionist and *palmera*[6] as well. Their marketing strategy is aimed at evoking the tourist's vision of flamenco and usually focused on stereotypical images of the dancer; red roses, castanets, frilly polka dot dresses, and imagery which arouses an air of mystery. Tourism bureaus, hotels, and tour companies all push the flamenco tablao as a necessary activity for any visitor to consume. The shows are noticeably missing locals in the audience—the prices are set higher than most Sevillanos can afford, plus they know where to go see it for free on the streets or at *peñas*. As a result of the primarily foreign and non-aficionado audiences, the crowd interaction is minimal, except for applause at the end of each 'piece'. This is something that performers sometimes feel is a disconcerting difference from when they play for Spanish audiences, although a few performers noted it made a nice change for audiences not to be talking during the performance (as often happens in Spanish bar settings). The repertoire performed in tablaos tends to be music from the lighter genres

---

[6] A *cuadro* member whose role is to clap *palmas*.

of flamenco, which are more easily accessible to non-aficionado tourists. The performers are often local flamenco stars, with famous visiting artists periodically making appearances. The aims of the performance are primarily to meet the expectations of the tourists, which involves playing the more upbeat flamenco *palos* and wearing these stereotypical clothes. Some flamenco aficionado informants have criticised the quality of performance at tablaos, but in my observations the performers are still top class. The most noticeable difference is the lack of *jaleo* and audience engagement, which changes the aura of the performance.

Many aficionados (local and foreign) at the very least question and oftentimes show outright hostility towards tablaos, citing that they devalue the culture by presenting an inaccurate version of the art complex. While I would dispute the complaint of cultural dilution (a point that will be discussed at length in Chap. 6), the tablao's importance to the culture as an economic vehicle is indisputable. The institution has significantly bolstered flamenco's status as not just a performance art and local subculture, but an industry as well. Although the jobs are not easy to win and are riddled with politics and nepotism, they are consistent and reasonably well-paid (for an arts job in a country in economic crisis). Indirectly, they have also encouraged foreign interest and mystique regarding the art complex, which periodically leads these visitors to take a dance class, go see another show, or buy a *traje de flamenco*.

For the most part, foreign interactions with tablao are limited to the audience side of the stage, whilst simultaneously making up the primary reason for the tablaos' existence. An understanding of the spaces in which flamenco occurs is vital context for the comprehension of the difficulties that native Sevillanos face in navigating the scene, constructing conflicting identities, and negotiating transnational interactions with flamenco ex-pats and tourists.

3.5   The Difficulties for Sevillano Flamencos

Although the data presented earlier in this chapter indicates that native flamencos have sovereignty over the Sevillano flamenco scenes, it is, nonetheless, a difficult road for them to traverse. Sevillano flamenco occurs on amateur and professional levels, as well as significant crossover between the two. While there is a fair amount of flamenco existing in Sevilla, to successfully make it as a professional requires not only a lot of dedication and luck but also the negotiation of a fair number of hurdles associated with national, regional, and transnational forces. To understand the transnational interactions that are an ever-increasing part of the scene, it is crucial to grasp how politics, socio-economic forces, tourism, local perceptions about the art complex, and conflicting views of national and regional identity are currently affecting the flamenco culture and industry in Sevilla.

Flamenco Perception

The first factor which creates difficulties for Sevillano flamenco artists is the perception of flamenco performers in Spain. While the non-aficionado view of flamenco is one that closely associates it with Spain and Andalucían identity, this is not a perception that is shared across the country or even the region. As will be discussed later, flamenco possesses a dubious link with the individual Andalucían identity. Guitarist Roderigo had significant insight on the assumptions made about flamenco performers:

> While the flamenco is more respected in Spain than abroad, the FLAMENCOS are not more respected in Spain, unless they are big names […] it's one thing to play flamenco, it is another entirely to BE flamenco. A flamenco is actually a person and not a very well looked at one. (Roderigo, personal communication, May 28, 2015)

Roderigo is in a unique position to understand this view, being Spanish-South African, living in England, but born in Granada. His words have been echoed by many informants, both Spanish and foreign, aficionado and non-aficionado. A young Sevillano guitarist informant, Cafuco, cleverly observed that:

> Until recently, the definition of "flamenco": in the dictionary was "unsavoury person". The dictionary had a pejorative connotation. Historically we have been conceptualized as drunks, addicts, *Gitanos*, etc. And if you

practiced flamenco you were [an outcast]. Now things are different [than the drug culture that flamenco used to be]. But it is very sad that in your own country dictionaries define you that way. In many pubs there are signs saying "*Prohibido el cante*"[7] which were also typical in the era of Dictator Franco. (Cafuco, personal communication, July 11, 2014)

This quote indicates the perception of flamenco amongst the broader Spanish population as well as residual resentment towards its culture left-over from the Franco regime.

An informant from Madrid who I met while dancing flamenco in Leeds imparted that when she worked in an office in Madrid, she never even told her co-workers that she was a flamenco dancer, for fear of their judgement of her. These traits are then applied to flamenco because of its inextricable link with *Gitanos*. This perception of illiteracy not only contributes to the negative view of the art form, but also results in promoters and agents trying to dupe performers with unfair contracts assuming that they cannot read (Aurora, personal communication, Jan. 11, 2014). While the *Gitano* community does have a notorious drug and alcohol problem (as do many marginalised communities the world over) this is neither a trait nor exclusive to the flamenco community, not necessarily applicable to it as a blanket statement. As a result of the *Gitano* link, even though flamenco is not exclusive to that community, drug abuse is an outsider's perception applied to those who are involved in the culture. The negative beliefs about those that practice the art are damaging to its legitimacy as a non-tourist performance art, furthermore it discourages locals to get involved in it (L. Perez, personal communication, Aug. 1, 2015).

A further problem, sort of on the opposite end of the spectrum, is the perceived mind-set of Sevillanos. Most Spain-based informants have, in some manner or another, referenced Sevilla as being a closed-minded city. This is also reflected in the feeling one gets when spending a period of time there—like it is operating on its own separate timescale, slower, isolated from the rest of the world, and existing in its own special bubble. While this may seem like a subjective and abstract statement, it is one

---

[7] Prohibiting flamenco-style singing.

that several Sevilla-based informants have echoed. Tablao singer Aurora states that:

> The problem is that Sevilla is a closed city. Madrid is an open city. Closed because we are very proud of our culture, our music, we think that our culture is the best. [...] There are a lot of other musics, a lot of cultures, a lot of artists. You want to think that you are the best? That is your problem. This is not reality. [...] I see Sevilla like a *cateto*. [...] 'Cateto' is an adjective that we use to name a person that just likes his own things and doesn't want to learn. [...] Sevilla is a very important place for flamenco, but it is not the only place. (Aurora, personal communication, Jan. 11, 2014)

While this evidence of certain feelings of cultural exclusivity maybe creates the idea that Sevilla flamenco is kept more 'pure' or 'authentic', the close-minded attitude has some problematic aspects. It creates a widespread narrow-minded view of flamenco's possible interpretation, something that was perpetuated in the first decade of the 2000s with its UNESCO Intangible Heritage designation. Firstly, this narrow mind-set limits what is artistically acceptable in a flamenco performance. Second, it exacerbates the concept of who can and cannot understand flamenco, and what they should look like—which enhances difficulties for outsiders, whether they be from another province or another country. Aurora, who is an internationally travelled singer with a much broader worldview, but significant insight into the Sevillano mind-set having performed there most of her adult life—states:

> I have a dancer friend who is Swedish with blonde hair and blue eyes [...] and because of her blonde hair, it is impossible for her to dance here. Because we are *catetos*, we can't understand that foreign people can be a good dancer or guitar player. (Aurora, personal communication, Jan. 11, 2014)

Although these conservative feelings towards outsiders may not, at first glance, seem to affect the careers of local flamencos, the implied restrictions on artistic interpretation creates some difficulty in their ability to express themselves. It seemingly curtails their capacity to differentiate their performance from what is already there, thus restricting available avenues for 'breaking into the scene'.

Impacts of Economic Crisis on Access

Another problematic aspect of the Sevillano flamenco model is the cost of tuition. As mentioned earlier, it is a commonly held assumption outside of Spain that the flamencos of Andalucía learn the art culture in their home, passed down through word of mouth and inherited through blood. While there is sometimes truth to this, plenty of Sevillano flamenco aficionados come from families without this background and attend classes similar to those that the foreigners do. However, the prices of tuition, in many cases, are set higher for foreigners and are unattainable commodities in a society in the midst of a ten-year-long economic crisis. It is difficult for local Andalucíans to afford these fees. For example, Fundación Cristina Heeren charges more than €3000 for a nine-month course. They offer a limited number of bursaries available for Sevilla residents and several other dance academies at the centre also offer similar discounts. Regardless, for most Sevillanos, tuition rates are incredibly expensive in the current economic climate. Rita imparted that this is going to create problems and knowledge gaps in the next generation of would-be flamenco stars—possibly a contributing factor to the slight animosity felt towards foreigners who can afford course fees (Rita, personal communication, June 2, 2015). While the high fees are to some extent emblematic of flamenco's foreign interest, their impact is a direct result of the economic crisis.

The most imminent problems that colour and influence the Sevillano flamenco scene revolve around the current economic situation and politics. Flamenco journalist and historian Juan Verguillos says:

> *Hombre*, now it is not easy for anyone. I do not think our sector is necessarily worse than others, but it is difficult for most people of the [flamenco] culture in general. It is now really very complicated [because] of the economic situation. (J. Verguillos, personal communication, Feb. 11, 2014)

In terms of the crisis, the complications of flamenco, or really any art form, are easy to comprehend: when a region (such as Andalucía) reaches unemployment figures ranging from 30% to 50% in 2014, commodities such as attending ticketed flamenco events all of a sudden are not a familial budget priority. Also, sadly inevitable are the government cuts to arts funding and closures of venues that previously ran shows—such as La Cartuja. Even successful performers, such as Aurora have had difficulties:

> It is very difficult, a strange time to make a performance because there is no money anywhere. For instance, in 'Carmen' [a flamenco version of the Bizet's opera], there are 60 of us. 60 to get planes, hotel, *dietas*. A lot of money plus the horse comes with us from Sevilla! (Aurora, personal communication, Jan. 11, 2014)

Aurora reports that with this flamenco company, which is internationally travelling and of fairly high level, she has not actually been paid in two years. The options for recourse are limited as the money is just not there and jobs in big companies are few and far between. Aurora reported that she had started singing in bars for the first time in her career—having always had enough work in tablaos, *peñas*, and theatres. Many other Sevillano flamenco informants conveyed that they have or would be going to Japan to teach for three to six-month stints, where there is a high demand for Andalucían flamenco teachers and performers. There has also been a noticeable influx of Spaniards (flamenco and otherwise) coming into the UK to try to find work. Despite the economic situation, tablaos seem to be staying open, as the tourist demand for flamenco has not diminished. However, due to the scarcity of performance opportunities, competition for these events is fierce. This is especially true if the artist is not an established performer, at least on a local level. Aspiring Andalucían guitarist Cafuco feels that chances are better for work outside of Spain:

> Because of the crisis and because there are so many people [trying to] do the same. Much flamenco. Flamenco is already international, and people from outside come to Spain to play, and do it well. And because of the economic crisis, many of them [the promoters] pay them the same as a native. And the person who asks for a little more has no chance because there are others who do it cheaper. Why do they do it cheaper? For those who come and are practicing and do not mind economic compensation. What matters to them is the art of practicing. (Cafuco, personal communication, July 11, 2014)

Cafuco, in this quote, is referring to competition from foreigners for performances, which often results in negative feelings towards foreign competitors who already have money and are perceived to be taking work away from Spanish flamencos. Unfortunately, in the UK Cafuco was not able to find enough flamenco-related work to stay. Aurora also reports significant competition from well-known flamenco performers who supplement their more prestigious performances in large theatres and concert venues with work in tablaos. Even though they cost more, a promoter is more likely to book them for a one-off performance because they know it will sell out. However, there are also political factors at work which have contributed to the competitive market for flamenco performances.

3.6 Sevillano Ex-Pat Flamenco Culture: A Construction

My first trip to Sevilla had me questioning if there was anything worth recording in a scene seemingly dominated by the tourist flamenco. It was not until I connected with Alicia that the intricacies of the Sevilla scene, including the seemingly hidden ex-pat scene, became apparent. Alicia, then 27, had moved to Sevilla at the age of 20. She had spent several years attending a ballet school in Birmingham, becoming acquainted with flamenco, and deciding that this was a dance for her. She moved to Sevilla without any specific plans a few days before Semana Santa (when Spain closes down for a week). She randomly stumbled across a class of Yolanda Heredia (the daughter of acclaimed *Gitano* singer Jesús Heredia), who took the more improvisational approach to flamenco that Alicia was seeking (as opposed to the normal routine-driven classes that attracts most foreigners). Alicia has been studying with Yoli ever since and has gradually been finding her way into the teaching and performance world of the Sevillano flamenco scene. Her original goal was to make it into the world of tablao performance. Recently she has been rethinking that particular path in favour of creating theatre projects and workshops that can be run in the UK. These projects initially resulted in Dot-Dot-Dot Flamenco, which was the collaboration between Alicia and two other British women (Yazmin and Maggie) who had also come to Spain to immerse themselves

Fig. 3.5 Foreign flamenco aficionados at T de Triana in Sevilla

in flamenco and stay. The Dots, as they called themselves, put together a flamenco show incorporating traditional flamenco *palos* with aspects of modern dance and marketed it to venues in the UK for a month each year in conjunction with a weekend of flamenco workshops. These workshops, uniquely, took place in conjunction with toque and cante workshops and culminated with a joint jam session with all participants.

The trajectory from paying student to professional is not an easy one for an ex-pat. Indeed, the battle with one's own body and mind to understand and internalise a physically, rhythmically, and conceptually challenging art form is nothing compared to overcoming the complications of cultural differences, economic crises, bureaucracy, and prejudice in the Sevillano flamenco world. These difficulties are what provide the glue and the ammunition for the creation of a diverse community of strangers from different countries who have come to one place in pursuit of their passion for flamenco (Fig. 3.5).

The Life of an Ex-Pat Student

Some come for a couple of weeks, others for a couple of months, and some change their plans and stay for years, scraping by on a meagre existence and a dream of professionalism (or at least greater proficiency). The members of Sevilla's ex-pat flamenco community have the ingrained belief that in order to become good at flamenco, they need to study in Sevilla—either for the good teachers, the superior musicians and singers, or simply for a better understanding of the culture. Most seem to come with a rather romanticised view of the scene, which is more often than not shattered quickly, especially if they attempt a professional existence. These foreign flamencos come to Sevilla to improve their *nivel*, as well as to absorb the culture. Most I spoke to had experienced a version of Spanish flamenco culture in their home country and had then flocked to their perception of the original homeland to discover how it really worked.

Many flamenco ex-pats, like Alicia, turn up in Sevilla with the ambition to learn as much as quickly as possible. Many, similar to my Sevillano friend Samuel, come to study at the prestigious Fundación Cristina Heeren—the largest flamenco school in Sevilla which boasts a broad curriculum including all four performance aspects of flamenco, as well as *palmas*, history, and Spanish. Unlike many other Sevilla flamenco schools, it has a comprehensive web presence with a well-laid out curriculum with obvious trajectories forward. This makes it easier for prospective foreign students to understand the offerings, which is a departure from many other independent teachers in Sevilla who, if they have an online profile at all, it is not up-to-date or only available in Spanish. The classes are attended by students from a wide range of countries, supplemented by a few locals who have received scholarships to help cover the pricy tuition. Adding to the international flavour is the fact that, while the school employs mainly local flamenco stars, the concept was created and financed by American flamenco enthusiast, Cristina Heeren. Many students stay at the school for a particular duration—maybe a series of months or a year, taking as many classes as they can cram in, and practicing in whatever tiny accommodation they have been able to afford. ('Cristina Heeren Foundation', 2014). Many of these have come with the idea of gaining enough knowledge (*nivel*) to return to their home countries as experts and revered teachers. Others, like Alicia, quickly discover that the formalised curriculum of Cristina Heeren, while a good starting point, is not inclusive enough for their broader goals. They search for a well-known teacher outside the school and, whilst still taking classes, begin to entertain aspirations of a professional career—perhaps in a theatre or tablao—within Spain.

The Life of an Ex-Pat Flamenco Professional

While most of the flamenco ex-pats are content with their short, class-oriented visits and will then return to their home countries to perform and teach, others, such as my friend Alicia, become attached to Sevilla and dream of a more professional existence there. Some want to do this for the prestige of becoming an exceptional performer and working in a tablao, creating their own theatre show, and winning regional competitions such as the *Concurso Nacional de Baile por Alegrías* in Cadíz. Others recognise that flamenco is not just defined by a single element (such as singing and dancing) but by how all the elements, including crowd participation and cultural ambience, combine to form the flamenco cultural complex. Sevilla is an excellent place for this.

There are very few places outside Andalucía, Madrid, and Barcelona where all flamenco ingredients exist at a professional level. It is extremely problematic to find experienced flamenco *cantaores*, in particular, outside of Spain, to perform for an audience who understand and engage with the *jaleo* performance conventions of an *espectáculo*. The ex-pats I interviewed report difficulties in returning to inexperienced dancers, musicians, and punters in their home countries and feel that they are unable to effectively progress in their own practice under those circumstances. So they opt to stay in Sevilla, where the flamenco culture feels like home to them. In Sevilla they also have the opportunity to take classes in their chosen discipline and to continue expanding their knowledge, while also learning more about the other aspects of flamenco. These ex-pats also stay because, oftentimes, they feel Spain—and Sevilla or Madrid in particular—is the best place to begin a performance career in an 'authentic' atmosphere.

While these ex-pat flamencos are from many different cultural backgrounds, they tend to develop similar routines in an effort to reach a similar goal—professional performance. Most of them maintain local mentors or teachers in order to continue improving their art, as well as to help them develop contacts within the city—as with many professional performance genres, with flamenco in Sevilla, it is not always what you know, but who you know. While some of them may have one-off jobs teaching private English lessons, most with whom I spoke to do not have consistent employment. This is due in part to the soaring unemployment rate in Andalucía, but also to their devotion to learning their art form. Those with whom I spoke cited doing just enough non-flamenco work to supplement their savings and were content to live in shared accommodation and eat cheaply. Many of them have living situations that are inconducive to practicing—either having non-flamenco flatmates or thin walls and intolerant neighbours. As a result, most of them rent out studio spaces—often just makeshift rooms above taverns—and sometimes splitting the costs with other ex-pat associates. All the informants reported practicing at least two hours a day in studio. In addition to this, they would spend time studying videos and other resources related to various techniques or *palos*. I met several people that, in addition to their normal dance or guitar classes, would take additional sessions about other aspects of flamenco. Of particular interest was a class offered by a *Madrileña* singer named Patri who taught classes specifically geared towards helping foreigners learn *cante*. This is significant because, as with many globalised music cultures, *cante* is often the most difficult to access for foreigners, and classes such as this would make one of the trickiest and culturally specific aspects of the art complex accessible. I have found that once these foreign aficionados enter and engage with the local scene, they realise that the most important aspect of flamenco is the *cante* and that if they want to understand and engage with the art form, they need to at least comprehend the mechanics behind it.

In addition to spending a large portion of the day practicing and studying flamenco, most flamenco ex-pats I met were engaged in some degree of self-promotion—in that they were networking to attempt to acquire gigs and connections. Without the presence of a performance engagement, this is carried out online and by attending various *peñas* and *juergas*. It is particularly common for students in classes at Cristina Heeren or studying *flamencología* at Universidad de Sevilla to meet up in public locales to practise with their course mates in groups that are composed of natives and foreigners. Important jamming and networking opportunities also occur at the events surrounding a *peña*, like the one described earlier in this chapter. This grass roots level of informal performance and networking enables ex-pats not only to hone their skills, but also to improvise and network with those that they may want to perform with in future.

Juergas, especially those at *peñas*, serve as important meeting points to network with the local flamenco scene whom ex-pat students have scant opportunity to play with otherwise. The networking opportunities, especially for dancers, extend to attending performances. As described earlier in this chapter, the final 'song' at the end of a typical flamenco performance (one that is reliant on crowd participation and not in a tablao or theatre), is a *fin de fiesta*. The importance of this occurrence is not only to network with performers and practice improvising, but also for showcasing talents to the public and venue owners who they might try to get gigs from in the future.

Performance Culture and Venue Options

The ex-pats that manage to attain performance opportunities spend a large amount of time promoting their upcoming gig. Usually that takes the form of Facebook badgering, but most will also create fliers to distribute. Popular distribution points are obviously the various flamenco schools around town, as well as local bars, but also include tourist information and hostels. These events, while seemingly less prestigious than tablaos, are also at least a third of the price of entry. It is interesting to note that not all of the tourist information centres are willing to allow the performer to leave fliers if they are not with a tablao. It is imperative for ex-pats to get a good audience at their performances so that they will be booked again and cover any costs. This is where I have experienced the most cohesion amongst the group—foreign flamenco students will flock to sit and watch their friends and associates perform, even if they do not know them, with the aim of supporting them and, often unknowingly, supporting the ex-pat cause in Sevilla.

Although it is not an easy engagement to acquire, there are venues where these ex-pat flamencos can periodically get a performance. Rarely will one of those be in the tablao or a theatre but in smaller venues or bars. On the topic of foreigner performances, Alicia told me:

> There are foreigners who have gone into the tablaos and done it … it's a lot about luck and who you fall in with. There are a lot of foreigners here and as with the Spanish dancers … there are all levels … us foreigners tend to dance in these places that aren't official because we can't get into the tablaos. (Alicia, personal communication, Jan. 7, 2014)

Alicia started her performance career at one such small venue called Bar Sol—a grubby local *taverna* with small rehearsal studios that rents a lot to foreign flamenco dance students. She recounts:

> They decided to put in a stage in my first year when I was here, to give us all an opportunity to perform. Because all of us young girls were coming from all over the world and practicing every day and going to class, but we had nowhere to perform for those first performances where you need to fuck it up and make mistakes—a safe place where you can do that. And these guys created a space for us. We did our own publicity and you know, all of our friends would come and see the show. (Alicia, personal communication, Jan. 7, 2014)

This statement brings up the point about how performance experience is necessary in flamenco in Sevilla. Since so much of the envisioned full flamenco experience is based on all four components being present, as well as the quasi-improvisational nature of it, performance experience at the lowest level is considered crucial to those with professional ambitions. Alicia tells me:

> I started dancing in these small places, like Bar Sol. And because I rehearsed so many hours [there], they obviously gave me a lot of performances […] and actually I really owe it to them. There was a time when I was dancing […] every other week […] and I really learnt so much because there is so much you learn only performing. (Alicia, personal communication, Jan. 7, 2014)

This is a sentiment echoed by most prospective professional flamenco dancers I met (note: not those only pursuing it as a pastime). However, the venues available for that level of performance, especially amongst for-eigners (bearing in mind that, unlike some Sevillano aficionados, perfor-mance amongst the family and in fiestas is not an option) are often difficult to find. In fact, as a researcher it took getting to know an actual insider in the ex-pat flamenco community to gain awareness of these performance venues—they are not well-publicised. Bar Sol has been forced to close its performance space due to complaints from the neigh-bours, as has La Cartuja, a church-turned-venue which ran a 'Miercoles a Compás' weekly flamenco performance where Alicia performed (Alicia, personal communication, Jan. 7, 2014). According to my informants, these venues come and go. Maybe a restaurant or bar saw its lucrative value and decided to put on a weekly or monthly show for a while, but, not being flamenco lovers themselves, lost interest eventually. Other ven-ues get shut down or forced to cancel flamenco performances by less-than-understanding neighbours. Still, when I was conducting my research in Sevilla there were a handful of small, non-tablao venues with regular *espectáculos* for a minimal entry fee. Dissimilar to tablaos, these small venues are not widely attended by tourists and were willing to accept foreigners as performers though.

It is important to note that most aspiring flamenco ex-pats are women coming at it from the dancing side. During my trips to Sevilla, I fre-quented a number of ex-pat oriented performances. Caja Negra was a modern-looking bar with a stage on the far end of La Alameda. The man-agement hosted shows two nights a week, featuring a mixture of native and foreign artists (primarily featuring dancers). The owner of this bar also owned a venue called Sala Garufa, a large roomy venue north of the city centre. Another popular ex-pat performance venue of note is T de Triana, which is a cosy bar with an elevated stage located in the former *Gitano* neighbourhood of Triana—on the opposite side of the Guadalquivir River from the city centre. It was an event started by a Chilean flamenco dancer, Flor, who decided 'we' (the ex-pats) did not have anywhere to dance. She asked the manager and he agreed to try a one-off flamenco night. A sizable intake of the ex-pat community came out to support the night, so the bar agreed to run it once a week. Now the event happens every Thursday and is free entry. They pay the artists (two dancers, a singer, and guitarist) at least €30 each. The guitarist and singer are Sevillanos and play every performance, while the dancers rotate out. The dancers do not have rehearsal time with the *tocaor* and *cantaor*. It is treated like a tablao—the dancers specify what *palo* and how many *letras* they wish to perform then go on stage. Alicia remembers:

> It is a brilliant experience. The idea is it doesn't matter if you are foreign or from here, they are not prejudiced. [...] It's just about dancers who don't have enough experience on stage and need it. [...] You just turn up, get on, and do it. That kind of experience you can't get anywhere else. (Alicia, personal communication, Jan. 7, 2014)

I attended T de Triana one evening and it was packed with people, even though it was at the end of the Christmas holidays. Although there were clearly some tourists that had found their way to Triana, most of the clientele seemed to be foreign aficionados and locals. It was a great atmosphere with a lot of *jaleo*. At the end of the performance, there was the traditional *fin de fiesta*, where I recognised a few of the dancers who got up from previous experiences, including my Taiwanese friend, Chian, who I would later interview about his plans to gain a high *nivel*, specifically in *fin de fiesta bulerías* improvisation (Fig. 3.6).

Fig. 3.6   Performance and Fin de Fiesta at T de Triana, Sevilla

There are several other little places, including one called La Carbonería which is perhaps the only one of these ex-pat venues that is advertised to tourists. Most of the ex-pats I spoke with do not consider it a very good venue to perform in. It is always packed mostly with the tourists and I did not get the impression that it treats artists very well. Another performance option explored by a couple of the bolder ex-pats is the option to perform on the street, although most stick with indoor venues or go back to their home countries.

Peña de la Niño de Alfalfa (described at the beginning of this chapter) is one of the more prestigious venues that *guiris* can acquire a performance opportunity at in Sevilla. They are considered more traditional in style and will often hold annual cante and baile *concursos* to decide who will represent the club in the city's annual competition. Peña de la Niño de Alfalfa is a relatively new establishment by Sevillano standards, having opened in 2010. Dancers must bring their own ensemble and provide their own publicity, but they get paid on the door. Alicia reports that because the audience is primarily local aficionados:

> It's a little bit more scary, because they know what you are supposed to be doing but [...at Niña de Alfalfa] they're really not prejudiced at all [against foreigners], really accepting and supportive. (Alicia, personal communication, Jan. 7, 2014)

Performance is an important aspect to ex-pats who choose to remain in Sevilla—both in the short-term goal of becoming a better flamenco dancer by learning to perform and in the grander scheme of becoming professional in the homeland of flamenco.

Difficulties for Ex-Pats

In talking to multiple ex-pat informants who aspire for permanent residency in Sevilla, it is clear that the ultimate goal does not involve the occasional, hard-won performances in one of the few small venues described above, where the clientele is primarily other ex-pats. Alicia told me:

I've stopped trying to advertise and get performance in all those shitty little bars now. I couldn't be fussed about working there—it didn't seem to be a step forward. Ever since I formed together with the Dots[8] it is like we have banded together—three British girls trying to accomplish the same things. (Alicia, personal communication, Mar. 14, 2015)

The goal for many, however, is to develop a professional career in a tablao, have their own studio, or perhaps join a touring company. Getting to that level is more complicated than the comparatively easy task of emailing smaller venues for a spot on a waiting list without being asked many tricky questions about nationality. To achieve the higher echelons, it is more than a question of skill. As mentioned above, as with many other aspects of the arts, there is some element of 'knowing the right people' and, in a town like Sevilla where families are close-knit and certain surnames are strongly linked to flamenco, this can cause difficulties for an outsider. Beyond that, there is a certain amount of prejudice to overcome regarding physical attributes and nationality—as demonstrated in the first section by Maru's quote.

There are four abstract characteristics of the Sevilla flamenco scene which create difficulties for these ex-pat would-be flamenco performers: nepotism, the economic crisis, ethnicity, and physical characteristics. The first factor, nepotism, arises because Sevilla is a fairly close-knit society where families have been living in the same locality for generations and, as a result, there is an 'everybody-knows-everybody' vibe to the flamenco scene. There is a certain saturation of the flamenco market, even amongst native dancers, and often in order to get into a tablao, dance company, or even a job teaching in a dance studio; it takes connections (J. Verguillos, personal communication, Feb. 11, 2014). These connections are not likely to be in place for an ex-pat who has only been in the city a year or two, as these connections exist outside the realms of dance classes (that most foreigners base their working and social life off of) and even *peñas*, although this desire for connections is one of the motivations for describing the post-*peña juergas* described above. French dancer Manuela imparted:

---

[8] Referring to Dot-Dot-Dot Flamenco Company.

Fig. 3.7 Manuela flamenco busking on the street by Torre del Oro and the Punta de Triana

It is difficult. There is a lot of tablaos, but to enter in, you have to have friends. […] Now there are so many dancers it is difficult. […] I know people in the tablaos but they aren't close to me. I have contacted but am still waiting. […] There are some programmes in *teatros* that give artists the funding for shows […] but it is mostly for the best-known artists. It depends on the level of theatre. If these programmes permit you to perform in the best theatres it will be based on the names. If it is a smaller theatre, they might give you a chance. It is still difficult. You really have to sell yourself. (Manuela, personal communication, Jan. 8, 2014)

Manuela was able to create her own performance opportunities by busking on the street with her *tocaor* (Fig. 3.7).

Shortly after my conversations with her, Manuela opted for a six-month stint teaching in Tokyo due to lack of opportunity in Sevilla. The level of nepotism inherent in the scene means that foreigners who wish to breach these barriers have to not only spend excessive amounts of time practicing, but also have to devote significant effort to networking outside of their classroom, which is daunting in a city as tight-knit and saturated with foreign tourists and ex-pats as Sevilla.

The second factor is that of the current economic situation in Spain. The crisis began in 2008 and only in March 2015 has been reporting mild economic growth (although unemployment figures and research funding still lag significantly behind). Since the crisis began, opportunities for flamenco performances have lessened and a lot of the government arts funding that was responsible for putting on shows and festivals has been cut (Aurora, personal communication, Jan. 11, 2014). My informants have cited that there are fewer big performances and, as a result, bigger name artists have been pushed down into the tablaos and smaller theatres which otherwise might have been the proving ground for up-and-coming Spanish and excellent foreign artists (Aurora, personal communication, Jan. 11, 2014). Manuela conveyed:

> From what I can see, the payment is now not so good. And there is not so much work as before. So then we have big names in tablao. If you want to go to a tablao now to perform you have to compete against the best artists. They need to go there too. And so people of the next level get pushed out. (Manuela, personal communication, Jan. 8, 2014)

Tourist tablao jobs became a difficult-to-obtain commodity because of the consistency of work (several nights a week at least) and higher pay rates.

Cultural Hierarchy: The Importance of Ethnicity and Appearance

While the two above-mentioned factors are significant, the most difficult factor that these aspiring flamenco ex-pats have to overcome is one they cannot control: idealistic concepts of looks and ethnicity amongst native Sevillanos and tourists. These are deeply seeded factors that are entrenched in Sevilla (and Spain's) concepts not only because of flamenco's image but also because of national identity and cultural exceptionalism. As early as the 1950s, American anthropologist D. E. Pohren theorised that non-Spanish aficionados would always need to remember that, regardless of their skill level, they will always be 'thought of, and referred to, as that fellow who performs well, or knows a lot, considering he is a foreigner' (Pohren 1962, p. 78). There is a history of Andalucíans assuming that they alone can properly perform and understand the art complex.

There are two primary grounds on which ethnicity creates issues: one being the perception that the foreigner's ability and feel is not as good because they were not born into the culture; the other is the importance of 'looking' Spanish, specifically in the presence of tourists. There is a not-so-hidden feeling amongst many Sevillanos, including some of those who do the hiring at tablaos, that flamenco is something so rhythmically and conceptually entrenched in the collective social history of the *Gitanos* and Andalucíans that a foreigner could not possibly do it as well—it would always be missing the heart, the *duende*. A number of ex-pat flamenco informants have noted various comments and attitudes about their arts and also the hindrance of gaining employment because of ethnicity. Alicia observed:

> I think there is a little [animosity] amongst them towards us. I have been with Spanish artists after a show and a singer has gone off on one "oh, these foreigners! Oh, not you. You're one of us." [...] It's a big barrier that hasn't been breached yet. (Alicia, personal communication, Jan. 7, 2014)

Even Manuela, who is French-born but of Spanish parentage has received similar comments:

> I think there is racism here [...] "she is an outsider. She can't dance well." This is especially come from the *Gitanos*—but not all of them. Normally those that come from traditional families and aren't so open-minded. Not as much with Spanish people, although Concha Vargas[9] said to a friend of mine once, talking about a foreign girl from the US, "she's no dancing so bad for a foreigner". So that's the mentality usually. (Manuela, personal communication, Jan. 8, 2014)

Both Spanish and ex-pat informants have referred to an unspoken ethnic hierarchy of flamenco performers, regarding who is preferred and respected: 1. *Gitano*, 2. Sevillano, 3. Spanish, and 4. Foreign (Pohren

[9] A prominent Andalucían *bailora*.

1962, p. 78; Manuela, personal communication, Jan. 8, 2014). The reasoning behind these designations relates to shared beliefs and myths about flamenco's origin and authenticity—that it was based largely on *Gitano* dance, Sevilla is one of the main *cuñas* of flamenco, and foreigners have changed and adulterated it (Malefyt 1998, p. 67). The paradoxes and realities of these theories of origin and authenticity will be discussed later in the chapter. Flamenco is seen as so attached to these ethnic designations that it is incredibly difficult for an outsider especially to acquire serious work. Rita, a UK dance teacher who formerly danced professionally in Andalucía, said of ex-pat performer prospects:

> No one will hire you, full stop, to work in the tablaos or companies. You have to be better than the best. [...] No one will hire a foreigner if they can hire a Spanish girl [...] nationality is important. [...] They feel it lessens the value of their art and identity if foreigners are doing it too. (Rita, personal communication, June 2, 2015)

These attitudes often encourage ex-pats to look more Spanish and acquire Spanish-sounding stage names (which sometimes they use permanently as their real names). While this may seem extreme, ex-pats who have been attempting professionalism often tire of constant ethnicity-based scepticism about their abilities. Alicia confides:

> I could pass for Spanish. This is one of the things that gets really old. People come up to you and say "oh, you're English! I thought you were Spanish! What are you doing flamenco for?" Blah, blah, blah. It gets wearing. I just think that flamenco is something that is so universal. You don't have to understand the words of the song to understand what they are singing about—human emotion. It's so obvious and it's something that is so direct and guttural that anyone can understand because it is completely an intuitive and instinctive thing. Obviously, most of us aren't going to have the same level as those that have 'lived' flamenco their whole lives. We get a bad name because of our nationality. We're struggling to catch up basically. Some of us put in the hours, but we're a minority. You're fighting against people's preconceptions. (Alicia, personal communication, Jan. 7, 2014)

These preconceptions are not only those of the Spanish but those of the tourists coming to see shows as well. Several informants report that, even though tablaos are mainly frequented by foreign tourists, the irony was that someone who 'looked' non-Gypsy and non-Spanish was not likely to be hired, especially as a dancer. Ex-pat dancers do not fit with tourists' image of flamenco, and as tourism is about the 'created experience' which meets idealistic (however imagined) expectations, hiring a blonde-haired, blue-eyed foreigner was not a likely scenario. This is primarily applicable to *bailoras* as, in the tourist *espectaculó* they are the focus.

Dancing, being the aspect of flamenco most accessible to foreigners is also the aspect that the majority of these flamenco ex-pats are engaging with. Being a singer as a foreigner is the most difficult, not only because of the unique, non-Western vocal techniques, but also because of the importance of grasping the distinct Sevillano accent, lingo, and cultural references (Aurora, personal communication, Jan. 11, 2014). Guitarists have the easiest path, as they can get by on playing talents and there are fewer of them compared to the dancers. Also, as they aren't the focal point of a Sevilla tablao show, their looks aren't as important.

While there are a few foreigners that have made it into the Sevillano tablaos and theatres—such as Canadian dancer Chloe Brule and Dutch guitarist Tino van der Sman—it is largely an area that is inaccessible to ex-pat flamencos as a result of ethnic prejudice. Several informants referred to feeling that the Sevillanos felt the ex-pat flamencos were robbing their culture. Alicia imparted:

> I do understand there's a kind of fear that the foreigners are going to take over flamenco. We're going to do it badly and it's going to lose the flavour from here. I think if we are going to take it back to our countries, most of us feel we owe it to flamenco not to do it half-heartedly. (Alicia, personal communication, Jan. 7, 2014)

Despite Sevillanos' fears and perceptions of foreign interest, the attitude reflected by Alicia is the one most often stated by ex-pat flamenco devotees—that they are coming to learn and perform flamenco with a viewpoint to respect the art complex and do it properly. I have also found that many Sevillano flamencos have not expressed major concern with foreign flamenco performers—that attitude has come primarily from Sevillanos and *Gitanos* who do not claim flamenco as something of their identity and non-Spanish tourists.

Ex-Pat Cultural In-Roads

Despite the insurmountable difficulties cited with regards to attaining professionalism on the Sevillano flamenco scene, my informants have noted recent in-roads that foreigners have made into the flamenco scene, although these seem to have mainly come as a result of placing well in one of the many *concursos* outside of Sevilla. 'Occasionally one of us— God it sounds like a clan!—gets a really good opportunity to dance at one of the big *peña* s like Torre de Macarena—where you are performing for Sevillanos and aficionados—your hardest customers' Alicia informed me, but these opportunities are few and far between. Both Alicia and Manuela advise me that the best way to get publicity and recognition towards a job is to do well in these *concursos*. Lately, several foreigners have had success in these. For example, Jasaila, a Cuban girl, had recently won the Perla de Cadíz *concurso*; she has since danced in some of the tablaos. Flor—a Chilean girl who opened T de Triana—has won a prize at Villa Rosa *concurso* in Madrid and since got into the Companía Andaluz Danza. 'These were really important moments for the clan', Alicia tells me. There have also been recent instances of a Japanese dancer coming in second place at Concurso de Las Minas (Alicia, personal communication, Jan. 7, 2014). This Japanese dancer comes back once a year to Sevilla, takes classes to acquire new material then goes back to Japan where she can have a career as a revered performer and teacher.

Despite the in-roads that can be made at the *concursos*, there is still a long way to go. Alicia imparts an opinion corroborated by several other informants—'The Japanese girl never would have actually won at Las Minas. Second is ok. But they couldn't let a Japanese girl win. Look at what that would say about flamenco!' It is clear from various informant comments that, although foreigners are often gaining grudging acceptance in some Andalucían flamenco circles, factors such as economics, ethnicity, and physical aesthetics still cause significant roadblocks.

3.7 External Influences on Sevillano Flamenco

There have been several recent developments external to the local Sevillano flamenco scene which have nonetheless affected the art complex. The effects range from employment opportunities (or lack thereof) to actual aesthetic shifts. These factors are tourism (as discussed in Chap. 2), the 2007 Revised Andalucían Statute, and flamenco's successful bid for UNESCO protective status.

Flamenco Conflicts with Tourism

Flamenco has a complex, love-hate relationship with tourism, specifically in more populous Andalucían cities, such as Sevilla. It exists across Spain in the form of tablaos geared (and priced) for tourists. These venues are advertised at tourist offices, hotels, transport hubs (bus and train stations), and essentially anywhere a tourist might be likely to find themselves. Aoyama captures this conflict in her work on consumption and globalisation, suggesting a global paradox in the cultural industry (including tourism), specifically with regards to flamenco. She observes that one side of the argument sees the need to maintain a 'place-based identity' and the other the need for regional cultures to establish export markets for survival. She further demonstrates that contemporary cultural exchange is not a unilateral global-invading-local scenario, but a process of consumers 'interpreting, appropriating, and adopting a cultural commodity in their own terms' (Aoyama 2007, p. 103). This validates my observations in the Sevillano flamenco scene. Tourism creates both opportunities and difficulties for local Sevillano professionals. The opportunities are primarily of a financial and employment nature. The difficulties are along the lines of aesthetics, transmission, and ideas about identity creation.

The paradox of the promotion of flamenco for national tourism is that Franco's inward-facing policies were known for austere Catholicism, hatred of liberal democracy, and anachronistic isolationism, as well as brutality (often resulting in 'disappearances') towards his political and moral enemies. This is especially significant when speaking about the flamenco scene because *Gitanos* and Andalucíans typically fell into these categories. For example, in 1943 the Guardia Civil (Franco's military police), passed a law specifically advocating the persecution of *Gitanos*, such as observing their dress and arresting them if they did not carry the proper horse-trading licences (Barbaret and García-España 1997, p. 177).

Andalucíans received similar levels of mistreatment, as the province, specifically urban centres such as Sevilla and Malaga, were strong supporters of the Republican government, which Franco overthrew using the province as an important battleground. Under Franco, political opposition and freedom of speech of any kind were harshly repressed. Due to its association with *Gitanos* and Andalucíans, Franco's secret police saw flamenco as a form of cultural dissent and political commentary. They repressed this, especially in lower-class neighbourhoods, by illegalising many concerts and *peñas*, as well as general flamenco singing in bars. Essentially, lighter, more frivolous forms of flamenco thrived as a diversionary art, primarily for tourists, whilst those that claimed it as their identity were persecuted (Washabaugh 1997, p. 53). During this time, that which was seen as authentically *Gitano* or Andalucían was condemned. Due to the rise of tourism (which included the marketing of flamenco) and its effect on city real estate prices, *Gitano* communities were expelled and thrown out of their neighbourhoods into slums outside of city limits, such as Sevilla's infamous Tres Mil development ('Flamenco's repression and resistance in Southern Spain', 2014).

While tourist interest plays a significant role in flamenco's widespread visibility in Spain, it also creates some points of friction both amongst those that like it and those that do not. Across Spain there is residual resentment towards flamenco amongst non-aficionados because of its association with *Franquismo* and the national identity they were assigned during his brutal dictatorship. This results in some consternation directed towards its usage as a representation to tourists. Within the aficionado community, many feel that since flamenco transmits a cultural heritage that reflects a history of Andalucían suffering, it should not be a form of light entertainment (Ortiz Nuevo 1985, pp. 14–16). There is also a belief that tablaos trivialise the art, reducing its cultural meaning to a girl in a frilly dress prancing about to an exotic dance. This contrasts with the *peña* which is not about objectifying music and dance, but about creating social space where flamenco can be celebrated, and creativity can flourish (Malefyt 1998, p. 65).

In speaking with my informants, the feeling towards tablaos was one of economic necessity but not necessarily artistic merit. The performance is changed for the tourist audience to one that is less dependent on the more sombre, reflective *palos*. It also tends to be more dance-focused, since most foreign visitors will not understand the lyrics or appreciate the raspy, free form singing style of *cante jondo*. Furthermore, there does not tend to be *jaleo* (audience participation) in tablaos due to lack of cultural knowledge amongst the punters. This omission alters the experience for both the audience and performers, who respond to the crowd energy. These artistic and atmospheric changes are felt by aficionados to cheapen the experience and negate its artistic merit.

On the other hand, there is certainly evidence that flamenco's survival, or at least its thriving, have been due in part to the tourist industry. Aoyama tells us that in the modern world arts and cultural complexes, such as flamenco, do not survive on their own—they are compelled to by a multitude of actors with 'broad and varying representations in various parts of the world' (Aoyama 2009, p. 85). According to her, flamenco thrives because of a combination of local interest, identity maintenance, tourists, and government subsidised artists at state-funded events (Aoyama 2009, p. 80).

There seems to be some evidence of this in that, by many accounts, flamenco had all but become obsolete, at least as a performance art, by the time the Spanish Civil War began. Many flamencologists maintain that without its promotion into the tourist realm, flamenco would have mostly died out (Heffner Hayes 2009, p. 40). In the early part of this century, flamenco tourism and its supporting industries have been worth about €120–150 million a year, which includes schools, tablaos bars, accommodation, events (festivals, *peñas*, theatre shows), and merchandise (recordings, clothes, etc.) (Aoyama 2009, p. 88). The largest concentration of the industry is in Sevilla, with a small enclave of guitar manufacturers residing in Granada. While a significant number of beach-motivated tourists attend flamenco shows, a certain percentage are also only there for flamenco—an estimated 626,000 in 2004, with overall tourism numbers rising from 7.9 m to 8.5 m since then (Aoyama 2009, p. 85). There is significant evidence that tourism plays a crucial role in the survival of flamenco, as mass tourism intensifies the interdependence between regional culture and economics. Even some local Sevillano researchers support this theory (Aoyama 2009, p. 96; J. Verguillos, personal communication, Feb. 11, 2014).

It seems clear, both through Aoyama's research and my correspondence with those working in the industry that, while tourism may change how flamenco is presented, it is crucial at least to the economic survival of those who practice it, if not to the art form itself. Despite the difficulty attaining work in a tablao, it is really the only steady flamenco work, especially in Andalucía. Because some local aficionados see it as an opportunity to gain work, it seems plausible that more Sevillanos are engaging with flamenco because of the tourist interest and, thus, the art form is strengthened.

Tourism has played such a decisive role in popularising and influencing flamenco, specifically by shifting the focus of the art complex from the *cante* to the dance, and in the styles that are performed (Aoyama 2007, p. 106). Tablaos and other tourist flamenco locales serve as an important place for transnational encounter. It is where foreigners develop their perceptions about flamenco, which will influence the expectations they have when attending shows in their own country. These experiences will thus influence how the art complex is interpreted on a glocal level. In Sevilla, tablaos will feel compelled to meet previously developed tourist expectations in order to attract punters. Abroad, glocal scenes will develop around perceptions of authenticity in Andalucía. Even foreign aficionados who know otherwise are forced to comply with these expectations in order to attract students and audiences. It is, therefore, imperative for Sevillano flamenco shows to recognise their role as transnational culture bearers and providers of quality standards, as what they exhibit will serve as a benchmark for the glocal flamenco culture.

Flamenco Politico

Although it may seem strange that politics could have a hand in affecting the flamenco scene, it has been an underlying trope throughout its history. Notably, there has seemingly been an increase of this influence in recent years. There are two primary developments in the last decade which have affected Andalucían flamenco, and by proxy, Sevilla: firstly its inclusion in the Revised Andalucían Statue of Autonomy, which included the creation of the Instituto Andaluz del Flamenco (IAF) and officially making flamenco a marker of regional identity (Machin-Autenrieth 2013, p. 133). The second political development was the successful bid by Spanish and Andalucían factions to have Flamenco acquire UNESCO Intangible heritage status.

Revised Andalucían Statute of 2007

Beginning in the 2000s, Spanish regional governments sought to revise their statutes of autonomy, which had been put in place in the early 1980s during the post-Franco transition to democracy (Machin-Autenrieth 2013, p. 135). This movement, in what political scientists Keating and Wilson refer to as the 'second wave of decentralisation' (Keating and Wilson 2009, p. 549), was a response to leading political party Partido Popular's centralist policies coupled with persistent identity issues overhanging from the 'first wave of devolution' (Machin-Autenrieth 2013, p. 135). Andalucía's revised statute was approved in 2003 and finalised in 2007 after both a regional and national parliamentary referendum and ratification.

The revised statute included competencies on a wide variety of issues, such as European integration and regionalised health care (Keating and Wilson 2009, p. 549). However, the statute also sought to partition out cultural difference and a regional identity which became a major controversial element (Machin-Autenrieth 2013, p. 136). The new statute sought to characterise Andalucía as *'hecho differential'*,[10] utilising their historical identity and unique culture (Keating and Wilson 2009, p. 550). Article 68 states that the Junta de Andalucía possesses 'exclusive competence [responsibility] regarding the knowledge, research, development, promotion, and diffusion of flamenco as a unique element of Andalusian

---

[10] 'Something different'—a marker of distinction from the rest of Spain, warranting autonomy.

cultural heritage' (as quoted in Machin-Autenrieth 2013, p. 134). Flamenco satisfied the quest for *hecho differential* because, although it had strong associations with Franco's tourism and nationalism campaign, it was felt that it still 'epitomised regional identity' and filled the role of distinctiveness.

To achieve the broad, sweeping goals of Article 68, the IAF was formed in 2005 as part of the *Consejería de Cultura*. Its responsibilities were for the conservation, promotion, and diffusion of flamenco inside and outside of the province. In an interview with flamencologist William Washabaugh, the body of IAF (previously known as AADF), Francisco Perjuo Serrano said that the institution is the "only official governmental institution charged with the responsibility for articulating music and politics by advancing an understanding of flamenco through investigation, study, teaching, and promotion" (Washabaugh 2012, p. 94). Andalucían flamencologist Cristina Cruces Roldán concurs that prior to IAF flamenco had little institutional support and was mainly a 'Fragmented system where foreign and provincial governments provided their own support' (Machin-Autenrieth 2013, p. 137). The significance of this will be discussed later in the chapter.

UNESCO Intangible Heritage

On the back of the Revised Andalucían Statute's inclusion of flamenco came the nomination (driven by the IAF) of Andalucían flamenco to UNESCO as an object of Intangible Cultural Heritage. The IAF emphasised that "flamenco reaches out to the world with its universal style while still serving as an Andalusian cultural marker" and was one of the primary drivers behind flamenco's nomination (Washabaugh 2012, p. 94). It was supported and accepted by the Andalucían parliament and regional governments of Extremadura and Murcia, as well as receiving backing from elements of the Spanish government, such as the Ministerio de Cultura and Consejo Nacional de Patrimonio. Similar to the Revised Statute, most of the rhetoric surrounding the nomination rested on flamenco as Andalucían in origin and radiating out to the rest of the world (Machin-Autenrieth 2013, p. 143). The IAF instituted an extensive publicity campaign called 'Flamenco Soy' which was intended to draw attention locally and internationally to the nomination and to drum up support. Its aim was to create emotional community support for what they viewed as Andalucía's most important cultural manifestation—flamenco. The campaign included promotional stands around commercial shopping areas where there was a support petition to be signed as well as merchandise. It also included a website with information about the campaign and an online petition, available in Spanish, English, French, and Japanese. In order to qualify for an Intangible Cultural Heritage designation, a nation-state must demonstrate a cultural practice/tradition that meets five key criteria:

1. To meet UNESCO's Definition of ICH, including one or more of the 5 domains
2. To contribute to the visibility of ICH as a marker of cultural dialogue, diversity, and human creativity
3. To safeguard the element
4. To show support from the community for the element
5. To inscribe the element in the state's own ICH inventories. (Machin-Autenrieth 2013, p. 146)

In terms of the first criterion, flamenco was demonstrated to have met four out of five of the ICH domains, in that it is a diverse tradition that "affords identity" to many communities and individuals, such as *Gitanos*, performers, and public and private institutions. The second criterion was met, by proclaiming that the nominating body would present flamenco at local, national, and international levels. To meet the third criterion, numerous safeguarding measures were proposed to be enacted by agencies such as the IAF. Some examples of these include maintaining a stable performance schedule and providing aid to the sector to continue conserving and promoting digitalisation (Machin-Autenrieth 2013, p. 147). Six key areas for further development were noted: Evaluation, protection, research, education, promotion (in the form of festivals and performances), and coordination. Promotion was the most important measure, with the file proposing €15 million to spend on promotion and support for flamenco events and festivals not only in Andalucía, but on an international scale (Machin-Autenrieth 2013, p. 148). Criterion four and five required the nomination to be supported by the communities and government involved, which was demonstrated by the petition. These criteria were all demonstrated in the UNESCO file and the nomination received a vast outpouring of support from flamenco performers and *peña*s across Spain, as well as the regional governments of Andalucía, Murcia, and Extremadura. It was accepted by UNESCO in November 2011.

Impact of Statute of Autonomy and UNESCO Designation: Outcries

Although these political moves come across as institutionalised, protective measures that hypothetically aim to shelter flamenco from the evils of globalisation and situate it as a defining feature of Andalucían identity, they have not been without their opposition. The Statute of Autonomy, for example, sparked major debates even before it was finalised regarding the use of flamenco for political purposes and issues of music ownership (Machin-Autenrieth 2013, p. 137). Additionally, there is a significant rumbling about how the UNESCO designation has actually harmed the artists who perform it and restricted the art form. There are three main groups from which these outcries have emanated: other regional governments in Spain (namely Extremadura and Murcia), non-flamenco Andalucíans, and regional flamenco performers.

Although flamenco is widely assumed to have its origins firmly ensconced in the Andalucían *Gitano* and *Payo* social life, there are other places where even the staunchest Andalucíanist will acknowledge has a hand in the creation of flamenco—namely Murcia and Extremadura. During the formation of the Revised Statute of Autonomy, there was an extensive outcry from members of these provincial governments regarding Andalucía's perceived appropriation of flamenco. Several key political figures of those regions even said publicly that flamenco's inclusion in the statute was unconstitutional. Extremadura's councillor for culture, Francisco Muñoz Ramirez, and President Juan Carlos Rodriguez Ibarra were particularly vocal in the press, arguing that Extremadura and Murcia were also critical in flamenco's geography with their specific palos, performance practices, and history. The feeling was that Andalucía was seeking exclusivity in flamenco (*Hoy* 2006). Murcia hosts one of the most prestigious annual *concursos* in La Unión—Festival Internacional del Cante de las Minas (Machin-Autenrieth 2013, p. 139). While Andaluz politicians and members of the IAF tried to quell these concerns by stating publicly that they only controlled Andalucían flamenco, detractors still viewed it as symbolic of Andalucía's monopoly on flamenco development and its close association with regional identity (Machin-Autenrieth 2013, p. 140).

Interestingly, even though the UNESCO declaration gave detractors of regionalisation more evidence to query how the Andaluz government could claim exclusivity over a deterritorialised tradition's development, the nomination was actually formally endorsed by the Extremadura and Murcia governments. Extremadura and Murcia are mentioned in the text of the nomination, but the monopoly Andalucía has over flamenco development is evident in that the majority of the safeguarding measures proposed apply to Andalucía institutions (Machin-Autenrieth 2013, p. 150). It seems that despite this, Extremadura and Murcia were happy to endorse the bid.

Regional Flamenco Professionals

Somewhat surprisingly, significant objections against both UNESCO and the Statute have been voiced to me by Andalucían flamenco professionals—that is, those that technically are the ones being protected. Although it got a fair amount of support from them at the time, many of the Sevilla-based professionals and aspiring performers reported negative feelings towards flamenco's use as a political tool, issues surrounding preferential treatment of big flamenco stars, and its institutionalisation. Tablao singer Aurora imparted:

> The *patrimonio*[11] is the worst enemy of flamenco. This definition, this political title that someone has given to flamenco is the worst enemy.

---

[11] In Andalucía, the UNESCO recognition is referred to as 'Patrimonio'.

> Because I think it is impossible to mix feelings and culture, artistic ways, impossible to mix with politicos, money, power, it is impossible. (Aurora, personal communication, Jan. 11, 2014)

Aurora's objections, which demonstrate a resistance to stylistic elements of art being dictated by governmental authorities, are shared by other flamenco performers and aficionados with whom I spoke.

The UNESCO declaration, as mentioned above, seemingly grants the guardianship of flamenco to the Andalucían government and allows them to make decisions regarding its safeguarding and definition. The idea of placing flamenco into a box of what is traditional and what is not is problematic. This is firstly because, even amongst Sevilla-based aficionados, the definition of what falls under the heading of 'flamenco' and, even more controversially, what constitutes 'good' or 'traditional' flamenco varies almost on an individual level. The controversy is only exacerbated when the debate includes someone from a *Gitano* background or from a different Andalucían city. Spain, despite being a hypothetically unified country, has cultures that vary almost on a city-by-city-by-town level. Local performers from Sevilla claim to be able to tell if a guitarist, for example, is from Jerez by miniscule stylistic variations in their playing—and often maintain that they are doing it wrong! Under those conditions it does not seem plausible or fair to generalise such a varied tradition. Secondly, relegating flamenco into a musical museum of sorts limits the artistic variations which naturally occur in any art form when a performer tries to differentiate their performance from that of another. Strict definitions restrict creativity and the artist's ability to exercise the individuality that is so integral to flamenco. Furthermore, flamenco developed over the last several centuries from the influences of the many different races who have passed through southern Spain, and thus to put it in a box is to break from tradition.

Objections to Political Motivations

Other objections came from feelings of doubt regarding the motivations of politicians. Many, including an informant who works for the regional Sevilla government, feel that the government's appropriation of flamenco was part of a political agenda. They felt that the government's desire to help and protect flamenco really fell under the category of uniting people under a regional identity without helping the artists. Aurora imparted:

> For me, Tenley, I think that this was a political maneuver. For us, flamenco has not changed since this Patrimonio Humanidad. I think it's all political fact, to earn points from the people. For me, is no changes. [Nor] for flamenco artists. I think if flamenco was an important culture for politicians there would not exist this tax of 21% [on artists]. For you, I think it is very important. You try to protect this thing and to make it easy for the rest of people to come to see your treasure. But here [in Andalucía] flamenco is nothing. Just the moment [for the politicians] to take a picture, go to the newspapers, say 'Oh, I'm the mayor of Sevilla; flamenco for us is the best'. A lot of artists and the mayor in the middle of the picture. Ok you have taken a picture, bye. Tomorrow there is no flamenco, so I [the mayor] don't want to make a picture. I want him to help flamenco, not me, FLAMENCO. But if you put tax of 21%, this is not a help. It is a knife to kill us. And I think this is a social or politician fact. […] I don't see any change since we became Patrimonio Humanidad. … I don't have a job now. I have 3 days here [in the tablao]. This is Patrimonio Humanidad for me. I started singing when I was 5 years, now I have 39. […] This is the worst moment in my flamenco life. Salvador, my boss, he depends on Ministerio Cultura, Ayuntimiento Andalucía. These people were supposed to pay him 2 years ago and he can't pay me. He can't because there is a lot of money owed €150 or something. So this is Patrimonio Humanidad. The money of this title, I don't know where it is. (Aurora, personal communication, Jan. 11, 2014)

Aurora's quote demonstrates frustration both with the general state of flamenco being institutionalised by people who do not really care about the art, but also with the governing body—Ministerio de Cultura—promising money to support artists and then not paying them. Because of this, fewer performances can happen. Additionally, Aurora refers to the 21% tax that the government places on performers, which is crippling them financially.

Sevilla-based flamencologist Juan Verguillos corroborates Aurora's observations that flamenco is closely linked with public administration these days. He informed me:

Most artists work for the government, because the festivals are organized by municipalities or regional governments […] as they are in crisis, all others are in crisis with them. […] [The IDF] is part of a political organization, and well, it is also in crisis like all other political institutions. Now they have no budget, practically, they cannot do much because they have limited resources, except engage in promoting it. (J. Verguillos, personal communication, Feb. 11, 2014)

It is worth noting here that there is an unfortunate and recent precedent for Spanish governmental entities supporting the art form but not the artists themselves—for example inflicting high taxes on performance income. This was a notable feature of the Franco regime. Throughout his reign, Franco's administration constructed flamenco into a symbol of national identity through extensive tourism campaigns, whilst simultaneously brutally persecuting poor Andalucían and *Gitano* artists who lived the art form. I find in my conversations with flamencos that this is never far from their thoughts about artistic regionalisation and national identity.

Flamenco Festival Promotion and Interference with Career Progression

There is some debate about the government's value even in promoting the art of flamenco. Civil servant and flamenco aficionado Patricio informed me:

I think sometimes what you get is a name, a little to somehow give some validity to the pricy ticket of a flamenco event—especially overseas. For example, recently in Russia there was a presentation of a flamenco festival and the IDF supported it. They participate in organizing the concerts. For example, if there are seven or eight concerts in a festival, they might pay for one of them, and in return, their logo is on the festival. (Patricio, personal communication, Jan. 9, 2014)

The real-life workings of these festivals and their relation to the IDF were described to me by several informants—including international touring performers Aurora and Catalina. They describe three levels of flamenco artists: first level of international flamenco stars, such as Estrella Morente, Miguel Poveda, and Paco de Lucía; a second level of regional flamenco performers, such as Aurora and Catalina; and a third level of up-and-coming performers. Before the IDF and Patrimonio Humanidad, local and regional flamenco festivals would hire performers from all three levels, giving those in the second and third tiers the chance for exposure, the opportunity to compete in *concursos*, and the capacity for moving up to higher levels (Catalina, personal communication, Mar. 19, 2013; Aurora, personal communication, Jan. 11, 2014). Since the Patrimonio Humanidad, this ladder system has changed. My informants report that the way festivals (regional, national, and international) work now is that they will contact the IDF for funding. The IDF will say 'ok, we will give you €40,000, but you have to spend €35,000 of that on Miguel Poveda, or someone else from that first level'. After spending that, the festival only has €5000 to spend on the other performers and can no longer afford any but the artists in the beginner's level. The festival rarely has a choice but to take this option because maybe their previous budget without IDF aid was €20,000.

Seemingly, the reason for the IDF taking this more elitist route is to put forth the best artists as the face of flamenco; their idea of the most representative of the culture. However, what these measures really accomplish is removing the rungs of the ladder that enable the second-level artists to climb to the first tier. Because of this, Aurora tells me:

> I think Patrimonio is good for these artists in the first level. For example, Estrella [Morente] is a social media star in flamenco more or less. Lady Gaga of flamenco. She of course is important for Patrimonio Humanidad. But these are the artists that the politicians show, but flamenco is more than these persons. I love Estrella and Miguel, Arcangel because they are fantastic. But there are a lot of artists and a lot of people in flamenco that need help. Estrella doesn't need nothing; her daddy was one of the best singers in the world. I do. [...] There are meteoric singers like Poveda and Estrella, but the culture is the same for all artists. So we in the second level [...] we are a lot of artists suffering to have recognition of the person that governed flamenco theatres. If I want to put on a performance in Teatro Central in Sevilla, I need a lot of papers, permissions, things that Estrella doesn't need. (Aurora, personal communication, Jan. 11, 2014)

This quote represents a conundrum created by institutionalisation and attempting to place flamenco into a sort of musical museum. Institutionalisation has resulted in a government organisation being granted the capacity to make decisions regarding aesthetic representation regarding an art form neither currently nor historically specific to the region. Furthermore, even within the region in question, opinions regarding authenticity and artistic value are contested on an almost individual basis.

The governmental entities that are creating such sweeping aesthetic designations are being viewed with a certain degree of hostility because they are not seen to be supporting the actual artists. Therefore, these definitions of authenticity are being viewed by actual practitioners with hostility. Further problems with institutionalisation arise because the government is in the midst of an economic crisis and cannot support the programmes it initially promised UNESCO, demonstrating the problem with making the continuance of an artistic tradition dependent on economics and political power. Finally, in an effort to support and demonstrate the 'best of flamenco' to the outside world, the IDF and the Andalucían government has seemingly granted preferential treatment to the bigger artists—described by some as the Flamenco Mafia—and have crippled the middle tier of performers. In so doing, the Statute of Autonomy and the UNESCO Patrimonio Humanidad, whilst raising flamenco awareness outside of the region, seemingly do more harm than good on a micro level.

Non-flamenco Andalucíans

During the period of time when the statute was being debated, there were people contesting the politicisation and nationalisation of flamenco at an Andalucían level. Machin-Autenrieth states that this indicates problems with the use of culture for the consolidation of regional identity (Machin-Autenrieth 2013, p. 139). This is somewhat problematic because, as mentioned earlier in this chapter, flamenco is an art that is actually only a form of identity to a minority of the population. Others may dance the odd Sevillana at a feria or a wedding, but rarely beyond that. In his virtual study of the Plataforma por Andalucía Oriental (PAO)—an online forum that discusses issues regarding regionalisation in Eastern Andalucía—there were many controversial reactions to the perceived regionalisation of flamenco (Machin-Autenrieth 2015, p. 14). Most objections focus on a lack of self-identity with flamenco, thus feeling it should not be part of a unified Andalucían identity. Many merely rejected flamenco development on an institutional level, viewing it as regional nationalism and equating it to Franco's often unpopular programme of Spanish Nationalism (*Franquismo*) (Machin-Autenrieth 2015, p. 15).

Objections are in part along the lines of the government spending millions of Euros to promote flamenco during a prolonged economic crisis (Machin-Autenrieth 2015, p. 16). Other questions of institutionalisation arose around how Andaluz government could presume to claim exclusivity over the development of a Spanish, and now universal, tradition. One PAO member is quoted to have written 'Flamenco belongs to its aficionados, not governmental institutions'. Prominent flamencologist Gerhard Steingress problematises government interference with flamenco, emphasising that it is a universal art form that can transcend Andalucían regionalism. He surmises that 'while it seems evident that the majority of the population considers it [flamenco] to be a consistent element of the Andalusian cultural system, this does not necessarily mean that they identify with it or consider it a "marker" of their identity as Andalusians' (Steingress and Baltanás 2002, p. 51). These objections are echoed by many Sevillano non-flamencos that I have interviewed in the course of my research. For example, an informant, Manuel, who is a Sevillano in his late twenties imparted:

> I like to have flamenco in Sevilla. But my musical taste, my daily music is rock, pop, blues, rap. […] I do not hear flamenco in my house. […] it's like bullfighting. I personally find it repulsive. I do not like it, but it is typical of my country. Something old that still exists. (X. Manuel, personal communication, Feb. 23, 2014)

This quote emphasises the paradoxical relationship that Sevillanos seem to have with flamenco—it is something many believe is from their culture, but not personally relevant to them so should not be institutionalised. It is for these reasons that many non-flamenco Sevillanos (and Andalucíans) have launched into outcries against both the art form's usage in the Statute of Autonomy and as a UNESCO protectorate.

3.8 Conclusions

This chapter has provided a description of some of the complex identities which make up the Sevilla flamenco scene. In doing this, I have described the basic structure, performance locations and occasions, and difficulties for those who practice it. These depictions often differ from the assumptions of those not directly associated with the scene. The chapter also introduces the ex-pat flamenco community and the complex relationship it has with the local Sevilla scene. These individuals are often assumed to not be able to understand flamenco properly by local aficionados. However, foreign interest is an economic necessity, in some respect, for the maintenance of Sevillano flamenco. Andalucían artists often reach towards foreigners for employment opportunities through tablaos, overseas workshops, and short tours abroad. Finally, I discussed several external influences which affect the current flamenco scene, which take the form of touristic and political factors. This dissection of the Sevilla scene is important when attempting to understand the culture that foreign flamencos experience. The flamenco experience they have in Sevilla has significant bearing on the culture that they then strive to emulate when they travel to their home countries. Chapter 5 discusses this phenomenon further with regards to Flamenca Britannica—the UK flamenco scene.

References

Actividades. (n.d.). *La Federación Provincial de Sevilla de Entidades Flamencas.* Retrieved from https://www.sevillafederacionflamenca.com/

Aoyama, Y. (2007). The Role of Consumption and Globalisation in a Cultural Industry. *Geoforum, 38*, 103–113.

Aoyama, Y. (2009). Artists, Tourists, and the State: Cultural Tourism and the Flamenco Industry in Andalusia, Spain. *International Journal of Urban and Regional Research, 33*(1), 80–104.

Barbaret, R., & García-España, E. (1997). Minorities, Crime, and Criminal Justice in Spain. In I. H. Marshall (Ed.), *Minorities, Migrants, and Crime: Diversity and Similarity Across Europe and the United States* (pp. 175–197). Thousand Oaks: Sage Publications.

Bartal, Y. (2014). *Flamenco's Repression and Resistance in Southern Spain.* Retrieved from http://www.truth-out.org/news/item/27946-flamenco-under-attack

Cristina Heeren Foundation. (2014). Retrieved from http://www.flamenco-heeren.com/en/

Extremadura critica que Andalucía quiera la exclusividad del flamenco. (2006, June 8). *Hoy.* Retrieved from http://www.hoy.es/pg060608/actualidad/regional/200606/08/estatuto-andalucia-flamenco.html

Heffner Hayes, M. (2009). *Flamenco: Conflicting Histories of the Dance.* Jefferson: McFarland & Company, Inc.

Keating, M., & Wilson, A. (2009). Renegotiating the State of Autonomies: Statute Reform and Multi-level Politics in Spain. *West European Politics, 32*(3), 536–558.

Machin-Autenrieth, M. (2013). *Andalucía Flamenca: Music, Regionalism and Identity in Southern Spain.* Unpublished Doctoral Thesis, University of Cardiff, Wales.

Machin-Autenrieth, M. (2015). Flamenco ¿Algo Nuestro? (¿Something of Ours?): Music, Regionalism and Political Geography in Andalusia, Spain. *Ethnomusicology Forum, 24*(1), 4–27.

Malefyt, T. D. (1998). "Inside" and "Outside" Spanish Flamenco: Gender Constructions in Andalusian Concepts of Flamenco Tradition. *Anthropological Quarterly, 71*(2), 63–73.

Ortiz Nuevo, J. L. (1985). *Pensamiento político en el cante flamenco.* Sevilla: Editoriales Andaluzas Unidas.

Pohren, D. E. (1962). *The Art of Flamenco.* Jerez de la Frontera: Editorial Jerez Industrial.

Rice, T. (1994). *May It Fill Your Soul: Experiencing Bulgarian Music.* Chicago: University of Chicago Press.

Steingress, G., & Baltanás, E. (2002). El Flamenco como Patrimonio Cultural o una Construcción Artificial más de la Identidad Andaluza. *Revista Andaluza de Ciencias Sociales, 1*, 43–64.

Washabaugh, W. (1997). Flamenco Music and Documentary. *Ethnomusicology, 41*(1), 51–67.

Washabaugh, W. (2012). *Flamenco Music and National Identity in Spain.* Surrey: Ashgate Publishing.

4

Madrid: The Consummate Professional Scene

Perhaps one of my most memorable flamenco experiences occurred when a friend of mine, Paco, attended a flamenco performance in a small bar called La Candela. After the show, the manager, Octavio, whom we had befriended, invited us into the basement which, as it turned out, was only for invited guests. It was unlike any VIP lounge I had ever been to before and, in fact, was an underground cave with whitewashed stone walls, a dirty stone floor, stone benches, and a few rickety tables. Surrounded by a thin veil of cigarette smoke (illegal indoors in Spain), we sat down with our drinks and gradually a few others began to trickle into the little room. Most of the clientele, I later found out, were *Gitanos* stopping by after working in the tablaos. Everyone sat around chatting, drinking, and smoking (a habit which, despite a nationwide ban, was clearly allowed in this part of the venue) and then someone started lightly clapping *palmas*. The room was soon packed with patrons, who had been invited into the private cave by Octavio. Soon, the *Gitano* next to me began to sing, while people clapped a *bulerías* rhythm or knuckle-tapped on the table. The rest of the group in the small grotto moved into a rough circle where the first singer had been sitting, and some paid attention while others continued their quiet conversations.

© The Author(s) 2020
T. Martin, *Transnational Flamenco*, Leisure Studies in a Global Era,
https://doi.org/10.1007/978-3-030-37199-9_4

After the singer stopped, there were cheers from the onlookers but the *palmas* continued. Soon another *Gitano* picked up the musical mantle and began another *letra* of *bulerías*. Paco and I began chatting with the first singer, whose name was Miguel, and was about our age. Paco mentioned that he was a flamenco guitarist and soon one of the bar staff went off to fetch a guitar. He returned with a beat-up, five-stringed instrument, which Paco accepted and began to quietly pluck. One of the *Gitanos* came over to Paco and asked if he could play a *soléa*. The *cantaor* sang a few *letra* and then someone else went back to singing *bulerías*, while Paco expertly matched his pitch modulations and shifting rhythmic pattern. The *Gitano* that Paco had played for came over and told Paco that he felt some rhythms had been misinterpreted and demonstrated various corrections he should make. All the while the music and clapping persisted. There was a loose structure to the proceedings, with singers swapping *letra* whilst others clapped, tapped, or shouted encouragement. In between songs, Paco would attempt to retune the battered guitar, fruitlessly pleading with the five strings to stay in pitch as the room became increasingly humid. The most notable characteristic was that the performance appeared largely improvised with lyrics sung on the spot in the style of, for the most part, a *bulerías palo*.

I sat slightly outside of the circle, looking in, sipping my *vino tinto*, clapping palmas, and rapping a cajón pattern on the table with my knuckles (an action referred to as *a golpe*). Periodically, I would shout *jaleo* with the rest of the non-singing Gypsies. I hadn't wanted to interrupt the spell of the musicians and singers. I was absorbed by the raw *duende*[1] of this *juerga*, which was pure improvisation, often lacking in the correct compás, but full of enthusiasm and passion from both performers and audience—an often-blurred line in this setting. I felt lucky to be in the setting of a private flamenco jam session. An outsider, along with Paco (who had been invited down for the first time that evening) allowed in by expressing a love of flamenco and displaying enough knowledge to appreciate the *juerga*. The impromptu *peña* lasted well into the next morning, with a constant flow of individuals wanting to get up and improvise. As I left the grotto, saying farewell to Paco and my new friends,

---

[1] A term for a heightened state of emotion or connection with the music being performed/danced.

Fig. 4.1   Underground at Candela

one of the younger *Gitanos* who I had spoken with earlier and explained my research turned to me and said 'Chica, if you seriously want to learn about flamenco, you're going to have to move a little bit closer, Sit inside the circle.' Unlike in Sevilla, some aspects of a foreigner 'sitting inside the circle' of flamenco are easier in Candela (Fig. 4.1).

Candela—a small but historically significant flamenco bar in Madrid's Barrio Lavapiés. My brief encounter with Candela's *juerga* was truly a fortunate experience because, while these impromptu jam sessions are not uncommon in the taverns and *peñas* in Andalucía, they are something of an anomaly in Madrid. Madrid, the capital city of Spain, is located in central Spain, approximately 300 km from the Andalucían border. Flamenco is not a native tradition in Madrid and, on the whole, residents do not feel a particular affinity to it. However, its central location and status as a cosmopolitan capital city have, since the mid-nineteenth century, turned it into an important surrogate home for flamenco culture. It is now the meeting place for Spanish professionals from across the country, as well as students from around the world and those associated with the recording industry. Most of the biggest flamenco stars, as well as aspiring professionals, make their home, at least

part-time, in Madrid because of access to increased performance opportunities, funding, other performers, better recording studios, and Spain's
biggest international airport. Unlike the scene in Sevilla, Madrid flamenco enjoys an almost purely professional existence. Its history is one of
a commercialised rendition of flamenco—where the art is played primarily in public, most of the time for money. This is in direct contrast with
Sevilla and other Andalucían locales, where the art originated as an
inward-facing culture—one practiced informally amongst family and
friends in private, at festivals, and at *peñas*. Of course, as mentioned earlier, these commercial performances also exist now in Andalucía (and all
over Spain). Madrid lacks this private version of flamenco. Similar to
Sevilla, Madrid does boast a large foreign flamenco student population,
with a large portion of them studying at the esteemed flamenco school,
Amor de Dios. Foreign students interact with Spanish professionals both
as students and, from time-to-time, as fellow performers.

This chapter will demonstrate Madrid's unique position as a city where
professional flamencos from all over the country and for various reasons
come to teach (primarily foreign students), perform, record, and develop
creative projects which might not be possible in Andalucía for reasons
including resources and marketability. Their activities create a significant
portion of flamenco's interaction with the global community through
recordings distributed, performers sent abroad, and students who learn in
Madrid and then go back home to transmit their knowledge. As a result
of these global interactions, Madrid represents a crucial point of study
when considering foreign perceptions of flamenco and what is transmitted in its global journey. Ultimately this chapter will explore the historical
and current dynamics of the Madrid flamenco scene, foreign interactions
with it, and how this impacts what ex-pat flamenco students carry back
to their home countries with them.

4.1   Flamenco Madrileño: Una Historia

There is a relative lack of scholarship devoted to the Madrid flamenco
scene, with many key histories of the genre leaving it out altogether. In
the 'popular imaginary', Andalucía is the homeland and the only

important aspect of flamenco's development. One possible reason for this is that, while flamenco in Andalucía emerged in a private, familial context, it developed almost entirely in a public, performative and commercial context in Madrid (Washabaugh 1996). In fact, there is little evidence of flamenco existing in a private setting in the capital (Hernandez Girbal 1933, p. 70). The commercialisation aspects of the art complex are generally treated as impure and insignificant in comparison to the private version, which is perceived as more authentic. Ironically, it is this commercialisation that creates traces of flamenco, through mentions in print media, legislation, and advertisements, which enables a somewhat clearer picture in Madrid than in Andalucía where the art complex largely was an oral tradition for most of its formative years. Despite the lack of attention paid by scholarly researchers, flamenco's history is closely tied to its reception and evolution in Madrid.

Internal Andalucían Migration

While it is unclear when exactly flamenco arrived in Madrid, it is likely that it stemmed from the mass internal migrations of Andalucíans (as well as other regional residents) to Madrid in the 1840s and 1850s. This occurred as a result of the 1836 and 1850 disentailments, where land expropriated from the church was made public and put up for auction (Cruces Roldán 2003, p. 52). This resulted in a mass exodus from rural regions to the cities, with Madrid receiving the highest proportion—up to 1500 people a day by 1850 (Carballo et al. 2008, p. 43). Madrid's population grew from 200,000 in 1830 to 500,000 in 1900, largely a product of this internal immigration boom (Llano 2018, p. 34). Andalucíans represented only 8% of rural immigration, but they provoked noticeable cultural changes which made them the focal point of an increased moral panic that took place in the city in the latter half of the nineteenth century. Flamenco, because of its distinctive musical and aesthetic features became synonymous with rural immigrants' cultural difference (not just Andalucíans) to concerned Madrileños (Llano 2018, p. 24). The first specific use of the term 'flamenco' in reference to the art complex, at least in the capital, occurred in a newspaper in 1853—prior to this, it had primarily been associated with Gitanos and the lower classes, which were in many ways glorified by the middle classes (Machin-Autenrieth 2017, p. 22). This marked the transition of flamenco from the private to the public realm.

The Restoration Era (1874–1931)

Spain's Restoration Era (1874–1931), marking the return of the Bourbon kings to the throne, was a significant period for the development of flamenco, specifically in Madrid which, due to the immigration and population boom, was fast becoming a centre of culture. This period is considered one of the most artistically significant in Spanish history, which featured substantial expansion of popular culture. This in part took on *costumbrismo* features—an idealistic combination of folkloric and popular traditions from Spain's regions, such as Andalucía (Harney 2006, pp. 156–157). The Restoration period also featured the rise of *cafes cantantes*—a key feature of what is considered the 'Golden Age' of Flamenco (Llano 2018, p. 20). These were performance venues often with multiple stages which featured a variety of types of music styles ranging from chamber music to flamenco. The first one of these opened in Madrid in 1867—just after the railway connection between Andalucía and the capital had been completed (Escribano 1990, p. 45). While this type of performance space existed in Andalucía and a few other major cities in Spain, Madrid boasted the highest number of *cafes cantantes* (Álvarez 2007, p. 37) and by the 1880s flamenco was among Madrid's most popular forms of entertainment. There are abundant references, both in literature and in periodicals, regarding *cafes cantantes* (and other performance venues) in Madrid, indicating the capital's prominence in the development of commercial flamenco as popular culture in the nineteenth century (Washabaugh 1996, p. 22).

Among the reason that *cafes cantantes* are significant is that they were, most likely, the first venues to actually put flamenco—a genre typically on the streets or in private—on a stage (Washabaugh 1996, p. 42). This transition came with aesthetic changes, including more refinement in timbre and less controversial lyrics—a cleansing that made them more palatable to middle-class audiences. It also came with a change in the ambience of flamenco performance as well. Testimonials indicate that everyone at a pre-café cantante flamenco event was an active contributor; however, when the art complex moved to a stage it became a spectacle watched by a paying audience, which coincidentally increased its accessibility to the uninitiated and its popularity (Washabaugh 1996, p. 42). This method of presentation both celebrated the street-music version of flamenco and suppressed some of the intent and passion behind it, whilst overshadowing the non-professional Andalucían rendition of the art complex.

The advent of the *cafes cantantes* marked a turning point for flamenco where the *cantaor* became a paid position, most of the time by wealthy classes, who hired them to perform at their fiestas, *juergas,* or other cafés (Belarde and Navarro 1985, p. 133). Uniquely, these were patrons who typically had limited or no pre-existing cultural connection to flamenco. The flamenco performances typically took place in the main hall of the *cafes cantantes,* many of which could hold up to 1000 people. The cafés were a place where audiences from across the social class spectrum mingled, although divides still occurred due to the better seats being more expensive (Llano 2018, p. 55). After the conclusion of the show, wealthier patrons would continue the party by holding juergas in the back rooms (or *reservados*) of the café (Ortiz Nuevo 1975, p. 219). *Juergas* were all night private parties hosted by a wealthy *señorito*[2] which featured flamenco, abundant (often free) alcohol, and sometimes prostitutes (Mitchell 1994, pp. 42–44). Some *señoritos* became known as professional *juergistas* for the regularity and notoriety of their *reservado* parties. The typical *juerga* included a *señorito* (who sponsored the event), a *cantaor*, *tocaor*, and various friends and followers. Oftentimes particular *cantaores* would 'gather a *peña*'—consistent following of aficionados—and these would become regular attendees at *juergas* that particular singer performed at—an example of this are the *peñas* of Antonio Chacón and Juan Breva, both of which are still in existence in Jeréz and Malaga respectively (Llano 2018, p. 54). *Juergas* were not exclusive to Madrid but

---

[2] Sons of wealthy landowners who moved to Madrid in the mid-nineteenth century when cafés and taverns were on the rise and were notorious for a debaucherous lifestyle.

gained particular notoriety there, in part because of the presence of national newspapers in the city, which spread rumours of scandals on a nationwide level. While the *juergas* were private events and largely devoid of journalists in attendance, testimonies from attendees contributed to the bad reputation of these events. For example, Chacón's *peña* gained a reputation for their longevity and excessive debauchery (Álvarez 2007) while Juan Breva's followers acquired the nickname 'the knights of Breva' because of their tendency to carry weapons and insight violence (Llano 2018, p. 54). This is fairly significant for flamenco's reputation moving forward, as its association with these paid *juergas* placed it in the company of a variety of social ills which has shaped stereotypes about the culture since that time (Cruces Roldán 2002, p. 84). Other attendees reported that *cantaores* refused start performing until they were very drunk (Blas Vega 1990, pp. 91–92). The infamy of these events prompted an increase in news of 'flamenco-related crimes' in local and national press, the earliest of these journalistic attacks occurring in the late 1880s. Newspaper sources suggested that *juergas* led to public disorders and reported on excessive drinking, weapons, and prostitutes (Llano 2018, p. 54). The earliest examples of journalistic attacks on the *cafés* and associated *juergas* were in the late 1880s, with publications like *El Motín* reporting them as 'permanent focuses of infection where young people get physically unnerved and morally debased' ('Frutos de la Restauración' 1888). These journalistic attacks would continue until the early 1920s, in conjunction with the continued expansion of Madrid's popular culture, contributed significantly to the rise of a social phenomenon known as *flamenquismo* (Llano 2018, p. 20).

Flamenquismo

The increase of flamenco in Madrid in the latter half of the nineteenth century caused an increase is social disquiet and became associated with alcohol abuse and violence. Social critics, in their publications, referred to it as 'the expression of a deviant lifestyle' which they began to associate with *flamenquismo* towards the end of the 1880s (Urbano 1995). Essentially, *flamenquismo* referred to a collection of cultural aspects associated with Andalucía, as well as *gitano* and flamenco culture; however, by the turn of the century the term expanded to refer to a variety of perceived social problems (not always related to flamenco) and degeneration that critics perceived in Spanish society (Llano 2018, p. 28). The allegations of anti-*flamenquismos* implied that flamenco was inextricably linked to a criminal underworld and incurable moral degradation, which in turn influenced public perception and shaped the music culture's development (Mitchell 1994). While *flamenquismo* began as a term to describe particular flamenco and Andalucían styles of dress and lifestyle, the connotations behind the term, particularly as it was utilised by late nineteenth-/early twentieth-century social critics, soon became negative. The opposition to *flamenquismo* was heavily associated with Andalucían immigrants.

The antagonism towards flamenco and *flamenquismo* was stoked by numerous journalists and criminologists. For example, *La Epóca*, in an 1888 article, characterised *flamenquismo* as a national moral crisis and called for a ban on 'juergas that are accompanied by singing and by the Gypsy contortions of *bailoras*' ('La Plaga Flamenca' 1888). These criticisms were echoed by many other newspapers, some of which seemed particularly concerned with *flamenquismo*'s ability to cross social classes, and how that can blur morals and identities. They seemed particularly concerned with flamenco's rural influences on Madrid and how that might obstruct modernisation (Llano 2018, p. 23). Criminologists, most notably Salillas in his document *Hampa*, reiterated stereotypes about *gitanos* and sought to link flamenco with criminal underworlds and sinful decadence. He also echoed the concern that *flamenquismo*'s lack of respect for social boundaries was a destabilising threat to the class system (Llano 2018, p. 42). The journalistic critiques are likely an extension of *mala vida* literature (the first of which was Cervantes' *La Gitanilla* in 1613) which consisted of stereotypical representations of the Gypsy in literary and theatrical realms (Llano 2018, p. 38).

The criticism of flamenco and *flamenquismo* during this time period also sparked impassioned defences of the art complex and of Andalucía, with claims that it was misrepresented. Most notably this is seen in the work of the 'father of flamencology', Antonio Machado y Álvarez (otherwise known as Demófilo), whose *Coleccion de Cantes Flamencos* (1881) marked the first attempt to collect and classify flamenco song. Demófilo stated that 'music derives its identity from the land in which it is born, and that it loses its supposed authenticity as the communities that perform it migrate elsewhere', implying vulgarity and corruption in Madrid's flamenco as opposed to the purity in Andalucía (Llano 2018, p. 28).

The people attracted to flamenquismo far outnumbered those that criticised it, although the latter had better access to the press. This is evidenced by the continued popularity of *cafes cantantes, juergas,* and flamenco itself throughout the late nineteenth and early twentieth centuries. Despite, or perhaps because of, this popularity, authorities began to take legal measures to control crime in Madrid, many of which took direct aim at flamenco-hosting establishments. Connections (real and fabricated) were able to grow freely due to the city having the largest number of *cafes cantantes* in the country (16) (Álvarez 2007, p. 37). As these associations grew, Madrid's authorities deduced that specific legislation and police control were necessary to control criminal activity rampant in the city's nightlife. Beginning in the 1880s, a series of regulations were passed aimed at limiting the activities and operating hours of taverns and cafés, which also had the effect of limiting flamenco performances (Llano 2018, p. 48). The reasoning for these limitations was based on the idea that sexy waitresses, flamenco, prostitutes, and heavy drinking triggered social disorder. Owners of these establishments retaliated by holding protests and forming unions, but ultimately found ways to dodge police through legal ambiguities and bribery (Llano 2018, p. 58).

In late 1900 and early 1901, Madrid's governor Antonio Barroso created legislation that more specifically targeted flamenco with statutes that forbade singing, dancing, and gambling, as well as placing damaging restrictions on café licences. He was likely under the influence of the anti-flamenquismo campaign, which was particularly strong at the turn of the century. There were rapid and vehement protests from artists and by late 1901, Barroso amended his decree to permit singing and dancing under approved conditions, but all noise had to cease by 2 am. *Juergas* in the *reservados* were completely banned in the early morning hours (Llano 2018, p. 63). Late night *juergas* continued anyway which prompted more stringent regulations on Madrid's nightlife establishments in the following decade. Those that directly harmed flamenco included a temporary closure of *cafes cantantes* in 1908 and a ban on *reservados* in 1909 (Escribano 1990, p. 82). Protests from artists, owners, and aficionados alike eventually prompted a loosening of these regulations in 1911, but this was in part because crime had gone down as a result of legislation aimed at drinking habits.

Post-World War I

After World War I, 'Flamenquismo', once considered disdainful, grew to become viewed as the basis for a lucrative entertainment industry, which drew a mixture of praise (from entrepreneurs, government ministers, and tourists) and revulsion (from aficionados) (Llano 2018, p. 16). This dichotomy would continue to the present day. Two developments in particular both demonstrate flamenco's move into industry status and the conflict between aficionados and those that would use flamenco as a commercial tool. These occurrences, which happened concurrently to some extent, were: *ópera flamenca* and the *Concurso de 1922*.

Ópera Flamenca

The first of these developments to materialise was *ópera flamenco*, which essentially was a cross between flamenco, French cabaret, and jazz (Washabaugh 1996, pp. 43–45). While it is difficult to pinpoint an exact date for its materialisation, Escribano (1990) suggests that it evolved from an 1893 theatre show in Madrid's Teatro Barbieri. It was a variety show that included performances of *cuplés*[3] by German singer Augusta Berges and, in later shows, Madrilena Pilar Cohen (Escribano 1990, p. 59). Flamenco was introduced to this variety show most notably by Amalia Molina and Pastora Monje Imperio, with its singing style taking inspiration from French cabaret performances (Washabaugh 1996, p. 44). Throughout the first few decades of the Twentieth Century, *ópera flamenca* developed into an excessively presented production with

---

[3] *Cuplé*: 'a complex hybrid of commercial flamenco, jazz, French cabaret, earlier Spanish theatrical genres with music, such as the zarzuela and tonadilla, and Latin American rhythms' (Baliñas 1999).

flamenco performances accompanied by orchestras and oftentimes interposed with jugglers and magicians (Washabaugh 1996, p. 43). The shows were relatively incongruous, with little connection between each musical or theatrical number, beyond the emphasis on flamenco (Lavaur 1976).

Ópera flamenca shows further altered 'authentic' flamenco in order to attract a broader audience to the spectacle. These theatre shows also increased their popularity by creating a carnivalesque atmosphere, attracting audiences who were not just watchers but part of the performance, eroding the boundary between spectator and performer (Washabaugh 1996, p. 44). *Ópera flamenco* was exceptionally popular with Madrid's public but wholly reviled by flamenco aficionados, whose writings began to combat the previous negative associations with *flamenquismo* (Llano 2018, p. 92). Somehow it was easier for pro-flamenco journalists to defend flamenco as an element of Spanish identity against the perceived foreign threat of French-influenced *ópera flamenca*. Notable amongst these critics of foreign influence were composer Manuel de Falla and poet Federico García Lorca, whose revulsion of *ópera flamenca* prompted them to organise arguably the most influential event in flamenco history: the 1922 Concurso del Cante Jondo in Granada (Llano 2018, p. 92).

1922 Concurso del Cante Jondo

The 1922 Concurso del Cante Jondo was proposed and organised by intellectuals, led by Falla and Lorca. This was essentially meant as a competition between amateur flamenco *cantaores* performing a capella *cante jondo*, which the organiser saw was the root of flamenco and Spanish identity. Falla and Lorca strove to draw a distinction between what they saw as a bastardised commercial flamenco (which was associated with *flamenquismo*) and the more pure *cante jondo*—which they portrayed as 'rural, ancestral, Andalusian, and mostly Gypsy' (Llano 2018, p. 78). They considered *cante jondo* to be a forerunner to Andalucían song and flamenco to be a corrupted form of *cante jondo* (Llano 2018, p. 84). The *Concurso*'s organisers purported that *cante jondo* had been spared commercial usage in taverns and the negative effects of urbanisation, and that where flamenco and flamenquismo had an inherently criminal nature, *cante jondo* was aesthetically pure and morally regenerative (Llano 2018, p. 97). Occurring in the midst of *ópera flamenca's* heyday, the *Concurso* was intended to be a celebration of authentic culture standing in opposition to the opulence of commercial flamenco in the theatre or the earlier *cafes cantantes* (Washabaugh 1996, p. 45). The competition displayed a similar aversion to flamenquismo as social critics in Madrid had done up until World War I—a critique that was aimed at Andalucían culture and migrants as a whole (Llano 2018, p. 79).

Significantly, the *Concurso* was meant as a defence against *ópera flamenca* and foreign cultural invasion. This was a reaction to the rapid modernisation that was occurring in early 1920s Madrid. The city was in a period of economic prosperity and cultural transformation, with European culture and jazz becoming increasingly popular. The revival of a perceived 'authentic' flamenco—in the form of *cante jondo*—to concerned traditionalists seemed like an antidote to the foreign musics, *flamenquismo*, and *ópera flamenca*. National newspapers began to hype the event months in advance, which served to further make a case for flamenco and *cante jondo* as a symbol of Spanish identity, as well as situating Madrid (as the home of national newspapers) as an arbiter of national cultural value (Llano 2018, p. 80). There were a series of journalistic debates between the *Concurso* organisers defending the value of *cante jondo* and others who lumped it in with *flamenquismo* and commercial flamenco. These discrepancies came in part because non-aficionados had some confusion about the difference between *cante jondo* and flamenco (Llano 2018, p. 82). There was also concern, particularly from Andalucían journalists, that the competition would only reinforce negative stereotypes about the art complex and the province.

The *Concurso del Cante Jondo* took place on June 13–14, 1922, against the picturesque backdrop of Granada's Alhambra Palace. The jury was made up with renowned performers of the time, including Antonio Chacón, Pastora Pavón (La Nina de los Peines), Manuel Torre, Juana la Macarrona, and Andrés Segovia. They were to compete in a variety of *cante jondo palos* categories including (1) *Siguiriyas gitanas*; (2) *Serranas, Polos, Canas, Soleares*; and (3) *Martinetes-carcelaras, Tónas, Livianas, Saetas Viejas*—which were *cantes a palos secos*, and therefore unaccompanied. They were forbidden from performing *Malaguenas, Granainas, Peteneras,*

Sevillañas, *Rondenas*, and other *palos* which were not considered old enough or emotionally intense (de Falla 1950). The competition was won by 72-year-old Diego Bermudez (El Tenazas) and 12-year-old Manolo Oretega (El Caracol). The competition received exceptional reviews from journalists and attendees alike.

The competition was not meant purely for Andalucían competitors or audiences. Among the invited guests to the *Concurso* were foreign intellectuals, such as John Brande Trend, a Cambridge University Spanish professor (Llano 2018, p. 85). Interestingly, the reaction to these international attendees from journalists would precede arguments made against foreign performers demonstrated in my ethnographic research. Several newspaper articles in the wake of the *Concurso* made a point of commenting on their presence, implying that foreign audience members could not truly enjoy the competition beyond a superficial level because they didn't possess the cultural background to differentiate between *cante jondo* and *flamenquismo* (Llano 2018, p. 86). Mora Guarnido, a journalist who supported the competition, condescendingly reported "for the foreigners who have come to the competition, and who do not have any pressure or predisposition to feel anti-flamenquistas, the celebration has been beautiful and transcendental" (Mora Guarnido 1922). In underestimating the foreigner's ability to fully engage with the *Concurso*, columnists such as Mora Guarnido shifted the insider/outside division from aficionado/non-aficionado to Spanish/foreigner, inadvertently strengthening the nationalist flamenco narrative. It is important to note that neither Falla nor Lorca explicitly condoned the designation of insiders being Andalucían or Spanish and outsiders being foreign, as that would undermine their message of flamenco's universal cultural value (Llano 2018, p. 86).

Despite the success of the *Concurso*, it seems that much of the point of differentiating commercial flamenco from *cante jondo* did not get across in Madrid. Commercial flamenco in the form of *ópera flamenca* and other theatre shows continued to be popular. A prime example of this lack of understanding was the hiring of El Caracol—one of the competition winners—by Agencia Teatral in Madrid to simply show audiences his certificate signed by *cantaor* Antonio Chacón ('Diversiones publicas' 1922). Additionally, a few months after the Granada competition,

Madrid's Club Parisiana replicated the event by hiring El Caracol and several of the judged performers from the *Concurso*. The event was entitled 'La Fiesta del Cante Jondo'—falling back on old flamenco stereotypes instead of displaying the cultural introspection intended by the *Concurso* (Llano 2018, p. 90). Similar to the still popular *ópera flamenca*, the event was structured like the varieties spectacles so reviled by Falla and Lorca. This is evidence that the *Concurso* clearly did not change the practice of flamenco, as a primarily commercial art, in Madrid, even in the immediate aftermath of the event.

The competition succeeded in bringing aspects of *cante jondo* into the realm of popular culture, as well as setting stylistic parameters that generations of aspiring *cantaores* would view as authoritative, in terms of how particular styles should be performed. It also positively influenced the overall public view of the art complex, as intended. By the mid-1920s, flamenco performance venues were no longer viewed as dens of iniquity, but simply as venues for consuming popular culture. Even venues which were notorious for rowdy *juergas* in the early 1900s, such as Villa Rosa, were viewed with a sense of nostalgia (Blas Vega 2006, p. 143). While the *Concurso* managed to disrupt the commercialism that was taking over flamenco, it also marked the beginnings of a folk culture becoming oppressive (Washabaugh 1996, p. 46). It not only set a barometer of authenticity for flamenco, but also set the scene for flamenco's use as a national signifier and tool of cultural oppression by the Franco regime.

The Impact of the Franco Regime in Madrid Flamenco

Developments in Flamenco, especially in Madrid, throughout the duration of the Franco regime (1939–1975) were largely shaped by the administration's policies to nationalism, tourism, and people who practiced flamenco. This has in turn significantly shaped the practice of flamenco and attitudes towards it in present-day Madrid. Franco, when he assumed power after a three-year long civil war, was exceptionally concerned about regionalism, in part because his Republican opponents had regional leanings. He decisively eliminated political support for cultural diversity in the early years of his rule by executing leaders of prominent regionalist movements—in Andalucía that included prominent supporters of flamenco as Andalucían identity such as Blas Infante Perez de Vargas and Federico García Lorca. National unity and centralism were the regime's narrative and cultural activities to the contrary were suppressed and censored (Machin-Autenrieth 2017, p. 27).

Madrid became the primary cultural hub, in a way that it had not in the past, in a manner that marginalised and persecuted Andalucíans, Catalans, and Basques. For Andalucía, centralist rhetoric was something they had been fighting periodically since 1868, which is linked to their historic concerns for cultural and political autonomy (Washabaugh 1996, p. 79). Music, and flamenco in particular, was a favoured way to differentiate a unique Andalucían identity. Flamenco had long been associated with regionalism and republicanism and as a result, the more traditional renditions of the art complex (those advocated by Lorca, Falla, and the ethos of the 1922 *Concurso del Cante Jondo*) were forbidden, as was singing in some bars (Machin-Autenrieth 2017, p. 27).

At the same time, Franco saw the value in flamenco as a symbol of national identity, as discussed earlier in this book with regards to his tourism campaign. From the 1940s to 1960s, flamenco was further cleansed and turned into a Spanish (as opposed to Andalucían) tradition appropriate for representing the country both internally and internationally. This was a movement known as *nacionalflamenquismo* (Chuse 1993, pp. 106–107). Part of this was a neo-classical revival movement which sought to valorise and reassign meaning to folk traditions and practices, which included a focus on the stereotypical *Gitano*. Ironically, despite the regime's persecution of Gitanos, the *Gitano* narrative was actually supported because it went along with Franco's core beliefs of family values and patriarchy, and also helped them appear tolerant to the outside world (Machin-Autenrieth 2017, p. 28).

Because of this cleansing of what was permitted in a performance, as well as the art complex being both a symbol of national unity and a tourist commodity, flamenco's presence in Madrid began to take new forms. After the Civil War, a period known as the 'Second Stage of Flamenco Opera' began, running from approximately 1940 to 1954. This differed from the earlier renditions of *ópera flamenca*, in that it was more of a folk music variety show, with a high proportion of acts consisting of

Andalucían song and flamenco (Blas Vega and Ríos Ruiz 1988). Similar to the earlier rendition of *ópera flamenco* the shows utilised elaborate orchestrations and a significant amount of the content was *cuplé*. Although several flamenco artists who headlined these spectacles (such as Pepe Marchena, Manuel Vallejo, and Juanito Valderrama) are now considered masters of 'traditional' flamenco, significant hybridisation occurred to appeal to a broader audience. The folkloric approach marked the final stages of *ópera flamenco* (Mora 2008, p. 328).

Interestingly, while the rather elaborate *ópera flamenca* was having a revival, aficionados in Madrid were developing their own performance scenarios which were subdued in order not to attract the ire of the regime. Since the end of the Civil War, they would meet in Madrid's taverns and discuss flamenco. This led to the development of the first flamenco clubs (or *peñas*) in legal spaces where fans would come and see influential flamencos in a more 'authentic' performance environment than the public theatre shows (Escribano 1990, pp. 102–103). The first of these clubs— Pena Charlot—opened in Madrid in the early 1940s and was a place where fans celebrated *pureza*—a celebration of the traditional and rejection of the commercial and superficial (Murillo Saborido 2017, p. 23).

The Advent of the Tablao

To recap, in 1953 Franco's Ministry of Information and Tourism conceived a series of branding ideas with which to market Spain to foreign visitors. These included beaches, history, and flamenco and in 1957 that translated into an official tourism campaign—'España es Diferente' (Storm 2013, p. 543). To accommodate these cultural policies, a new type of performative space evolved in Madrid specifically designed for the tourist-oriented flamenco show—the tablao. The tablaos was a return somewhat to a traditional form of flamenco—devoid of variety acts, juggling, and excessive orchestration but cleansed to fit with the values of the Franco regime. While they attracted some aficionados, they were primarily geared towards tourists. The first tablao opened in Madrid in 1954— Zambra—and was closely followed by La Taberna Gitana and El Corral de Morería (Machin-Autenrieth 2017, p. 27). The tablaos were, to some extent, based on nostalgic perceptions of the nineteenth-century *cafes cantantes* (Blas Vega & Ríos Ruiz 1988). The primary difference was that tablaos were exclusively flamenco, whereas the *cafes cantantes* offered a variety of different musics (Blas Vega 2006, p. 63). The tablao experience offered scripted performances starting between 11 pm and 12 am and ending as late as 3 am, with the possibility of a private *juerga* afterwards. These were often accompanied by typical Spanish food and alcoholic beverages. Madrid, as the de facto administrative, economic, and cultural capital, had the greatest number of tablaos—16—most of which were prominently located in the city centre. At its height, Franco's cultural policy also involved exporting the show abroad, as evidenced by the star artists from Zambra being sent abroad to represent Spain in the 1964 New York World's Fair (Murillo Saborido 2017, p. 30).

Tablao owners were not aficionados but entrepreneurs with artistic advisors who recommended particular performers (Grimaldo 2010, p. 14). There was often a connection between them and the Franco regime and ministers would periodically visit the venue to censor what was performed. The owners' main goal was to showcase the typical Spanish woman, so as to represent the tourism campaign, and thus had a habit of hiring dancers with questionable talent but exceptional beauty (Diéguez 2008, p. 68). Part of the incentive for tablao entrepreneurs was the state support provided to such venues from their outset in the mid-1950s (Murillo Saborido 2017, p. 69).

Prior to the tablao, the flamenco performer's employment options were primarily to either be hired for a private party or become part of a famous artist's company. The availability of state funding for the tablao and the regularity of shows provided relative economic stability in the form of a daily salary. The fixed salary was an innovation of the tablao (Cruces Roldán 2003, pp. 249–250). The centralisation and stability of tablaos caused more artists from across the country to move to Madrid. This migration was further encouraged by the laws preventing flamenco song in taverns in Andalucía and Madrid's prohibition on singing in unapproved venues, both of which changed how performers made money (Murillo Saborido 2017, p. 31).

According to Blas Vega, the success of the tablao rested with its specific marketing to a new audience of tourists, where previous venues had not had a defined clientele (Blas Vega & Ríos Ruiz 1988, p. 720). Although the shows were aimed at foreigners, local aficionados attended as well. The entrance price of tablaos was, however, aimed at tourists and thus not typically attended by lower economic classes. The spectacles were intended for white middle and upper-class men and women. Typically, youth were not present—probably in part due to the high prices, but also music preference as this was a time period when Western pop music was gaining popularity (Bethencourt Llobet 2011, p. 7).

The performance aesthetics over time changed slightly due to fluctuating trends in flamenco performance, as well as economic factors. In the late 1950s and early 1960s *cuadros* were fairly large. First the house *cuadro* would perform a set, then the headline act would perform, then the house *cuadro* would perform a final act (Murillo Saborido 2017, p. 47). As the tablao progressed, the number of performers decreased and the main performer gained more clout. The profession of this main performer (*bailora, cantaor/a, tocaor*) altered as the format progressed as well. At the outset of the tablao's invention, the *bailora* was the main attraction. The primary requirements for this role were to be beautiful, tall, and well-dressed. During the Franco regime, a *bailora* was also required to work in other artistic endeavours associated with the administration, such as singing in the Women's Section, which was a choral and dance troupe focused on communicating and instilling the values of Franco to the general public (Murillo Saborido 2017, p. 56). From the 1950s to the mid-1960s the flamenco guitar had the least esteem in the tablao and primarily served as a rhythmic accompaniment. This may have been in part to a number of prominent guitarists going into exile after the end of the Civil War (such as Sabícas and Mario Escudero), which resulted in the stagnation of the flamenco guitars progress as a solo instrument in Spain (Torres 2005). At the end of the 1960s, the dancer diminished slightly in importance with public interest shifting to singing and guitar, which gave the latter room to further develop as a solo instrument (Diéguez 2008, p. 76).

Towards the end of the Franco regime, Andalucían summer festivals began to gain prominence. While there would not be festivals devoted specifically to flamenco until the 1980s, these summer festivals prominently featured *peñas* and flamenco performances. As the number of festivals in Andalucía increased, as well as public funding for them, up-and-coming flamenco stars began to perform there instead of in the tablaos. This resulted in a slight deterioration in the quality of tablao acts, as artists could live solely off the festival circuit (Murillo Saborido 2017, p. 25).

4.2   Madrid's Current Flamenco Geography

Madrid's current flamenco geography is an echo of its historical developments since the mid-nineteenth century, with particular similarity to the Franco-era scene. It is crucial to note that in Madrid flamenco developed mainly in public contexts and that even in private *juergas* it was a commercialised art form—evidence of flamenco in a private familial or non-commercial cultural context is rare (Hernandez Girbal 1933, p. 70). This is in direct opposition to Andalucía where, while flamenco does certainly exist in a commercial format, it evolved in a private and non-commercial fashion and has roots in the cultural practices of the region (Washabaugh 1996). As a result of this, the Madrid flamenco scene primarily consists of varying types of commercial endeavours, many of which are specifically geared towards foreign aficionados and tourists.

Madrid's flamenco geography consists of three main types of institution:

1. permanent performance venues
2. festivals
3. flamenco schools

In the course of numerous field research trips, I explored each one of these avenues.

Permanent Performance Venues

The category of permanent performance venues includes tablaos, concert halls, theatres, and other small venues. There are also numerous flamenco dance companies, recording studios, and equipment shops based in the city. Tablao *bailor* Esteban describes Madrid as a typical capital city which has many alternatives for performance, including tablaos, theatres, smaller bars, concert halls, and art galleries (Esteban, personal communication, Jan. 15, 2014). This allows established and up-and-coming performers ample opportunities to showcase their skills and develop their career—providing they have the right connections or the knowledge of how to gain those connections.

The most prolific of these permanent fixtures are the tablaos, which are robustly promoted by tourist agencies and are the face of flamenco in Madrid. There are approximately 20 tablaos in Madrid, primarily located in the city, around *Barrios* such as Chueca, Lavapiés, Plaza de España, and Latina (https://www.flamencotickets.com/madrid-flamenco-shows, n.d.). Some are established having traced their routes to Franco-era venues, such as El Corral de la Morería—founded in 1956 by Manuel del Rey. Some, such as Villa Rosa (founded in 1911) reach back further into Madrid's commercial flamenco history to the *cafes cantantes*. They each have one or two shows a day, often offering a drink or dinner with the ticket price. The ticket prices start at between €15 and €50 and increase depending on where your seat is and if you choose a dinner-inclusive experience.

Tablaos have several styles of decoration. The older café cantante or Franco-era tablaos tend to utilise elaborate adornments and imagery that hark back to that era, such as tile murals, aged paintings of flamenco dancers and matadors, and ivy vines draped around the room, with the aim of evoking a passive nostalgia of *la edad de ora de flamenco*. Other newer venues, such as Las Tablas and Cardomomo, are sparsely decorated, often consisting of merely a black room with the tablao's name above the stage, so to conjure a feeling of modernity and progress.

The tablaos, similar to those in Sevilla, are almost entirely aimed at tourists—both in terms of the price (which is out of reach for many Spaniards due to over a decade of a shaky economy and high unemployment) and in terms of the type of flamenco show on offer and expectations of the audience. This differs from earlier forms of this performance fixture, as *cafes cantantes* were aimed at Spanish non-aficionados and Franco-era tablaos, while aimed at tourists, were financially accessible to Spaniards. I found in Madrid that tablao *cuadros* often were slightly larger than those in Sevilla—often with more than one singer, dancer, and guitarist and usually with a percussionist. Stylistically, artists tend towards the more upbeat *cante chico* song styles (such as *bulerías* and *alegrías*), as these are typically better received by tourist audiences. Similar to tablaos in Sevilla, there is little expectation that the audience will involve themselves with the proceedings, beyond applause at the end of each piece.

A difference between Madrid and Sevilla tablaos, in my experiences and the observations of my informants, is the feeling that more creativity can be applied in interpreting various flamenco styles. For example, an informant, Esteban, who also organises theatrical flamenco concept shows and tours them, was hired to perform a series at Las Tablas, which is near Plaza de España. He reported that:

> Las Tablas entrusted me with the power to [do a show for a month]. The guitar and the cantaor are from the tablao itself [...] but they are not part of my company. What happens is that I have adapted my dances or my dance concept a little to that tablao, to do something different, not the typical tablao. (Esteban, personal communication, Jan. 15, 2014)

The show itself, which Esteban invited me along to, departed from concepts of authenticity typically on display in tablaos. It did this through the artist's style of dress, the props utilised, and creative interpretation of the music and dance itself. Esteban wore a plain pair of black trousers and a button-up blue shirt. In the course of the show, he used a crooked cane and a chair to accent various parts of the routine and the compás. He also had different lighting combinations for varying parts of the routine and had sections that the only sound emanated either from the dancer's feet or from the props. While this may not exactly be as edgy as the jugglers and orchestras of flamenco opera, the addition of props and lighting concepts in particular stretch the boundaries of what is expected in a flamenco show, both from tourists and aficionados. Despite this, Esteban's concept references earlier imagined connections with flamenco performance—in particular the use of a cane and a capella *cante*. These elements remind the aficionado of alleged *gitano* performance styles from flamenco's earliest developmental stages which accompanied a capella *cante* with accoutrements such as a cane or an anvil. 'Everything is traditional, but it is wrapped in lights, in different details to make it cooler—

the cane is traditional, the music is traditional, but it is wrapped in a modern energy' Esteban described his concept (Esteban, personal communication, Jan. 15, 2014). It is something a little different, while still with allusions to perceptions of flamenco authenticity and history. This demonstrates Madrid's, especially in the tablao circuit, approach to flamenco—allusions to authentic perceptions but with an openness to innovation.

The artists that perform in tablaos typically are in a pool for that particular venue and are rotated for each performance. Periodically a headline artist, such as Esteban, will be brought in for a set time length to curate a performance. These headliners are nearly always dancers and are often internationally known so as to bring in more interest to the tablao. Because of the regularity of performances, tablaos periodically require substitutes to their performer pool, which allows them the opportunity to enter the regular performer pool. Typically, these better-known and connected international artists spend their time performing in festivals and theatre shows, which typically will only hire famous, recognisable flamenco artists. The plethora of tablaos in Madrid, in particular, offers younger performers the opportunity to hone their performance technique and acquire consistent income. My teacher and informant Bandolero (a professional flamenco percussionist) reported that 'Cardomomo, Casa Patas, all these tablaos have young people eager to do things, because the "top" artists already go to theatres and festivals' (Bandolero, personal communication, Feb. 18, 2014). The problem with this is that, because of the economic crisis, more of the top-level artists are forced to sporadically perform in tablaos. This means that the competition for the tablao spots is fierce. Esteban points out that, despite the number of tablaos, Madrid is a very closed circle, with each venue having its set team of dancers, singers, and musicians. Esteban reports 'it is difficult to move from one circle to another circle as normally the tablaos label you if you are a long time in a particular tablao, then it is a little complicated to break that barrier so that other tablaos count on you' (Esteban, personal communication, Jan. 15, 2014). This creates some difficulties in career progression and also pigeonholes an artist into a particular working situation. The economic crisis has necessitated newer venues, such as Cardomomo, hire younger dancers who don't have to be paid as much, which is often a sacrifice in the quality of the performance.

Smaller Performance Venues

There are a number of, often ad hoc or one-off, performance venues in Madrid that allow artists who haven't gained access to tablaos to attain performance experience. Most of these are general performance spaces which, similar to the *cafes cantantes*, host a variety of musical genres in their programme. Esteban describes these as 'alternative venues, outside the circle of the tablaos', which consist of rooms, small spaces, bars, art galleries, and concert halls where the owners are willing to programme flamenco which allow younger artists to showcase their art and developing performers to pitch their newest projects (Bandolero, personal communication, Feb. 18, 2014). These smaller performance venues often allow aspiring artists to book the venue for a small fee, which allows them to put on their own production with the hope of making a profit or at least breaking even. A dancer informant, Donya, described the experience of putting on her own events:

> I started to organise shows at a place called Arte Bar because I couldn't get any work in a tablao due to my immigration status. That's closed now—the Ayuntamiento[4] doesn't allow shows there any more, in the past year they have been strict about closing restaurants that don't have a permit to have live music. Arte Bar was the kind of place where we learned how to be on stage—you showed them you knew how to dance then they would give you dates and you would organise the night—bring your own guitarist and singer and whomever else was dancing with you. The place held a capacity of 40–50 people. I started every 3 months, then once a month, twice a month. We had to print out fliers, go give it to tourist places. There were nights when we had ten people watching and we would do it anyways. [...] There were times when I had to pay the guitarist out of my own pocket. (Donya, personal communication, Feb. 15, 2014)

Donya's experience echoes that of many of my informants—that it is possible to make use of the smaller venues and put on one's own programme, but there are risks involved. Similar to experiences elaborated on in Sevilla, smaller, self-run performances must be self-advertised and self-

---

[4] Regional government.

funded, receiving little in the way of help from the tourist office. These venues often have government regulations put upon them that makes it difficult for them to stay open—another similarity to earlier times in flamenco's history in Madrid. Several informants, for example Beatriz and Donya, noted smaller venues which had put on flamenco shows closing down—such as Arte Bar and Soléa. Nevertheless, other small venues pop up to replace them, allowing artists to put on their own shows. These are an important aspect of the Madrid flamenco ecosystem.

Norwegian guitarist Beatriz described her experience at Soléa, where she had her first Madrileño performance:

> The first gig I had was in this really shady place—the Soléa. It was closed several years ago now. It was like a bar where people would go to drink and sing. [...] So I just went there one day with the guitar. [...] And somebody asked me if they could borrow the guitar and I ended up playing. The boss saw me playing and she asked me to work there. And that was a very enriching experience because you are playing for everybody. Pitingo came and sang and some other really good professional singers. People would sing all these different styles and all, so you would learn a lot. (Beatriz, personal communication, Feb. 16, 2014)

The experience she imparts demonstrates another variety of small performance space in Madrid—the jam session. As described by Beatriz, these are events where anyone can come and perform flamenco. In the case of Soléa, this consisted of a house *cuadro* accompanying any *cantaor* who wanted to sing. While Soléa is now closed, I attended a similar event at Café Berlin, near Calle Gran Via. Café Berlin hosted a flamenco jazz band, which featured a basic backing band (bass, drums, congas, guitar, keys) and then people could get up and solo with them. I attended the first one of these in 2014, and as of this writing, the flamenco jazz jam is still running. The first session was a sold-out event, but I somehow managed to make my way to sit in the front of the crowd. Similar to Beatriz's note about the presence of Pitingo and other well-known singers, my experience at Café Berlin was also star-studded. The event itself is run by Latin Grammy nominee Diego Guerrero and on that evening the backing band included prominent Cuban bass player Alain Perez and the soloists included Jorge Pardo (a flamenco jazz woodwind player who toured with Paco de Lucia) and Tomatito (an internationally renowned flamenco guitarist). The high concentration of professionals in Madrid makes it possible at events like these for aspirational flamenco performers to rub elbows, network, and perform with living flamenco legends (Fig. 4.2).

A final small performance venue of importance is that mentioned in the opening of this chapter—Candela, which is in Madrid's Lavapiés neighbourhood. This historic locale differs from any other that I encountered in Madrid. It was founded in 1982 by Miguel Candela, originally as Peña Chaquetón, meant as a meeting place for guitarists and flamenco enthusiasts (https://flamencocandela.com/historia/, n.d.). After a few years of running it as a *peña*, Miguel decided to convert the space to a performance venue called 'Candela'. The ethos of Candela was to host exceptional flamenco artists in an uncontrived setting, befitting of a tavern in Andalucía instead of the glitzy tablaos of the capital. Over the years

Fig. 4.2 Flamenco fusion with Diego Guerrero and European Jazz Musician of the Year, Jorge Pardo (flute)

Fig. 4.3 Performance at Candela

the venue has hosted a plethora of flamenco royalty, including Camarón de la Isla, Paco de Lucía, Enrique Morente, and Sara Baras. Unlike the tablao focus on dancers, headliners can be singers, guitarists, and percussionists as well. Candela is not meant just for aficionados; the general public is welcome and it is advertised online. It isn't a tablao and the entry price is between €2 and €10 depending, including a drink. It isn't advertised by the tourist agencies but has an online presence that enables an intrepid traveller to find out what is on and when. Octavio, the current manager, books acts which range from what would be considered traditional flamenco to avant-garde fusions. The list of artists ranges from well-known stars to relative newcomers to the scene and to the city. Oftentimes international artists will come to this venue to trial their programme before taking it abroad or to a festival. In addition to the diverse acts, Candela is notable for its cave-like, invite-only, grotto in the basement, which is guarded by a bartender. This is a place where local *gitanos* and flamenco performers come and have impromptu *juergas* (much like those from the café cantante era) until well into the next morning. Candela is an important and one-of-a-kind venue in a city full of commercial flamenco (Fig. 4.3).

Festivals

As mentioned earlier, festivals are a significant performance locale for upper level flamenco performers, most of whom are based in Madrid. There is one flamenco festival based in Madrid—Suma Flamenco Festival which runs throughout the month of June and began in 2005. The festival programmes the best flamenco acts in Spain, and they perform in several venues (primarily concert halls, theatres, and museums) across the city throughout the month (http://www.madrid.org/sumaflamenca/2019/entradas.html, 2019). The shows that are put on are often theatrical with some sort of thematic narrative running throughout, although some artists choose to do an unadorned flamenco set. In addition to the performances, Suma features one day of free classes at Amor de Dios—a flamenco school in Barrio Lavapiés—with one-hour sessions with a selection of the institution's high-profile dance instructors. It is interesting to note that only at this flamenco-specific series is one likely to find the art complex at a festival in Madrid. There are numerous cultural festivals in the city dedicated to saints and other important regional days, but it is highly unlikely to find flamenco at these events. This is simply because the art complex, as stated previously, is not a part of Madrid's inner culture, as it is in sectors of Andalucía, but primarily a commercial enterprise.

Importantly, since many of the most prominent performers are based in Madrid, the city serves as a meeting point and a springboard for artists to be booked for other prominent flamenco festivals. International festivals, such as those in London, Nimes, and Moscow, have pitched similar artists by Spanish governmental authorities. Ironically, this is one of the factors that makes it difficult for artists who don't have a robust international profile to move up in the flamenco world. The perception of artists such as *tocaor* Beatriz is that, despite some opportunities at smaller venues, the closed circle of the tablao and festival circuit (which many find too much of a departure from non-commercial flamenco) results in a fairly limited Madrid flamenco scene.

Peñas

Notably absent in the Madrid flamenco scene are the *peñas*. These flamenco clubs, while common in Andalucían flamenco hotspots, no longer exist in the capital. Their purpose in Sevilla is for local aficionados to appreciate flamenco in a relatively private setting, apart from the tourists and non-aficionados, as well as provide a space for *juergas* and promote homegrown artists. While *peñas* have previously existed in Madrid (and by some accounts, originated there), they have been closed down (Donya, personal communication, Feb. 15, 2014). There are places that try to emulate aspects, such as after-hours jams in the grotto at Candela, and infrequent post-show *juergas* at some of the tablaos, but the *peña* as a flamenco club concept does not exist in Madrid.

Escuelas de Flamenco

The third important category in Madrid's flamenco geography is *Escuelas de Flamenco*—or flamenco schools. There are numerous flamenco teachers in Madrid, such as Isabel Quintero and Amelia Vega. There are also several general dance schools that offer flamenco classes, such as Dance Classes Madrid, Mushi School of Music and Dance, and El Horno. According to my informants the school that has the most resonance and is considered the most comprehensive, influential school in Madrid is Amor de Dios, located in Barrio Lavapiés (Bandolero, personal communication, Feb. 18, 2014).

Amor de Dios, improbably located above a market, opened in 1953 by Antonio el Bailarín, an internationally touring dancer, most famous for his collaborations with Rosario, as a studio space for his company. The locale soon evolved into a teaching facility which has hosted most of the great flamenco teachers and taught many of the most influential dancers over the last half-century (http://www.amordedios.com/webad/El%20 centro/historia.htm, n.d.). While Amor de Dios is primarily dance-focused, there are also classes for *cante*, *toque*, and cajón. The teachers that were there when I visited represented a cross-section of the best-known past and present artists from across Spain. The classes covered a wide range of *palos*, as well as some specific to a particular technique—such as *zapateado* (footwork) or *braceo* (arm work). In addition to permanent teachers, such as Cristobal Reyes and La Tati, the school also can capitalise on artists who have a break in their touring or tablao schedule, or perhaps are passing through Madrid. These visiting teachers are hired to do short courses—usually lasting from one week to a month. The central location of the school (in the capital city) also makes it possible for dancers in the big companies (such as Companía Marco Flores and Companía Sara Baras) to continue to hone their skills at Amor de Dios when they are not touring. The school pitches itself as 'a non-academic, traditional school, which does not grant degrees but trains professionals for the stages', suggesting that its main client base comprises those that actually want to become professional. (http://www.amordedios.com/webad/El%20centro/historia.htm, n.d.).

Significantly, Amor de Dios also has a high proportion of foreign students, such as my friend Donya. *Bailor* Esteban, who has taught short courses there, describes the school as a multicultural space, where all kinds of people share flamenco with each other, since the vast majority of the attendees are from abroad. He was influenced by this opportunity because when he first moved to Madrid from Cadíz he was able to study with the great Antonio Canales alongside dancers from all over the world (Esteban, personal communication, Jan. 15, 2014). He felt that outside of the benefits of studying in a top-class environment, Amor de Dios functioned as a meeting place where Spaniards could interact with international aficionados and aspiring amateurs could learn from and socialise with elite performers. Similarly, cajón player Bandolero sees the importance of the school as it being a place where people see 'you' (the aspiring professional), a place of opportunity to be in the moment (Bandolero, personal communication, Feb. 18, 2014). By this, he meant that Amor de Dios' status as a meeting place affords it status as a place where an aspiring dancer could be 'discovered'.

I visited Amor de Dios on several occasions, once as a tourist, twice as a student of Bandolero's, and twice to audit Merche Esmeralda's classes. The place is bustling from 10 am to midnight with numerous classes happening concurrently, collaborators having a coffee in the sparse waiting area, dancers wandering between the locker room and the studios, and teachers waiting for their next class to start. There is a tenseness palpable in the often humid air of the studios and around every corner you might meet a genuine flamenco star.

Donya, a *bailora* from Canada, came to Madrid specifically to study at Amor de Dios with the aim of becoming a professional. While she has gained a lot from the experience, she cites several negatives that echo true across the entirety of the Madrid flamenco scene. She describes Amor de Dios as a 'step factory'—highly focused on complex choreography and especially with aggressive footwork, but less concerned about the emotion behind the dance (Donya, personal communication, Feb. 15, 2014). She felt that it was a good place for advanced dancers who had learnt technique at conservatory, but potentially dangerous for those that came at a beginner or intermediate level. This is in part because of the temptation of learning with prominent teachers. It is inspiring to be in their presence, but most aren't likely to turn one into a dancer. She thinks that the older teachers, such as Cristobal Reyes and Merche Esmeralda, pay a little more attention to detail when it comes to intricate technical issues with the body, as opposed to complex choreography. Many of the teachers, especially those visiting for short courses, focus only on teaching a routine without actually correcting student errors. This focus on technique is evident across the Madrid flamenco scene, an emphasis on perfection and elaborateness, but less concern about raw emotion, which is more common in Andalucía.

Donya says 'Amor de Dios is a big school with a lot of movements happening in it, you have the best artists, the best guitarists, singers, dancers, percussionists in that environment. That doesn't necessarily mean that it's the best place to learn'. She feels that Amor de Dios has a lot of malicious energy—as if everyone is competing with one another. In some ways they are, especially since most big flamenco dance companies are based in Madrid and their lead dancers are teaching at the school. This lends itself to a high feeling of competition amongst aspiring flamenco students, not much camaraderie, and a high level of criticism of fellow performers (Donya, personal communication, Feb. 15, 2014). This feeling of competition is one mentioned by other informants regarding the Madrid flamenco scene as a whole. Since the scene's entire existence is based on a commercial context, the existing jobs are highly sought after and battled for. Nevertheless, Amor de Dios is one of the most important junctures in the Madrid flamenco scene. It is a place to see and be seen, to gain credentials from the most influential professional dancers and teachers, and to facilitate collaborations. Most importantly it reflects the most significant features of the Madrid flamenco scene: professionalism and commercialism.

4.3   Professionals in the Madrid Scene

As alluded to previously, Madrid's status as the commercial centre of flamenco has resulted in a high density of flamenco professionals making Madrid their base. This has been a prominent attribute from the advent of the *cafes cantantes* in the mid-nineteenth century. By 1900, Madrid had firmly displaced Sevilla as a centre for flamenco performance, with famous artists such as La Argentina (*bailora*) and Antonio Chacón (*cantaor*) heading the long list who relocated to the capital (Washabaugh 2012, p. 64). This trend has continued to the present day, with established and aspiring flamenco artists from all over Spain, and indeed the world, making their home in Madrid. Some of them make Madrid their main place of employment, while others use it as a springboard to exclusively international projects. Internationally performing *bailora* Merche Esmeralda describes the capital as:

> [...] a place that has always been very important in flamenco because Madrid has for a long time been the cultural centre of Spain. So if an artist wanted to succeed in the flamenco world they had to come here. Andalusia is important because it gave us flamenco, but instead when you want to project yourself, it had to be [here] because this is where the world of culture has moved, including the tablao. Madrid has had a great ability to collect the great figures of flamenco and that has given much prestige [...] to Madrid. (M. Esmeralda, personal communication, Feb. 17, 2014)

The capital is home to the most tablaos (which offer consistent work), theatres, and small performance venues of anywhere else in Spain. It also is home to government institutions which offer artistic funding for projects. Finally, it is home to Amor de Dios and most of the major flamenco and Spanish dance companies. This makes it a place of interest for those wishing to sustain a career in flamenco. Paquito, a flamenco bass player, agrees that everyone, historically, came to Madrid, including Camarón de la Isla, Paco de Lucia, and Gerardo Nuñez—legendary artists known even outside of the flamenco world. He believes that if you want to work and develop your art in an innovative way, you've got to come to Madrid (Paquito, personal communication, Jan. 10, 2014). Performers who want to create projects meet and go abroad from Madrid or even across the country to festivals (Donya, personal communication, Feb. 15, 2014). Four of my informants in particular represent the types of professionals resident in Madrid and capture how they interact with the flamenco scene. The following brief bio-ethnographies will demonstrate the typical professional experience in Madrid through the eyes of Esteban (a *bailor*), Paquito (composer and bass player), and Merche Esmeralda (a *bailora*).

Esteban: The Young Professional

Esteban, in his early 30s when I met him, was born in Cadíz, on the southern tip of Andalucía, which is one of the important cities in flamenco's origin story, being a port town. He started dancing at age 6 and performing at 13. At the age of 17 he began dancing on Cadíz's tablao circuit and got booked for international tours in the US by the Junta de Andalucía.[5] Upon returning to Cadíz, he began to develop a project— *Tierra Cantaora*—with a prominent flamenco guitarist named Manuel Morao. After completing a run of that show in a Cadíz tablao, Esteban decided to move to Madrid to increase his working opportunities (Esteban, personal communication, Jan. 15, 2014). When I met him he had lived in Madrid for 13 years, gradually building a series of performance networks that includes many of the tablaos across the city, as well as numerous internationally performing artists and foreign flamenco enthusiasts. In fact, I first encountered Esteban at an event in Birmingham hosted by the hub of the flamenco community there—Ana. Esteban had been hired to do a performance and then a series of weekend workshops. His status in Madrid has enabled Esteban to develop numerous international connections, spending his time developing projects to tour Spain

---

[5] Andalucían provincial government.

and then take abroad, in conjunction with teaching workshops all over Europe, as well as in Japan and the US. From his base in Madrid, he also collaborates with numerous renowned artists, such as Olga Pericet, to tour conceptualised flamenco theatre productions at Spanish flamenco festivals, such as those in Malaga and Las Minas (in Unión). After meeting Esteban in Birmingham, I met up with him again in Madrid to watch his show at Las Tablas, described earlier. His current schedule involved him finishing that run and then performing in another Madrid tablao, Casa Patas, for a month. He doesn't teach consistent classes, but short courses in Madrid or weekend workshops abroad (Esteban, personal communication, Jan. 15, 2014).

Esteban represents the flamenco professional who has moved from elsewhere to Madrid to forward his career. He considers flamenco his main form of employment and it is something that he feels as a significant part of his identity (Esteban, personal communication, Jan. 15, 2014). He engages directly with the Madrid flamenco scene through his tablao performances, but also develops his own projects which he tours around theatres. While he doesn't consistently teach, he does short-term work. Significantly, he has direct interactions with foreign aficionados and audiences, therefore shaping how they dance and how they understand flamenco. This, plus his considerable international teaching and performing, will have impact on how flamenco scenes are manifested abroad.

Paquito: Professional Bassist

Paquito, unlike the other flamenco professionals I met, does not consider himself *a flamenco*. He does not assume the art complex as his identity. He was born in the Basque country—a place with its own rich music culture and very little flamenco. Paquito describes his musical education as 'classically trained' and, in fact, attended the Vienna Conservatoire, where in addition to classical he started playing jazz (Paquito, personal communication, Jan. 10, 2014). Also during his time in Vienna he began playing in his first flamenco group, alongside a German guitar player.

Paquito had of course heard flamenco before, but it wasn't until coming to Vienna that he began to take an interest in it and teach himself.

After finishing in the conservatoire, Paquito moved to Madrid. Here he began to establish himself as a jazz and flamenco bass player, as well as performing in orchestras. He started to play with important flamenco musicians, such as pianist Chano Dominguez and guitarist Gerardo Nuñez, who are well known for experimenting with jazz in their flamenco compositions (Paquito, personal communication, Jan. 10, 2014). He has now been playing with Gerardo for 15 years and has since done tours with many other Madrid-based flamenco legends, such as Rocio Molina and Carmen Linares, all over the world. He was between international tour dates when I met him in Madrid. He believes that what made him able to attain rapid success in the Madrid flamenco scene is his prowess on the double bass. This is not a traditional flamenco instrument, although electric bass has been used in flamenco fusion and jazz, most notably by Carles Benavent. Because of this, Paquito views himself as somewhat a pioneer—forging a role for the double bass in flamenco culture. He feels that his many accomplishments 'makes me original in every sense, in New York, in Bangladesh, in Madrid, wherever I go and because of this I feel I have the legitimacy to explore the bass and believe in myself' (Paquito, personal communication, Jan. 10, 2014).

In addition to performing alongside flamenco greats, Paquito also has two of his own ensembles—a jazz quintet and an Ultra High Flamenco. The former he describes as jazz musicians that play flamenco structures and compás with jazz concepts and the latter is a flamenco group that has jazz improvisation structures. He imparted that in Madrid flamenco and jazz musicians understand each other—the two scenes have a proverbial meeting place in the city (Paquito, personal communication, Jan. 10, 2014). He believes in 'codes'—musicians understanding tacit cues when at the jam sessions that are popping up around the city. These blurred lines inform Paquito's view that flamenco is not just a culture, it is an industry label that guides audience expectations of his work. That is why his flamenco jazz group, Ultra High Flamenco, has the name of the art complex in the band name. Alongside his already busy jazz and flamenco performance schedule, Paquito also composes film music for various documentary film projects.

Paquito represents a particular faction of flamenco artists—those who don't necessarily identify with the art complex but instead consider themselves, as in his case, a bass player who can perform flamenco among other things. This is in opposition to the concept of a *flamenco*, who assumes the art complex as the primary aspect of their identity, as a performer and otherwise. Obviously, he still excels as a flamenco artist and has indeed had much success, but it is just one of several of his creative outputs. Paquito attributes part of his success to his knowledge of flamenco performance codes which enable him to interact with top flamenco artists (Paquito, personal communication, Jan. 10, 2014). He is able to do this through his instrument of expertise—the double bass. In 'authentic' flamenco ensembles—those considered normal in tablaos and in Andalucía—the guitar, with the possibility of some percussion, is the only instrument. Yet, in the Madrid flamenco scene Paquito has forged a role with some of the more prominent, internationally travelling flamenco artists, as well as within his own flamenco jazz ensembles. Paquito's flamenco jazz fusions also represent a departure from perceptions of authentic flamenco. While he is not, by any stretch, the first to combine the two styles, he exemplifies a type of flamenco artist that pushes the flamenco art complex beyond its usual boundaries. These variations are possible in Madrid, which because of its lack of a historical cultural connection is more open to innovations.

It is important to note that while he is Spanish, Paquito considers himself a relative foreigner to flamenco. In his words 'I didn't grow up with it, I am not a flamenco, I play with them and I am considered almost like one of them because I understand the culture, but I am as foreign as a French guy' (Paquito, personal communication, Jan. 10, 2014). Interestingly, Paquito didn't learn flamenco in Spain—he started performing it when he was living in Vienna. Part of his inroad to acceptance into the flamenco world is that he has been able to present himself as Gerardo Nuñez's bass player, which is a high accolade both in the world of 'traditional' flamenco and flamenco jazz (Paquito, personal communication, Jan. 10, 2014). Of final significance is Paquito's relative lack of engagement with the Madrid scene itself. He creates projects there and networks, but primarily he uses it as a springboard for international projects.

Merche Esmeralda: International Traveller and Film Star

Merche Esmeralda, in her late 60s when I met her, is, without exaggeration, a flamenco star, whose career spans from the tumultuous years of the Franco regime to today and across every continent except Antarctica. I was privileged not only to watch Merche teach several classes but also to interview her during my fieldwork in Madrid. Merche was born in 1947 in Sevilla. She did not grow up as part of the dynastical flamenco families, and instead started singing *cante* at Academia Sevilla de Adelita Domingo. She described her early interactions with flamenco to me:

> I started singing because two of my uncles were aficionados who moved in the flamenco world and my grandmother was a beautiful general singer. I liked to sing but when I went to study with Adelita Domingo I found I did not have good voice power and then when I discovered the dance, I saw that I was more passionate about that. (M. Esmeralda, personal communication, Feb. 17, 2014)

Following her switch to dance, Merche's career accelerated quickly. She made her performance debut at the age of 12 in Sevilla's Youth Galas. She then became a professional performer in the Spanish National Dance shows (which incorporated a variety of approved folk traditions) which were prominent in Spain during the Franco years. By her mid-teens, Merche premiered as a tablao *bailora* in both *El Duende* in Madrid and *El Guajiro* in Sevilla. At the age of 16, she premiered as a solo dancer and started performing at all the major Andalucían flamenco festivals, whilst completing tablao seasons at *Las Brujas* in Madrid and *Los Gallos* in Sevilla (M. Esmeralda, personal communication, Feb. 17, 2014). Her prominence in the tablao scene prompted an invite in that same year to perform at the wedding of the Moroccan King Hassan II's nephew in Casablanca (M. Esmeralda, personal communication, Feb. 17, 2014). Then in 1968 she won the National Dance Prize at the *Concurso Nacional de Arte Flamenco de Córdoba*—an event which was meant as a successor to the aforementioned 1922 *Concurso del Cante Jondo*.

After her success in the 1968 *Concurso*, Merche began appearing on television and went on her first international tours. From 1974 to 1980 she balanced these tours while performing in Madrid tablaos such as Las Brujas, Café de Chinitas, La Venta del Gato, and Los Canasteros. In conjunction with the tablao work and the tours, she taught lessons and continued to develop her television career. Her television career included stints on Radio y Televisión Española (RTVE) programmes such as 'Flamenco' and '300 million'. In the early 1980s, she entered the National Ballet of Spain, where she danced flamenco roles in their repertoire throughout that decade. Merche's prominence on television and in the tablaos led to roles in several films which truly brought her image to a worldwide level. The most notable of these were those by Carlos Saura—*Sevillañas* and *Flamenco*—and *Alma Gitana* by Chus Gutiérrez.

Of note are the numerous foreign dignitaries Merche reminisced about performing for—sent as Spain's flamenco representative to the world. She has danced for royalty, such as the King of Spain and the Emperor of Japan. She also reminisced fondly about her tours in the US:

> In 1987, I was at the Metropolitan [Opera] in New York, dancing a Soléa[6] with the National Ballet in La Medea. It was wonderful. The Americans fell to the ground: they applauded me and called me by my name. Here, I got to know the widow of Kennedy—Jacqueline. And the man who stepped on the Moon—Armstrong. And also, that nice president of the United States who ate peanuts—Jimmy Carter—when I danced at the Kennedy Center [in Washington D.C.]. (M. Esmeralda, personal communication, Feb. 17, 2014)

She also lists performances at the Kremlin during the Cold War among her many accolades. Merche considers herself very lucky to have had these opportunities to connect with people all over the world through dance. After decades of travelling, Merche founded her own company in 1996 and constructed the show *Mujeres*,[7] which included collaborations with Madrid-based *bailoras* Eva Yerbabuena and Sara Baras—both influential and international names in the flamenco world. In 2014, when I

---

[6] A flamenco *palo*.
[7] Translation: 'Women'.

met Merche, she had largely retired. In addition to maintaining a performance career, she had worked at the Spanish Dance Conservatory and the Royal Conservatory of Madrid until 2013 (M. Esmeralda, personal communication, Feb. 17, 2014). As of 2014, she taught a few classes at Amor de Dios, counting my informant Donya as one of her pupils. Merche takes a considerably traditional focus to flamenco dance tuition, with a high level of focus on individual body parts and their movements. She also sings in class so that students gain an understanding of how their dance fits in with the *cante*.

Merche represents several layers of the Madrileño professional flamenco world. Firstly, her development as a performer spans the decades of the Franco regime when he was developing his tourism campaign and coalescing ideas about a Spanish national identity—one of the ways that this manifested was in the Spanish Dance Performances in which Merche participated in her teens. Secondly, from an early age her career moved from her hometown of Sevilla to Madrid. The migration of her career to Madrid was the catalyst for a major leap forward in her career—one which led to first national recognition at the country's major festivals, and then an international presence that entailed her being almost a flamenco ambassador. Thirdly, her international presence, not only through her tours but through her films (well known to flamenco aficionados all over the world), has played a significant role in shaping a global perception of the flamenco art complex. Finally, throughout her career, Merche has maintained a constant connection with Madrid—through teaching, tablao appearances, and national television presence. This maintenance of both local and global influence is what makes Merche, and similar level of artists, a unique part of the Madrid flamenco scene.

A Professional Haven

Madrid's historical connections with commercialised flamenco has made it somewhat of a focal point for professional flamenco performers ranging from aspiring professionals to international stars, as well as artists like Paquito who play flamenco professionally but do not consider themselves a *flamenco*—at least not as a primary part of their identity. This concentration of high-level artists in one place engenders a sense of openness and creativity within the scene, which encourages collaborations. It also results in a high level of competition for the more secure and lucrative opportunities. Esteban imparted that there are many young people in Madrid dancing at a very high level with a lot of ambition (Esteban, personal communication, Jan. 15, 2014). This is a sentiment echoed by foreign dance students as well. Similar to informants in Sevilla, professional flamencos in Madrid described a hierarchy of performance scenarios that had narrowed since the onset of the economic crisis in 2008. The highest echelon of performers is a very small group and, as mentioned previously, festivals tend to book only artists from this level of performers and these are also the ones promoted by governmental departments to international festivals. Percussionist Bandolero imparted that consecrated artists such as Tomatito, Diego el Cigala, and Estrella Morente will never have any problems even in periods of crises. Even if they have less work, they will never have to go to tablaos because all the festivals would hire them (Bandolero, personal communication, Feb. 18, 2014). As in Sevilla, that means the tablao scene is really the only other place for permanent employment, outside of teaching. Some students cite the problem that teachers seem less than enthused about teaching, merely demonstrating choreographies but not actually providing meaningful, specific instruction to students (Donya, personal communication, Feb. 15, 2014). Others report that tablao performers, who maybe feel their talents would be better afforded in a theatre show or festival, often appear bored and lacklustre and sometimes leave out aspects of the dance, like *braceo* (Donya personal communication, Feb. 15, 2014).

Regardless of the shortfalls that come from oversaturation and competitiveness, Madrid's status as a scene with a preponderance of high-profile professional flamencos make it an important juncture for transnational interactions. Despite not being considered one of the *cuñas* of flamenco, some foreigners (especially those with professional ambitions) flock to the capital to study with living legends, such as Merche and La Tati. Thus, this atmosphere of professionalism and technical perfection and innovation are among the values that foreigners take with them when they travel home. If they teach and perform in their home countries it will be the Madrileño version of the art complex they transmit, which as noted is a more technical and commercial interpretation of the Andalucían rendition. Additionally, Madrid's status as a place where jet-setting artists situate themselves to develop projects and collaborations to then take abroad is also evidence of its influence on foreign flamenco perceptions. This is crucial because often these high-profile artists and collaborations are the only shows that get funding to take their shows elsewhere and thus shape audience expectations of the art complex when it is emulated by foreign cosmopolitan hubs.

4.4 The Flamenco Ex-Pat Experience

Of course, one of the reasons that there is such a commercial flamenco presence in Madrid is attributable to the foreign interactions with the scene. These foreigners are there as tourists primary; however, while many non-Spanish aficionados choose cities in Andalucía such as Granada, Sevilla, and Jeréz when they travel to experience flamenco abroad, the Madrid scene also receives a fair number of aspiring flamenco students and performers. There is a high proportion of foreign students, particularly at storied institutions such as Amor de Dios. Navigations of the Madrid scene are fairly different from Sevilla, because of the high preponderance of professionals and tablaos, acceptance of modern interpretations of flamenco, as well as the lack of *peñas* like Niña de Alfalfa, which provide opportunities for younger performers. There are two main types of foreign flamenco aficionados that I encountered engaging with the Madrid scene: the student and the aspiring professional. While these lines sometimes blur, I have these to be the primary designations of international flamencos in Madrid.

The Student: Donya

Like my initial expectations of Sevilla, my first trip to Madrid had left me with no real impression that there was much of a flamenco scene in Madrid beyond the tablao—obviously a misconception—much less one that included a foreign ex-pat element. Once again, it took a virtual introduction from Alicia to Donya to begin to grasp how non-native flamenco aficionados interact with the Madrid scene.

On a damp, chilly January night, I ventured out of my hostel to go to 'La Tóna'—a small venue attached to Barco Bar—just off Calle Gran Vía. La Tóna is among the small performance venues described earlier, which periodically programme flamenco, although their typical line-up includes a wide variety of music genres. I was there to see a performance by a *cuadro* of aspiring flamenco professionals, including Donya, whom I had only previously spoken to online. Donya, an Iranian immigrant from Canada, was performing alongside another female dancer, guitarist, percussionist, and singer—all Spanish. They performed two sets of what would be considered 'traditional' flamenco, with the dancers each doing a solo piece and then a duet in each half. The performance ended with a *fin de fiesta*—which is fairly unusual in Madrid (as most of the time the typical audience is composed of non-aficionado tourists). Several audience members got on stage to perform a few *pataitas* alongside the official performers. After the *fin de fiesta* concluded, the venue (essentially a small performance area surrounded by a handful of café tables) quickly emptied, with the exception of a few friends of the group. I went up to Donya and introduced myself. She invited me along to watch her class in the morning with Merche Esmeralda and we also set up a time for an interview.

Donya has a fairly unique background—born in Tehran and then immigrating to North America as a teenager with her family. When she was a child, there was (and remains to be) strict censorship on the possession of foreign audio and video recordings, as well as performance of Western genres in particular. She first heard flamenco courtesy of contraband Paco de Lucía and Paco Peña CDs which had been smuggled into the country. She was entranced not only by the music but by the fact that both recordings featured the sound of a dancer's *zapateado*. 'I was like, "oh my god, what is happening back there!"—this was not just music, this music had some energy to it!', she recalls. It was a few years later when her childhood friend's mother, upon returning from visiting family in Germany, smuggled back a VHS of *Riverdance* in the hidden pocket of her suitcase, that she actually saw flamenco *baila* for the first time. *Riverdance* features a performance by Maria Pages, a renowned flamenco dancer. Donya recounts, 'I was amazed how the body could dance and be rhythmic, produce music, movement, and dance at the same time' (Donya, personal communication, Feb. 15, 2014).

Of course, in Iran, beyond watching and listening to contraband recordings, flamenco was something that was largely out of reach for Donya. It wasn't until her family immigrated to Vancouver that she began to have a possibility of engaging with flamenco on a deeper level. 'When I started university [in Vancouver] I had student loans, so I used them towards my flamenco classes—it was ridiculously expensive ($25 each, plus $300 for the shoes), but it was a priceless experience for me', she reminisces. Her main goal was to get to Spain, but as a poor university student this seemed like a pipe dream. By a stroke of luck, in her third year she got a chance to study abroad in Barcelona for a year where she simultaneously studied flamenco with La Tani and Flora Albecín, well-known Barcelona flamenco royalty. Similar to other foreigners, she found that even though she had been studying flamenco in Canada for several years, her level in Spain was fairly rudimentary, especially when it came to understanding how the other elements (*cante* and *toque*) fit together with the dance. Nevertheless, she fell in love with Spain and became more enamoured with flamenco. Several years later, after starting a Master's degree back in Montreal, Donya became frustrated with not being able to engage with flamenco at the same level as when she was in Barcelona, so decided to return to Spain, this time to Madrid where she was able to find teaching work to supplement her flamenco studies.

While she was in Barcelona, Donya had heard all about Amor de Dios, described to her as 'the cathedral of flamenco where all the great flamenco dancers teach' (Donya, personal communication, Feb. 15, 2014). On her second day, still jet-lagged, Donya rushed over to the school above the *mercado* in Lavapiés and was the first one through the door at 10 am, full of queries about the classes available. One of the teachers, an older man, interrupted and asked 'what's your level? Come to my class in the after-noon and try it out—we do technique and some choreography, it will be good for you.' This was Cristobal Reyes—part of a flamenco dynasty that includes Joaquín Cortés, Antonio and Manuel Reyes, and ex-wife Juana Amaya. He is also a perennial fixture at Amor de Dios and theatres, both around Spain and abroad. Donya went to his class and really enjoyed it, but still found that her level fell way below those in her class, despite her years of study—perhaps because the class contained professional dancers from Joaquín Cortés' company. The other dancers had exceptional turns and footwork, and she felt very lost. Cristobal put her in the back of the class holding a ballet bar and doing *zapateado* slowly, teaching her the proper technique, which was looser and more comfortable than the way she had been taught, an old method now considered antiquated in the flamenco world. For the first three months, Donya cried every day, always feeling bad about herself. She felt the pressure of high levels of competition at the school, which included the other students in her class. They would look disparagingly at her technique and would block the mirror so Donya couldn't see herself while she was dancing. Cristobal was a great teacher and after a few months of toughing it out, Donya started advancing very quickly with such intensive focus on technique. After a couple years, Donya began studying with Merche, having always dreamed of learning from the flamenco star, but had been working at a primary school which conflicted with class times. After altering her work schedule, she was able to start taking classes with her five days a week. Donya found Merche's classes specifically, and her time studying in Spain as a whole, to be exceptionally valuable because of her focus on how the *cante* fits with the *baile*, as well as how the structure of various *palos* play out. These are things that are not spoken of specifically outside of the country in such detail (Donya, personal communication, Feb. 15, 2014).

In addition to her regular classes, Donya takes workshops from visiting artists at Amor de Dios—those that are in Madrid for a short time or who are often internationally touring so can't teach regularly. She finds those enjoyable, as a way to learn modern steps and choreographies, but as mentioned before these temporary technicians don't tend to make corrections to dancers' technique, just run through a three-minute choreography in a week and then collect their paycheque. Although her primary purpose in Madrid is to learn, Donya has tried to branch out and get performances. She has had a difficult route because, since she is not from an EU country, she is not allowed to work under normal channels in Spain—so tablaos and dance companies are not an option. As described earlier, Donya has been able to make use of smaller performance venues, like La Tóna and Arte Bar. She has also performed at cultural centres. Donya confided:

> from early on I understood that nobody was going to just offer me work— fix my path for me to make it comfortable—if you want to dance here, you have to make it happen for yourself because everybody is hungry for an opportunity here. There is a lot of competition. (Donya, personal communication, Feb. 15, 2014)

This entrepreneurial attitude led Donya to curate an education flamenco package with a friend of hers for visiting North American students. This event entails an hour lecture on flamenco and the mechanics of a performance followed by a 30-minute show. She also teaches private lessons to small children or to beginner students at Amor de Dios that need extra help. While she enjoys her classes, Donya confided that she is largely fed up with Madrid, but flamenco helps her survive the other frustrations about Spain. Her plan is to study at Amor de Dios for a couple more years and then possibly move back to Canada or another European country. She feels that from a business perspective, flamenco works better outside of Spain, although it is difficult to find a singer—a prospect which pains her.

Donya's story is symbolic of countless foreign aficionados who have chosen Madrid as their flamenco educational destination. The scene in Madrid, unlike that in Andalucía is one that has a public instead of private history. The performance opportunities are competitive and aimed at non-aficionado, paying audiences. They journey to Madrid specifically to study with the many stars who count the capital as their base. Most of them (especially if from outside the EU) will find difficulty starting a significant career in Madrid, both for reasons of employment law and because of the high saturation of artists competing for the same jobs. They have to, as Donya did, find ways of creating flamenco performance opportunities for themselves most of the time. Therefore, many of them come with the intent of returning home and emulating the Madrid version of flamenco in their home countries. Different from Sevilla, flamenco in Madrid does not include *peñas* or *juergas* (except for the exclusive one at Candela), which removes a lot of the improvisatory practice that was common in Sevilla performances and *peñas*. Interestingly, Donya does not harbour any illusions regarding flamenco's value outside of Spain—that it will be easier for her to make a career of it elsewhere.

The Foreign Professional: Beatriz

Another cold, rainy winter night in Madrid a few weeks later I found myself wandering through Lavapiés once again to Candela. I didn't know who was performing, just that it was a full *cuadro* plus a violin. I arrived at the small bar early, paid the €5 entrance fee (which included a free drink) and took a seat towards the front. Although the shows at Candela are advertised as beginning at 10 pm, they often don't start until 11:30 pm or so. At around 10:30 pm, I saw the artists show up at the bar and filter into the dressing room, while the percussionist set up his equipment on stage. Surprisingly, this included not only a cajón, but a large metal washtub, filled with water and with what appeared to be a large, halved, upside down dried pumpkin in it—all of which was miked up. I was intrigued.

Soon, the full ensemble came on stage, featuring one of the more eclectic-looking acts I had seen on a flamenco stage in Spain: a blonde, female *cantaor/tocaor*, a violinist (not a typical flamenco instrument), the aforementioned percussionist, and a striking, female *bailora* (who turned out to be Mexican). Later inquiries revealed that the reason the ensemble arrived late was that the *bailora* and violinist had been playing at the tablao Casa Patas earlier in the evening. Not only was the instrumentation unique, but also the international nature of the ensemble, and the female guitarist, which is not often seen in flamenco. The first half of the show was a solo set by the *cantaora/tocaora*, which began with a slow, soulful melody sung in a language which was not Spanish or English. After the first song, the guitarist/singer introduced herself as Beatriz and the *bailora* as Karen Lugo—a well-known internationally touring performer who bases herself in Madrid. Beatriz explained that she was Norwegian and her set combined flamenco with English and Norwegian folk songs that she composed. The second set started with the percussionist slowly pouring water into the tub, accompanied by a violin solo, which morphed into Beatriz singing and playing to a rapid *tangos palo*, accom-

Fig. 4.4 Performance by Norwegian tocaora/cantaora Beatriz and Mexican bailora Karen Lugo at La Candela

panied by the entire ensemble and energetic dancing, which included choreography that seemed modern. The second song was a duet on the guitar in a slow *bulerías palo* with the percussionist, who accented the cajón pattern by tapping the pumpkin in the water. The hour-long set featured creative arrangements of the folk songs and flamenco, with interesting, sometimes ambient, musical arrangements. The melodies were haunting and sometimes unlike any flamenco harmonies I had heard before (Fig. 4.4).

Karen's dancing incorporated modern techniques which at one point included a duet with Beatriz while she was singing a slow, soulful *cantes libres* in Norwegian. The show, similar to others I attended at Candela, seemed well-rehearsed and choreographed (not just in terms of dancing but between the performers), which is different than a lot of tablaos (both in Sevilla and in Madrid). Tablaos are often somewhat improvised, due to the performers rotating every night. This was more like a flamenco concept show in a theatre. The audience was packed into the small bar/performance space, which had once hosted greats such as Camarón de la Isla (and still, indeed, has a picture of the tragic flamenco hero in front of the stage). The crowd was composed of aficionados, such as me, as well as performers from tablaos and the Madrid-based Compañía de Marco Flores. The audience enthusiastically cheered for the ensemble as they finished the last number, clearly appreciating the many unique factors of the performance. This was fusion which is not usually as appreciated in flamenco's Southern Spanish homeland.

A few days later, I met up with Beatriz to chat about the spectacular show she had orchestrated at Candela that evening. She had started her flamenco explorations in Norway and as a dancer, although she had always written songs and played simple 3-chord harmonies on the guitar. When Beatriz saw the guitarist playing in her dance classes, she fell in love with the sound and asked the *tocaora* for lessons (Beatriz, personal communication, Feb. 16, 2014). She had never imagined making a career of flamenco. From 1996 to 2000 she was learning the art, while busking her own songs. In 2000, Beatriz decided she wanted to investigate flamenco a bit further. She applied for a grant from her town council and was funded to go to Sevilla and take flamenco guitar classes (Beatriz, personal communication, Feb. 16, 2014). Beatriz remained based in Norway, as she had a partner and a job, but she would go to Sevilla for two or three months.

Beatriz found her time in Sevilla challenging. Not from a musical perspective, but in terms of lifestyle—she was foreign, blonde, vegetarian, and a female guitarist. All these factors make one stand out in a place like Sevilla and she found them to create barriers (Beatriz, personal communication, Feb. 16, 2014). Beatriz also was always lonely in Sevilla, although she had an excellent guitar teacher. From 2000 to 2006 she would visit Sevilla for several months a year, whilst touring with a flamenco trio in Norway and working on a Bachelor's in Musicology in her home country. In 2006, by chance she ended up going to Madrid instead of Sevilla and from the first day it felt like home—someplace where she could be herself. There were vegetarian restaurants, people from all over the world, and an open-minded flamenco scene. In considering the difference between the two cities, Beatriz observed:

> in Sevilla they have the attitude that 'flamenco is ours'—foreigners can come and pay for classes, but they must never think it is theirs. Whereas in Madrid, people and things that are different *Llama la atención*.[8] People think it's cool—I am actually lucky to be so incredibly different here. (Beatriz, personal communication, Feb. 16, 2014)

Beatriz was happy from her first day in the capital. She was going to stay for a couple months, but within a few weeks she started to get job offers. In her six years in Sevilla, Beatriz had only performed once. She didn't even try to search for gigs in Madrid, they came to her. She remembers that her first gig was in a really shady place, called 'Soléa', which has since closed. It was a bar where people would go and drink and sing flamenco alongside a house *tocaor*. She also played for some flamenco classes. Over the previous eight years, she had moved permanently to Madrid as the performance opportunities turned into a viable career. Beatriz, who can work under Spanish employment law, now worked for two flamenco companies: Companía Estuaria and Companía de Marco Flores. These are two internationally touring flamenco companies which have performed at prestigious events such as Bienale Sevilla, Festival de Jerez, Festival de Nimes, and Festival de Albuquerque. Beatriz has also accompanied dancers at many of the important Madrid tablaos, such as Casa Patas. Beatriz also tours with Karen Lugo, which involved upcoming trips to Tel Aviv and around France. She confided:

> I just feel so lucky. If you had told me 10 years ago all the things happening in my life, I would never in my wildest dreams think I would be playing in

---

[8] Translation: 'Captures the attention'.

Spain. [...] I really thought I would spend my life coming here for classes and working as a flamenco guitarist in Norway. That was my reach. Then I came down here and things started opening up. (Beatriz, personal communication, Feb. 16, 2014)

Because of the connections she has made through her playing in the companies and in venues around Madrid, Beatriz has been able to collaborate with respected performers, such as Karen, when creating her own ensemble. This, in turn, has engendered access to influential venues, such as Candela, as a performance space. While she loves playing traditional flamenco, Beatriz feels that her project is a positive reflection of who she is—a Norwegian who, having grown up in Kenya, has English as her first language. These linguistic identities, combined with flamenco, which she feels is her life's calling, means that she has a personal, honest connection with her performance, thus reflecting her individual approach to the art complex. While this sort of fusion doesn't appeal to traditionalists, it flourishes in Madrid (Beatriz, personal communication, Feb. 16, 2014).

Beatriz's experience in Madrid reflects that of a select group of flamenco ex-pats who come to Madrid (including the Mexican *bailora* Karen Lugo) intending to learn and end up turning professional. She also demonstrates the Madrid scene's relative openness to outsiders, even those that look slightly different—a factor which she feels has been an asset in the city, while being detrimental in Andalucía. Beatriz observed that this difference is one of the aspects that makes her successful—there are not many female guitarists, much less those that are blonde and foreign. Beatriz's experience also demonstrates Madrid's relative openness to fusion, with her personal ensemble which incorporates Norwegian and English folk lyrics and melodies with flamenco rhythms. That sort of fusion would not have been acceptable in Sevilla. Overall, Beatriz's story exemplifies how in Madrid it is possible for an ex-pat flamenco to become professional and engage with exceptional levels of flamenco performances.

The Ex-Pat Experience

The flamenco ex-pat experience in Madrid is characterised by flamenco's status as a purely commercial existence. This results in them having access to a plethora of famous flamenco figures, first as teachers at Amor de Dios and then as possible future performance collaborators. The negative side of the scene is the high level of competitiveness and animosity reported amongst students, but also amongst aspiring professionals who are overly critical of fellow performers (Donya, personal communication, Feb. 15, 2014). This leads to a feeling of a less cohesive ex-pat community, unlike the one found in Sevilla. A positive difference from the Sevilla scene is the relative openness to foreigners participating in the flamenco performance scene. Madrid has a history of creative innovations to perceptions of traditional flamenco, which is much more so than in Andalucía perhaps due to the lack of an in-built cultural connection. This has led to a receptivity towards foreign performers but also fusion, such as that which Beatriz engages in, allowing ex-pat aficionados to access flamenco incorporating their own cultural identity. Through interviews and observations, I have surmised that flamenco performers in Madrid have relatively few qualms with the foreign aficionado's presence on the scene and with their ability to understand the art complex. Although some tablaos remain close-minded—primarily to meet tourist expectations—several important ones, such as Casa Patas, have hired foreign *bailoras* (e.g., Karen Lugo, Magdalena Mannion, and Yinka Graves), as well as guitarists like Beatriz. Esteban, originally from Andalucía, believes:

> The essential thing is that [*bailor/a*] is a sensitive person. If they feel identi-fied with what they hear, what they are seeing, I think it is possible for them to feel flamenco. It's not something Spanish, it's international. Flamenco is a World Heritage Site. (Esteban, personal communication, Jan. 15, 2014)

He takes a postnational viewpoint, that any foreigner who takes the time to appreciate the art complex properly, understand the meanings behind it, and, of course, practice hard will be capable of performing as well as a Spanish person.

Amongst Spanish flamenco professionals in Madrid there seems to be a genuine appreciation for foreign interest in flamenco. Percussionist Bandolero, in his observations touring and teaching, believes that often foreigners are more receptive to flamenco, as opposed to non-aficionado Spaniards. A feeling reiterated by other internationally travelling artists,

Bandolero feels that, despite its UNESCO designation, flamenco has not been granted the respect it is due—by the general public it is not viewed as traditional Spanish music, but as *fiesta* music, *flamenquismo* (Bandolero, personal communication, Feb. 18, 2014). Merche reaffirms this point in her observation that dance, in general, hasn't been protected or properly funded by institutions, unlike opera, theatre, and *zarzuela*.[9] In addition to an openness towards the foreigner's ability to understand the art complex, Spanish artists also see the financial benefits of foreign interest in preserving and sustaining flamenco. Bandolero sees there is a great importance in being able to export flamenco—both recordings and artists— abroad to access the foreign market (Bandolero, personal communication, Feb. 18, 2014). This in turn attracts people to spatial hubs, such as Madrid, to learn the art complex. Despite this lack of respect from flamenco outsiders, insiders on the Madrid scene are much more open to foreign involvement than Sevilla. As one informant describes it:

> Flamenco is a way of Being, a way of playing and presenting yourself. If you are respectful of these things, the foreigner can understand. *Pureza*, this concept of purity, is important everywhere because you have to know the tradition to keep it alive, but flamenco is really innovating right now and globalising, and that is important to its survival. (Paquito, personal communication, Jan. 10, 2014)

This makes the foreigner not only accepted in the scene, but also crucial to maintain flamenco, which is not otherwise respected in its home country.

4.5 Conclusions

Unlike Sevilla, flamenco's local presence in Madrid is well-documented, although often underestimated. This is largely because its development and existence has primarily occurred in public, commercial realms, as opposed to a 'private' art complex in its Southern Spanish homeland. As a result, there is less a feeling of collective cultural ownership, which

---

[9] A Spanish lyric-drama which resembles opera but includes dialogue and often includes themes about the social realities of Madrid in the late nineteenth century.

enables creative alterations to be made. As evidenced in the earlier part of this chapter, Madrid has a long history of commercialisation in flamenco, which persists to this day. It doesn't really have a 'private' usage, as it does in cities in Andalucía. This presence of commercialism has led to a migration of artists seeking a professional career to the capital—a phenomenon that has also occurred throughout Madrid's flamenco history. The continual relocation of major artists to the capital has made it a perennial professional centre for flamenco in Spain, with more opportunities for paid work across tablaos, theatres, companies, small performance venues, and in teaching. The dense concentration of artists, which far outweigh demand, has led to a high level of competitiveness, which keeps the scene from being as cohesive as that in Sevilla.

One aspect that sets Madrid apart from Sevilla is its open-mindedness towards flamenco. While not a complete rejection of *pureza*, it is accepting of variations and fusions, and is appreciative of difference. This is evidenced by the type of shows that get booked under the heading of 'flamenco', which includes combining it with different genres, incorporating modern dance, and utilising varying forms of staging, lighting, and technology. The cosmopolitan nature of the city has also led the scene to be more receptive to non-Spanish performers, as well as instruments that wouldn't typically be used in flamenco (like Paquito's double bass). Amongst professionals, there is an acceptance, and often voiced appreciation, for foreign flamenco aficionados. Foreigners are viewed as perfectly able to understand the art complex, as long as they are willing to put the work in to learn it properly. They are also valued for their role of consumers, which keeps the industry afloat. Despite the openness to variation and non-traditional approaches within the Madrid scene, there is nonetheless a feeling amongst performers that flamenco is more accepted outside of Spain than inside, which is one factor why performers utilise Madrid as a springboard to international tours and record releases. The capital is flamenco's window the world, with a large domestic and international flamenco scene, yet 'local' aficionados and aspiring professionals are often reticent to mention their interest to non-flamenco friends, family, and colleagues because it is not well-respected. Most of its negative reputation is historic, reaching back to the smear campaigns of the late nineteenth and early twentieth century related to *flamenquismo*. It is an art form that is looked down upon for its perceived association with *Gitanos*, drugs, and illiterate people.

The impression of flamenco that foreign cosmopolitan hubs experience and emulate when they return home is obviously somewhat different from that gained in Sevilla. The Madrid scene gives license to innovation and adaptation. This is reinforced by the touring theatre shows that often develop in the Madrid scene. It allows for fusion and diverting from the perceived 'traditional', which is valued in Andalucía. This tendency towards invention and creativity is second nature when flamenco moves abroad, perhaps for the same reason that it exists in Madrid: because of a dearth of in-built cultural connection to the art complex.

References

Álvarez, S. (2007). *Tauromachie et Flamenco: Polémiques et clichés, Espagne, fin XXIXe-début XXe*. Paris: L'Harmattan.

Belarde, F., & Navarro, J. G. (1985). *Sociedad y Cante Flamenco: El Cante de Las Minas*. Murcia: Editora Regional de Murcia.

Bethencourt Llobet, F. J. (2011). *Rethinking Tradition: Towards an Ethnomusicology of Contemporary Flamenco Guitar*. Unpublished Doctoral Thesis, Newcastle University, Newcastle.

Blas Vega, J. (1990). *Vida y cante de Don Antonio Chacón: La Edad de Oro del flamenco (1869–1929)*. Madrid: Cinterco.

Blas Vega, J. (2006). *Los Cafés Cantantes de Madrid (1846–1936)*. Madrid: Ediciones Guillermo Blázquez.

Blas Vega, J. Y., & Ríos Ruiz, M. (1988). *Diccionario enciclopédico ilustrado del flamenco*. (2 vols.). Madrid: ed. Cinterco.

Carballo, B. B., Pallol, T. R., & Vicente, F. (2008). *El ensanche de Madrid: Historia de una capital*. Madrid: Editorio Compultense.

Chuse, L. (1993). *The Cantaoras: Music, Gender and Identity in Flamenco Song*. New York: Routledge.

Cruces Roldán, C. (2002). *Más allá de la música: Antropología y flamenco (I): Sociabilidad, transmisón y patrimonio*. Seville: Signatura.

Cruces Roldán, C. (2003). *Más allá de la Música: Antropología y flamenco (II): Identidad, género y trabajo*. Seville: Signatura.

de Falla, M. (1950, 1972). El Cante Jondo (Canto Primitivo Andaluz). (in the Apéndice). In *Escritos sobre música y músicos* (pp. 137–162). Madrid: Espasa-Calpe.

Diéguez, F. (2008). *Historia de un tablao: Las Brujas. Sus gentes, susartistas y su época*. Cádiz: ed. Absalon.

Diversions publicas. (1922, August 8). La Época.

Escribano, A. (1990). *Y Madrid se hizo flamenco*. Madrid: Al Avapiés.

FlamencoTickets.com. (2019). Retrieved from https://www.flamencotickets.com/madrid-flamenco-shows

Frutos de la Restauración. (1888, July 8). *El Motín*.

Grimaldo, A. (2010). *Historia social del flamenco*. Barcelona: ed. Península.

Harney, L. D. (2006). Controlling Resistance, Resisting Control: The "Género Chico" and the Dynamics of Mass Entertainment in Late Nineteenth-Century Spain. *Arizona Journal of Hispanic Cultural Studies, 10*, 151–167.

Hernandez Girbal, F. (1933). *Salvador Sánchez "Frascuelo": Una vida popular: biografía novelesca*. Madrid: Sociedad General Española de Liberaría.

La Plaga Flamenca. (1888, July 9). *La Época*.

Lavaur, L. (1976). *Teoría romántica del cante flamenco*. Madrid: Editorial Nacional.

Llano, S. (2018). *Discordant Notes: Marginality and Social Control in Madrid, 1850–1930*. New York: Oxford University Press.

Machin-Autenrieth, M. (2017). *Flamenco, Regionalism and Musical Heritage in Southern Spain*. New York: Routledge.

Mitchell, T. (1994). *Flamenco Deep Song*. New Haven: Yale University Press.

Mora, K. (2008). *Las raíces del "duende": lo trágico y lo sublime en el cante jondo*. Unpublished Doctoral Thesis, The Ohio State University, Columbus, Ohio.

Mora Guarnido, J. (1922, July 11). El Cante Jondo. *La Voz*.

Murillo Saborido, E. (2017). *Los Tablaos Flamencos En Madrid Entre 1954–1973: Una Aproximación Académia a su Escena Musical*. Unpublished Masters' Thesis, Universidad Complutense de Madrid, Madrid.

Ortiz Nuevo, J. L. (1975). *Pepe el de la Matrona: Recuerdos de un Cantaor Sevillano*. Madrid: Ediciones Demófilo.

Storm, E. (2013). Un España más Española: La influencia del turismo en el imagen nacional. In L. J. Moreno & S. X. M. Nuñez (Eds.), *Ser españoles: imaginarios nacionalistas en el siglo XX* (pp. 530–560). Barcelona: RBA.

SUMA Flamenca. (2019). Retrieved from http://www.madrid.org/sumaflamenca/2019/entradas.html

Torres, N. (2005). *Historia de la guitarra flamenco: El surco, el ritmo y el compás*. Córdoba: ed. Almuzara.

Urbano, M. (1995). *La hondura de un antiflamenco: Eugenio Noel*. Córdoba: Ayuntamiento de Córdoba.

Washabaugh, W. (1996). *Flamenco: Passion, Politics and Popular Culture*. Oxford: BERG.

Washabaugh, W. (2012). *Flamenco Music and National Identity in Spain*. Surrey: Ashgate Publishing.

5

Flamenca Britannica: One Foot in Andalucía

5.1 Introduction

In the previous chapters, I examined the complexities within the Sevilla and Madrid flamenco scene, exploring its structure, performance contexts, and competing identities that characterise its manifestation. I discussed the socio-political and cultural factors that have influenced the local flamenco scene, as well as how globalisation has shaped those factors. Most notably, I described the transient ex-pat subculture that developed in conjunction (although not always in accord) with the local Sevillano flamenco community. I explored the transnational interactions (both present and historic) that transpire between local and foreign factions which have influenced flamenco's development 'at home' in Sevilla (Fig. 5.1).

These transcultural encounters become significant as we move to this chapter because it is the cross-cultural interactions at the 'local' level that most impact individual perceptions of flamenco which are transmitted abroad. What becomes especially important is the act of transit between Sevilla and, in this case study, the UK. This physical and conceptual journey across borders shapes the form that flamenco takes when moved from

© The Author(s) 2020
T. Martin, *Transnational Flamenco*, Leisure Studies in a Global Era,
https://doi.org/10.1007/978-3-030-37199-9_5

Fig. 5.1   Hebden Bridge flamenco

its 'original' context. Individual cosmopolitan hubs have a significant, if not dominant, role in flamenco's transmission in the UK. There are several factors that influence what occurs on the journey between the Andalucían and the UK culture which determine how flamenco is manifested across the border. The first is the individual's experiences in Sevilla (or other Spanish flamenco location), specifically if they believe they have encountered 'authenticity'. Another factor to consider is their motivations for returning 'home'—is it to teach, to practice, to perform? Is it permanent or temporary? Another factor which influences flamenco's development abroad is the transmitting individual's role in each location (Spain and home). Interviews revealed that these motivations often differ significantly. Finally, the most tangible alterations which happen to flamenco on this proverbial journey from Spain to the UK are the changes enacted to cope with cultural differences, involving aspects of the art form that might be 'lost in translation'. These are changes that the cosmopolitan hubs deem necessary and are often a compromise between their perceptions of 'authentic flamenco' and the concessions which must be made to suit student and audience expectations, as well as UK cultural norms.

This chapter reveals how Flamenca Britannica developed and is maintained through the efforts of these individual cosmopolitan hubs that transmit information gained through transnational interactions with the Spanish flamenco scene. The mode of UK transmission is significant because, unlike the 'human hubs' described by Kiwan and Meinhof, most of these flamenco culture brokers in the UK are British. Furthermore, many of them serve as the only flamenco aficionado (beyond the hobbyist level) in their general locality. On the one hand it is wonderful that there are dedicated individuals who learn flamenco in Spain and want to transmit it at home. On the other hand, it is problematic because most UK flamenco scenes feature only one person who is considered the expert. This presents issues not only with the continuity of a scene but also because these individuals create what oftentimes is the only perception that their students/audiences have of flamenco. If it is too diluted from the original, it becomes detrimental to the survival of the art form. Ultimately, this chapter offers insight into the factors that influence the development of a glocal flamenco scene in the UK and cultural identity.

This chapter is configured around one primary question: **What is the role of cosmopolitan hubs in the creation and maintenance of UK flamenco communities?** First, I examine what 'flamenco' entails in a UK context and how it has developed. Drawing upon ethnographic methods, interviews, and participant observation, I suggest a scene structure, history, demographics, and cultural norms that shape the appropriation of flamenco in the UK. Here, I also examine the flamenco characteristics that change 'in transit' when transmitted by human hubs in the UK.

Second, I differentiate between varying levels of participation (hobbyist, cosmopolitan hub/scene driver, and Spanish performer), which ties into the socio-cultural factors that inform the UK approach to leisure, especially in activities considered 'exotic'. In doing this, I provide insight into how the British approach leisure, tourism, and multiculturalism. All three factors influence how foreign music cultures are interpreted in a British context. Furthermore, I demonstrate through individual ethnographies how cosmopolitan hubs, the transient flamenco aficionados, are instrumental in the creation of local flamenco culture and networks in the UK.

Third, I examine the role of individual cultural brokers in the development of these local British scenes. I explored how these British aficionados have come to assume flamenco as an identity and something to transmit. I looked at the transcultural interactions of British cosmopolitan hubs (both at home and in Spain) which inform the development of a local UK scene, as well as influencing the counterpart in Spain. Here I also present a picture of who these individual cultural brokers are, specifically the roles they play in the British flamenco scene which often drastically differs from those assumed when amongst Andalucían flamencos. Specifically, I outline the importance and relevance of foreign human hubs (as opposed to Spanish) in the manifestation of flamenco in the UK, as well as an analysis of the factors that change as a result of their journey between Spain and the UK.

Finally, I propose a model for the UK flamenco scene—one that is relatively new for a music culture. It is a local (to Andalucía) subculture that has been transmitted abroad by human hubs who, in most cases, are actually UK nationals claiming flamenco as a surrogate cultural identity. Uniquely, these UK flamenco scenes reach towards Andalucía for inspiration as the ultimate authority on flamenco, instead of looking inwards at a definitive 'UK flamenco style'. Presumably, this is because of the foreign aficionados who recognise that to understand flamenco, one must reference the culture that surrounds it. As a result, I propose a glocal model which refers to perceptions of the 'original culture' (in Andalucía) for inspiration but is informed by regional cultural norms. While established for many years, the UK flamenco locales are still reliant on these individual brokers for transmission, continuity, and connection to Andalucía. This chapter provides insight into how the British approach multiculturalism, which often has bearing on how foreign music cultures are interpreted.

5.2   What Is the UK Flamenco Scene?

Around the UK, there exists small pockets of flamenco aficionados consisting primarily of British enthusiasts with a small population of relocated Spanish performers, most of whom are semi-permanent fixtures.

These entities, operating mostly independently of one another in a growing number of locales across the country, represent a faction devoted to the practice and preservation of a passionate and emotionally intense art complex existing independently of its Andalucían homeland. When I speak about the UK flamenco scene, it is in reference to a small collection of individuals across the country who are organised into groups dependent on locality. Flamenco exists in many locations across the UK, from predictable hubs such as London, Manchester, and Birmingham, to unlikely alcoves in Hebden Bridge and Matlock Bath. The scene is primarily situated around a particular dance class or teacher. Most localities only have one group—exceptions being in larger metropolitan areas, such as London, Bristol, and Birmingham. However, even in these cities, the groups are generally in different neighbourhoods. While there are rarely interactions with those outside of their localities within the UK, they do have intermittent contact, in one way or another, with elements of the Andalucían flamenco community. This will be demonstrated more fully in the following ethnographies.

Flamenco Groups

When I refer to the UK flamenco scene, I am mostly talking about a variety of mini-scenes that are loosely (or not at all) connected—however, they have similar characteristics, namely, that they are made up of a series of hobbyists pulled together by an individual culture broker. Despite their primarily autonomous existences, these groups consistently share several common characteristics. First, they are predominantly focused around a particular dance class, which is the main source of interactions (via classes, performances, or workshops) with flamenco. Second, these classes are principally composed of non-Spanish participants who approach the complex art form as an exotic hobby to be engaged with on a superficial, one-a-week level. Finally, in each locale there are individuals who have, for whatever reason, become infatuated with flamenco, to the extent that they have made it a way of life, often quitting jobs for periods of time because they recognised that the best way to understand the art form is to spend time studying it in Andalucía or Madrid. These individuals become revered as local experts and, more times than not, become the drivers or cosmopolitan hub of the individual flamenco scenes, which would often cease to exist without them. However, given that a large part of flamenco's meaning supposedly emanates from the history of collective suffering felt by the *Gitanos* and Andalucíans who practice it, it is important to consider the impact that an outsider cultural broker, such as these revered cosmopolitan hubs, can have on perception and appropriation of flamenco in the UK.

Groups existed in three formats: publicly run (by an institution), private businesses (by an individual), or as a *peña*. Publicly run groups were generally facilitated by dance schools or institutions such as Instituto de Cervantes. In this case, students pay a subscription to the institution and the latter would hire the teacher and advertise. In such cases, the teacher is generally not one of the scene drivers, but the classes are often part-organised by an individual in collaboration with the organisation. Private businesses are typically run by individuals (such as Rita in Oxford and Theresa in Liverpool, whom we will hear from later). They hold primary responsibility for finding a venue, advertising, and other logistical functions such as hiring musicians and scheduling performances. *Peñas*, in the UK format, operate as a sort of flamenco club that puts on performances—sometimes using professionals and sometimes students—and *juergas* which are flamenco jam sessions. They typically exist in locations with more than one dance teacher and pull in membership from across classes, as well as professionals in the area (who are often hired to perform). An example of this is Peña Flamenca de Londres. These first two group types are characterised by being the figurehead for weekly classes, which, as mentioned previously, forms the basis for UK flamenco sub-scenes. All three types feature the presence of a scene driver, who is often single-handedly responsible for the continuance and advancement of flamenco in the local community.

Group identity is defined by associating one's flamenco activities with a specific organisational entity. Some groups have formal membership, such as Peña Flamenca de Londres, which requires a yearly membership fee to attend events. Other groups, such as Flamenco Birmingham, are defined by whomever is attending courses or associated with the scene—such as semi-professional dancers and musicians.

Members and non-members alike are kept informed by group Facebook pages and email newsletters, usually run by the scene driver.

Group Activities

While membership is largely based on locality, there is intermittent cross-over between nearby factions—usually at events such as visiting artist workshops and performances. Singers and musicians, because of their scarcity, are often connected with more than one group. For example, Mike (a guitarist for the Leeds flamenco group) would often travel to Hebden Bridge to play for their classes. Activities they engage with out-side of class, depending on the location, include *peñas*, performance attendance, workshops, and the occasional class performance.

UK flamenco groups, although primarily class-centric, often have other activities associated with them. Some, such as Flamenco de Leeds and Birmingham Flamenco, hold *peñas*, every few months, attended by members, family, and friends. They also often have public class perfor-mances, with anywhere from one (the teacher) to fifteen dancers. Often groups are asked to perform by venues in the broader community. These smaller performances take place in pubs and restaurants, while larger class performances are often in large church halls, theatres, or town squares. Groups, particularly their leaders, often have interactions with community or local government organisations. For example, Paula (Hebden Bridge Flamenco) and Ruth (from Leeds Flamenco) periodi-cally taught flamenco history and dance workshops in local schools or for the Women's Institute (Paula and Claire, personal communication, Apr. 14, 2011). Claire from Deva Flamenco taught a weekly class for SCOPE to adults with disabilities.

Local Performances

Paid performance opportunities are not uncommon within the UK's fla-menco sub-scenes. Oftentimes a Spanish or Latin-themed restaurant or a pub will ask a local group if they want to perform for a one-off flamenco night (although the pay is usually low). They are specifically after a dancer, as this is in line with the UK perception of flamenco. Often these small venues do not understand why the dancer requests money for a guitarist and sometimes a singer and percussionist as well. The *cuadro* usually is contracted for several sets of 25 minutes, which involves a combination of instrumental, singing, and dancing. The typical audience is not familiar with flamenco, as is demonstrated by the lack of *jaleo* at these events. Even when instructed on how to clap *palmas* in the course of a performance, a British audience is reticent to participate.

The typical British audience conventions do not apply during a *peña* performance, as usually those present are students or flamenco aficionados. In that respect, they are comparable to an English folk club—while non-members may be present, most of the attendees are insiders with a basic understanding of the behavioural and musical norms (Finnegan 2007, p. 59). In fact, the audience members are supposed to be participants in a *peña*, with an awareness of the appropriate conventions of when voice and clapping are used. Most flamencos I have encountered in the UK have been British by descent and, if they do come to *peñas*, are interested in learning how to utilise *jaleo*. *Peñas* generally boast a relaxed, friendly atmosphere. Frequently they are more of a jam session than a performance, with attendees eating, drinking, and chatting in the background. The exception to this is when a visiting professional attends and performs; here it is an unspoken behavioural alteration that, instead of musicians and dancers joining in, everyone will respectfully watch.

Peña participation within these flamenco sub-scenes is akin to amateur ethnomusicology, with attendees striving to re-enact an Andalucían cultural phenomenon in order to learn and understand it. As will be discussed in the following ethnographies, most participants have never experienced flamenco in its Spanish homeland and rely on information from people who have—namely visiting artists and the cosmopolitan human hubs responsible for creating their particular flamenco scene. The UK *peña* creates an opportunity for students to perform amongst local aficionados and to link their local scene with its roots in Andalucía in order to create a better understanding for the premise of the music itself.

Group Components

Flamenco sub-scenes in the UK have typically featured similar components. As mentioned before, these sub-scenes usually focus around a particular flamenco class. Therefore, primary components include a teacher, students of varying experience levels, and a guitarist who not only plays for the class, but may have associations with other classes. Other elements, such as a *cajón* player or singer, are not common to every scene. The group driver can fall into any of these categories and it is not unusual for them to not be the teacher.

Most flamenco sub-scenes feature a professional flamenco teacher who regularly instructs one or more classes of amateur, hobbyist students. Most of the teachers I contacted were of British origin. During the course of my research, I encountered a handful of teachers who were of Spanish parentage; however, most of them were temporary fixtures and returned to Spain within a year or two. I attribute this in part to the difficulty of finding consistent work in flamenco in the UK, as well as inaccurate perceptions of the UK scene. The British instructors I encountered were usually university-educated, had previously held a conventional non-dancing career, and often had no prior dancing experience to flamenco. For example, Claire (Deval Flamenca) was formerly a librarian at Chester University and Paula (Hebden Bridge) taught languages at Bradford University. These educators (and others) discovered flamenco, became enthralled, and made it the primary focus of their lives. Many teachers, like Claire and Paula, quit their other jobs to devote themselves to the art complex. They learn through books, online resources, and workshops. A common characteristic is that they travel to Spain for lessons, for time frames ranging from two weeks to several years. This is the basis for how individuals become Cosmopolitan human hubs, carrying flamenco knowledge from its homeland to create scenes in its image in the UK. This does not always occur as a result of actually visiting Spain, with flamenco knowledge available online and from visiting artists. One of the primary differences between teachers and students is a desire to perform. Teachers generally had a strong desire to showcase their constantly developing talents and attract more students.

Students tended to primarily be women of British descent, although since the outset of Spain's economic crisis there has been an increase in

Spanish migrants which has resulted in an increase in Spanish students—most of whom are not from a flamenco background (Rita, personal communication, June 2, 2015). They range in age from mid-20s through to their 80s, as well as a few groups (such as Camino del Flamenco in Oxfordshire) boasting classes for children. For most students, interactions with flamenco occur only during this weekly class; some do not attend *peñas* or workshops.

Dissimilar to their teachers, most students are not inclined towards performance unless persuaded. Unless the students have aspirations towards paid work, most really just want to do it for fun. Instructors such as Paula, Claire, and Rita actually lose pupils once they start preparing for a performance, even though they are given the option whether to perform or not (Claire—2011, Paula—2011, and Rita—2015, personal communications). Several teachers, such as Paula, have theorised that since the British culture is generally not ostentatious and the prospect of performing an emotional dance for an audience which includes their peers is terrifying (Paula, personal communication, Mar. 27, 2011). One possible reason for this reticence might be that the majority of these participants do not define themselves by their flamenco involvement; it is simply an activity they engage with for a limited time.

Each sub-scene I encountered featured a few exceptions to student performance aversion. There are usually a few students who have fallen for flamenco to the extent that a once-a-week class is not enough involvement. Students like Elizabeth in Leeds, who is a mother of two young children and former primary school teacher, has become the hub of the Leeds flamenco scene. She does not teach the class but has revitalised the scene by facilitating bi-monthly *peñas* and workshops with visiting professional dancers. She practices for classes on a fold-out wooden floor in her kitchen and seeks out performance opportunities (Elizabeth, personal communication, Aug. 12, 2015).

Singers and Instrumentalists

Flamenco singers and instrumentalists (guitarists and percussionists) are hard to come by in the UK, especially outside of London. The reason for the lack of singers, as will be discussed later in this chapter, has to do with the difficulty of singing and improvising in Andalucían dialect for non-Spanish speakers, the complexity of flamenco singing techniques, and the intricate rhythms. Outside of London, I encountered only three singers. Flamenco percussionists are rare simply because there are not many classes focused on cajón. While the cajón itself is not a difficult instrument to play, the flamenco *compás* is not one that can be effectively learned by notation—it has to be understood within the context of the guitar, singing, and dancing.

Flamenco guitarists in the UK make for an interesting discussion. The best analogy is that there are many guitarists who play a bit of flamenco, but there are very few flamenco guitarists. There seems to be a certain type of guitarist that is attracted to learning a few showy flamenco *falsetas*, with no inclination towards playing for dancers or fully engaging with the culture. They are interested in learning the impressive technical side, but not in understanding the context. In flamenco, the role of the guitar is first and foremost to accompany and respond to the dancer and singer, keeping the *compás*. For this reason, I do not classify classical guitarists who have learned a few Spanishy-sounding riffs as part of the flamenco scene. There are several professional solo guitarists in the UK who play exclusively flamenco sets, but their interaction with the flamenco art complex is often peripheral. Flamenco guitarists seek out opportunities to perform with local dancers and often play in dance classes for practice or for a small fee. One potential explanation for the scarcity of singers and instrumentalists on the scene is that they generally require some degree of prior training on the instrument or in vocal techniques and, ideally Spanish language. This makes flamenco singing and guitar something that cannot be randomly picked up on a whim. Dancing, on the other hand, is often picked up as a hobby with no prior dance experience.

External Awareness Within Flamenco Groups

An interesting discovery in the early part of my research involved how little awareness existed within UK flamenco groups of the Spanish version of the culture, or even of other similar groups in their own countries. UK groups are essentially a local salute to a foreign cultural complex;

however, for most participants, cognizance of this is limited to information provided by local cosmopolitan hubs and teachers, with little individual initiative to learn independent of that. Direct interactions with Andalucían culture are typically limited to the local aficionados who travel to Andalucía or invite visiting Spanish professionals over. An example of this is Claire bringing *bailora* Maria de Suarez (from Malaga) to Chester to teach yearly workshops to Deva Flamenco (Claire, personal communication, Apr. 14, 2011). Overall, group contact with the Andalucían cultural complex comes primarily from second-hand information conveyed by human hubs (such as Claire) and aficionados. As will be discussed, with 60 or more years of flamenco classes, London has greater contact with the Spanish scene. Despite this, few actually go over to Spain—they rely on artists coming to them. For the most part, London students' interactions are still dictated by local cosmopolitan hubs (R. Ritchie—May 2015, Rita, June 2015, personal communications). There is, however, limited awareness of UK groups outside of London. For example, despite Peña Flamenca de Londres's heightened connection with Spain, the members I spoke with were not aware of the flamenco scenes north of Birmingham and were undeniably shocked that Leeds had one at all. The unfamiliarity with other similar organisations would not be so shocking except that there just are not that many flamenco entities in the UK, at least compared to other music interest groups. Outside of London, inter-group interactions are a little more common (although usually only occur if a significant flamenco teacher or performer is visiting). This will be demonstrated in the ethnography on Flamenco de Liverpool, in which students from several groups in northwest England converge for *peñas* and workshops. Interestingly, although London offers many excellent workshops and performances, hobbyists and aficionados north of Birmingham are usually more likely to fly to Spain for a performance than take a train to London (Paula—2011, Trish—2013, Claire—2011, personal communications).

Individuals in the UK Flamenco Scene

Finnegan, in her work with amateur musicians in Milton Keynes, utilises Becker's concept of 'art worlds' to describe 'musical worlds' as scenes that are composed of people whose actions are necessary to the production of a music scene (Finnegan 2007, p. 31).[1] They are characterised by shared practices, musical styles, values, social conventions, and 'modes of production and distribution' (Finnegan 2007, p. 32). Within these scenes, individuals situate themselves in a specific socio-cultural space and navigate the space utilising their knowledge of its shared values and behavioural norms to create a cultural identity. In the case of Flamenca Britannica, this identity (for most participants) is one that exists when they are in that particular social space. However, the parameters and cultural capital within these localised social spaces are generally determined by cosmopolitan hubs who assume flamenco as an integral part of their personal identity. The difference between these hobbyist and scene-driver personas will be discussed later in this chapter. Spanish flamencologist Enrique Baltanás, in his discussions about recent developments in flamenco, observed that:

> New flamenco tends onwards a great universality, towards an international and a cosmopolitan expansion but at the same time this new flamenco keeps inventing its own set of identities, either from the classic and well-known groups (Gypsy, Jewish, Moorish, Christians, etc.) or from additional, ad hoc ones […] [This has to do with] a procedure far too familiar in the realm of culture and art […]: the mutual exchange of influences between individuals, social groups and ideological currents. (Baltanás 2002, p. 159)

This quote is a step towards understanding the effects of individuals on scene creation in flamenco, specifically with regards to identity and aesthetics. Therefore, in order to grasp the nature of the UK flamenco scenes and sub-scenes, it is necessary to examine the role of the cosmopolitan hubs within them. Through transcultural interactions with the Spanish scene (both in the UK and in Spain), cultural capital gained in an Andalucían or Madrileño context, and a knowledge of UK behavioural norms, these British aficionados serve as cosmopolitan human hubs within the UK scene. The individual ethnographies in the remainder of

---

[1] See also Becker, H. (1984). *Art Worlds*. Berkeley: University of California Press.

this chapter will demonstrate how a foreign music culture (such as flamenco) manifests itself in a scene abroad (like the UK scene), as well as the influence of various foreign (British) human hubs in facilitating this process.

5.3   Ron: Tales of a Cockney Flamenco

I knock on the elegant front door, made from green, sculpted terracotta tiles. The door is answered by an elderly Chinese-British man with a smile and a sparkle in his eye. He introduces himself as Ron, in a thick Cockney accent. This is the man who every London flamenco I interviewed for the past four years told me I must speak with. He is the person who knew 'everyone' and whom 'everyone' had heard of, both Spanish and British, that had passed through the UK scene for the past 50 years.

As I enter his front hallway, I hear jazz coming from what turns out to be a 50-inch flat-screen TV. As he leads me through the front hallway to the sitting room, I notice the wall space is filled with art work, photos of Ron dancing, and photos of famous flamenco and jazz performers. After helping him to make cups of tea, he has me sit on one of the sofas so he can set up a video camera—he wants to make sure that I have copies of our conversation and that he can talk to me about some of the photos. Within the first few minutes of our conversation he has referenced his art, his love of flamenco, his trip to reform school for stabbing someone, his passion for jazz, and the fact that at the age of 31 he broke the Guinness World Record for jive dancing for over 24 hours straight. It is at this point I know that I am in for an eclectic afternoon.

Since I began researching the London flamenco scene in 2010, I have had people telling me to speak with Ron. Every single person, regardless of their age, who had at any time associated with the scene, viewed him as one of the ultimate authorities on the nature and development of the London flamenco community. His legend seemed to play a part in most narratives, both from native Londoners and Spanish visitors. Most informants cited the length of time that he has been active in flamenco and the related historical developments that he was part of as reasons to speak with him. Additionally, his extreme sociability, demonstrated largely by flamenco parties at his house, provided him with the opportunity to connect with people from the UK scene as well as artists from Spain. These factors combine to form one individual's part in shaping the history of flamenco in the UK. Beyond that, and perhaps most representative of the UK flamenco experience, is Ron's involvement in many different leisure activities, and his claim that he is not 'a flamenco' he just likes flamenco. It is not a source of identity for him. Ron is an example both of a cosmopolitan human hub, who has transmitted and developed the London flamenco scene, and a representative of British leisure consumption practices.

History of Ron

Ron was born in 1926 in the East End of London to British-Chinese parents. After a stint in reform school for stabbing someone, he was released because of World War II and went to work in the mines in Derbyshire. After the war ended and he returned to London, he began dancing—specifically jive. It was in 1951, though, that Ron first discovered flamenco.

He recounts:

> Well, I went to see Antonio and Rosario[2] at the Cambridge Theatre in, I think, 1951. In them days, they had been touring America and Spain doing recitals—so it wasn't just flamenco, it was Spanish dance, jotas, Peruvian, flamenco, a real mixture. The difference between those other types of dance and flamenco is that in the former you follow the music; in flamenco the musicians follow the dancer. So, I went backstage and talked to Antonio, who could speak a little English. I told him I wanted to dance flamenco and he said 'Don't think it's as easy as it looks!' I figured, already being a dancer and having rhythm, I'd have a routine nailed in a month. Sixty years later, I'm still learning!
>
> The next year I went to see some Indian dancing and bought a book called 'Dancers and Dancing'. There was an advert for Spanish dancing

---

[2] Antonio and Rosario were a world-famous Andalucían dance duo (including Spanish, Latin American, and flamenco styles) who left Spain in the wake of the Spanish Civil War and toured North America, South America, and Europe.

classes by Madame Lalagia. So, I found it, and she said to come along and see if I liked it. There were two other Spanish dancing teachers in London at the time—Elsa Brunelleschi and someone else whose name I can't remember. (R. Hitchens, personal communication, June 3, 2015)

Ron explains that Madame Lalagia's[3] reasoning for allowing him to come and see if he liked it is that so many people don't because it is contrary to their expectations. They want to do it for the fancy footwork, the clacking castanets, and the fiery dancing. Like Ron, they think they can learn a routine in an hour. However, flamenco is more complex than that. Learning the tools first is imperative—the body, the footwork, the arms, and the castanets—before a routine can be created. Many lose interest when they realise the work that goes into it. However, Ron stuck with it:

Because I said I would do it, I persevered, and it became a big part of my life. And, of course, after that I got "the fever". Each class had 45 minutes of exercises (arms, turns, castanets, etc.) then you learnt one step at the end. I kept thinking "when are we actually going to do some flamenco?!" Antonio came over to London again in 1954, but instead of Rosario, he brought an entire company of at least 50 dancers. It was out-of-this-world! They were only supposed to stay for a month, but flamenco was so popular in London they kept extending! (R. Hitchens, personal communication, June 3, 2015)

Flamenco, as well as other forms of foreign folk dancing was very popular in London during the post-war era. Important concert venues included the Cambridge Theatre and Palace Theatre. Even the Royal Albert Hall was holding annual folk festivals. The venues included performances from around Ireland and Great Britain, as well as Spain, Macedonia, and other parts of Europe. Ron performed flamenco in several of these prestigious events.

Alongside these prominent venues, Ron refers to several more casual venues that staged shows of both professional and amateur artists. Ron's

---

[3] 'Madame Lalagia' is Joan Evelyn Brind (1907–1999), and English dancer who, after studying in Barcelona and Madrid for a number of years, founded the Studio of Classical Spanish Ballet in London in 1951.

first performance experience came at 'The Acapulco', then a coffee bar on Hanway Street, which was near Cambridge Circus where Ron had lessons. He and his classmates would go after their weekly class:

> You would pay 2 and 6 to get into the basement, which included coffee and a coke and a night's entertainment. They had a flamenco guitarist and singer (who would also dance). The first dance you really learn in a flamenco class is Sevillañas, because it is a partner dance and has a set routine. This duo would play Sevillañas for us to dance to. (R. Hitchens, personal communication, June 3, 2015). (R. Hitchens, personal communication, June 3, 2015)

These coffee bars were typical of London during the post-war era, and a number of them offered foreign and folk music. The most famous of these venues was The Troubadour. The Troubadour was opened in 1954 by Michael and Shelia van Bloemon as part of the second Great London Coffee Revolution ("UK Coffee Revolution, the Third Wave?", 2013). It became known as one of the primary venues of the British folk revival (late 1950s and early 1960s) ("Troubadour London History", n.d.). They hosted the likes of Bob Dylan, Jimi Hendrix, Joni Mitchell, and Paul Simon (as well as *Private Eye* and the 'Ban the Bomb' campaign). However, alongside these Anglo-centric activities, were a number of foreign music and dance nights. Ron remembers:

> Once we knew a bit more, we would go to the Troubadour on Old Brompton Road, instead of The Acapulco. In them days, you had people who were interested in different types of dances. It was a place where everybody went because it was Earl's Court, where there was a lot of bedsits. They would come to this place, pay 3 and 6 for a night's entertainment and get food at a reasonable price. Wednesday night was flamenco night, Tuesday was French. There were other world music and poetry nights too. Us students would go there and there was pro guitarists and student guitarists. We would get up, practice dancing, and enjoy ourselves. (R. Hitchens, personal communication, June 3, 2015)

He points out that the world is much more intertwined now than it was in post-war London. People did not travel as much, and video technology was not widely utilised. 'When the war finished, here in London you had to go to the theatre to see a Mexican or an Indian show; if they got Ravi Shankar over, you wanted to know when you would see him again. TV and the internet enable that now', he says (R. Hitchens, personal communication, June 3, 2015). People were, therefore, eager to participate in other ways, such as putting on their own dance nights.

It was then that Ron met many other actors and musicians who were just starting out, such as Oliver Reed and Ken Russell. This led to a steady stream of radio and television appearances over the years, such as 'Monitor' with Ken Russell and the Russell Harty Show. Ron has always attracted attention because of his Cockney and Chinese background and his diverse interests.

Ron mentions some of the many venues that were putting on small nightly or weekly shows. The Antonio Restaurant in Long Acre, for instance, would book a group of three or four performers from Spain. Ron got his first flamenco job in 1955 at Casa Pepe in Pelham Court because some of these performers were headed back to Spain. The vacating dancer suggested him for an audition. Ron remembers:

> I went, not expecting much, without any flamenco boots, wearing crepe-soul shoes, with my braces undone. I looked a right state, but I got the job because I could improvise and had a good feel of the music. I learnt that improvisation was an important skill in flamenco. (R. Hitchens, personal communication, June 3, 2015)

He joined a troupe of Spanish performers—two guitarists, a singer, and another dancer. They did four twenty-minute shows, six nights a week for £9/week. Ron earned the nickname of 'El Bruto' because he was responsible for cracking the parquet floor with his jumping and stomping. He also went by 'Manolo':

> Because the Governor wanted me to have a Spanish name. But I never wanted to be Spanish. I wanted to be English and do Spanish dancing. I even got reprimanded for not picking up my wages there—the money wasn't important. Just the dancing. (R. Hitchens, personal communication, June 3, 2015)

Ron refers to many other little venues putting on nights like this, as well as recitals that were put on in peoples' houses. The interesting thing about these evenings was that the guests were not always flamencos; there would often be other types of music played on violins and pianos, different sorts of dances, and a combining of styles. One night, after performing at a wedding, Ron and, his girlfriend, stopped by a little Turkish restaurant they often frequented in Islington (the Sultan Ahmet). When questioned by the owner regarding their Spanish attire, his girlfriend revealed they had been dancing flamenco. The owner thought they were joking as Ron usually sat around playing backgammon. He then suggested they put on a flamenco night in his establishment. So, Ron created a group called 'Flamenco Place' and started running a flamenco night there on the first Sunday of the month, starting at 3 pm. There were no entrance fee and people brought their own wine and would pay three and six (3 *s* 6*d*) for a large plate of Turkish food.

Student dancers and guitarists from nearby flamenco classes came down to perform and practice. Sometimes professionals would attend and dance for fun. Even visiting Spanish dancers turned up periodically. The event would continue until about 7:30 pm, then the flamenco students and guests would head back to Ron's house where he had prepared chicken and jacket potatoes, supplemented by food and wine brought by guests. The flamenco party would continue until 3 am. Ron refers to this time period as one that brought together flamenco lovers, not only across London but transnationally. I recognise many of the names Ron mentioned, but most notable is Vivian, a professional journalist, who assumed the task of creating and printing the group's newsletter—'La Habladora'. She would later go on to begin London's prominent and long-lasting flamenco-meeting point—Peña Flamenca de Londres. Ron credits her with keeping the organisation going strong—now at 400+ members—since 1984. Ron's 'Flamenco Place' evening was the precursor to this.

Flamenco Parties at La Casa de Ron

These flamenco evenings and after-parties were also central to Ron's (and the London flamenco scenes) transnational interactions with Spain. From the comfort of his couch, we spent a couple hours watching DVDs of the many videos and photos Ron has from these occasions—some dating from the late 1950s. There are old photos, colours dulled with age, on his walls of some of the more renowned visitors:

> You see Mario Maya up there? And to his right is Carmen Vargas. Juan Amaya is the photo next to her. My friend Mark, a Scottish guitarist, went to Jerez last year and met someone who had been at my house twenty years ago! (R. Hitchens, personal communication, June 3, 2015)

We sit and laugh at more recent videos of Sara Baras eating melted ice cream on his stairs and Vicente Amigo laughing at Ron's practical jokes. Ron began these little informal flamenco gatherings as early as the late 1950s. He and his friend, Jingles, would go backstage after a visiting flamenco artist performance, compliment them on the show, and ask if they would like to come back to the house for food and drinks. Earlier that day, Ron would have acquired the food and begun making Tandoori chicken, rice, and spareribs. Jingles would pick the artists up and bring them back to the small semi-detached house in which we sat. Ron remembers:

> People would be packed in here. On the stairs, in the studio, because sometimes there were two companies in town at a time. José Greco[4]'s daughter was here (pointing to a black and white photo on the wall). Then of course, the people from the Spanish community in London would come, as well as my friends from the *peña*. We would all sit here eating, smoking, and drinking. Manuela and Rafaela Carrasco, Manolo Ti, La Tati, Cumbre Flamenco—they were all here. Then a guitarist would get a hold of an instrument and the singing and dancing would begin. They were so disciplined on stage but let loose once they got here! (R. Hitchens, personal communication, June 3, 2015)

Ron's parties became famous among the London flamenco community and visiting artists as a liminal space between performances to relax and

---

[4]José Greco (1918–2000), an Italian-born American flamenco dancer, known for popularising flamenco in the theatres and in films in the 1950s and 1960s.

let loose after a show. Generations of flamenco families passed through, for example, the Basiliscos in London, and the Farrucos from Sevilla. Ron reports that visiting Spanish are told when they come to London that 'when you are there, you will meet someone named Ron Hitchens, or "El Chino". You will go to his house and eat well and when he gets up to dance, you must watch him' (R. Hitchens, personal communication, June 3, 2015). This demonstrates the reverence that Spanish performers travelling to London developed for this Cockney aficionado. 'They all knew where I lived, even when they didn't know where Buckingham Palace was!', Ron tells me proudly. On a reciprocal note, the occasions brought the London flamenco aficionados, who may otherwise not have had any other association with Spain, into casual contact with 'the real thing'.

Ron is well known amongst the flamenco community for his antics at parties. Although an excellent dancer, Ron confesses that he never got on well with learning specific choreographed routines once he grasped the techniques. He has always preferred improvisation. However, his improv has often included a certain sense of humour. He recounts how he once had someone turn off the lights at a party so he could enter the room to start dancing. When the lights went up, he was completely nude except for shoes and a sombrero performing a particularly sombre *siguiriyas*. At Peña events, he often is called onstage at the end to dance. He finished by turning his bum to the audience and making it 'dance' in *compás*. Ron's flamenco parties and informal *peña* events offered a place for relaxed transcultural integration of flamenco (Fig. 5.2).

The Hobbyist

After a couple of hours of video and picture viewing (as well as a half dozen biscuits and a cup of tea), I asked Ron about what he got out of these events—all the time and energy that went into them was an admirable level of dedication. I also was curious if he ever felt that the Spanish professionals had questioned his ability because he was foreign. He replies that he had never felt that because they had never seen the extent of his

Fig. 5.2 The author and Ron Hitchens in front of his hand-sculpted terracotta door

dance abilities—he only ever got up and did a bit of *bulerías* at these parties. He explains:

> I've always done it [these parties] because I love to dance. It's not a business. I'm not looking for connections or a good name. I'm a moron in flamenco; I know nothing about its history. But I do love it. It's for fun.

Even though he is considered by many (local and foreign) to be one of the focal points (cosmopolitan hubs) of the London flamenco scene, Ron says that it is a hobby he can take or leave because he has other things in his life. He does not speak Spanish and does not miss flamenco now that he is too old to dance. Ron says that he took flamenco up as a hobby (as he has tango, salsa, jive, and many other things) because he loves to dance. Most of the time when he was performing for money, he would not even bother to pick up his wages because he already had a career selling shirts at Petticoat Lane Market. Ron clarifies:

> I love flamenco, but I am not A FLAMENCO. I don't live for it like those guitarists that practise three hours a day or the dancers who perform with a broken ankle. I just enjoy dancing and want to have fun. Its music and the greatest thing about music is you don't have to speak the same language. (R. Hitchens, personal communication, June 3, 2015)

This sentiment I have found to personify the British approach to leisure—one that devotedly dabbles instead of 'lives' a cultural activity. This is demonstrated by other British music culture researchers such as Miller (2013), Eisentraut (2001), and Finnegan (2007). Still, after spending eight hours in the presence of an entertaining and multi-talented Cockney flamenco aficionado, I leave Ron's house with the impression that I have met the heart and soul of the London flamenco scene. He is someone who brought it together for sixty years and single-handedly (if fleetingly) linked it with some of the biggest flamenco performers in Spain on an intimate level not experienced in normal performance interactions. He also brought the local London flamenco community together—first through his 'Flamenco Place' events at the Sultan Ahmet and subsequent contributions to Peña Flamenca de Londres, and second through his famous parties. In 2016 he started sponsoring a £300 bursary for young flamenco dancers through Peña Flamenca de Londres. Ron is representative of the influence of the individual in developing a local, but transnationally connected scene, as well as the British hobbyist approach to flamenco that will be demonstrated to be the norm.

Analysis

The story of El Chino, Ron Hitchens, is in many ways the story of Flamenca Britannica, at least in London. His story offers insight into several aspects of the British flamenco scene. First, he offers a view of how flamenco has evolved as a leisure activity in the UK (and London in particular). Ron also offers an example of how the British approach leisure activities in general and flamenco in particular. While Ron is a network creator, he is not one who claims flamenco as a sole identity. Despite this, he has represented an important transcultural link and human hub within the London flamenco community for over sixty years.

The Evolution of Flamenco as Leisure

Ron offers particularly poignant insight into the evolution of the London flamenco scene, as there are not many who have engaged with it from the outset of its adoption as a leisure activity in the post-war years, through its development into a global phenomenon. If we follow Ron's flamenco pathway, he starts off wanting to learn because he sees a show by Antonio and Rosario, who performed Spanish and Latin American folk dances—including flamenco. Ron began taking lessons from Madame Lalagia who taught Spanish folk dancing, of which flamenco was just one of the styles. There were two other Spanish dance teachers in London at that time (early 1950s) who offered similar agendas. Ron references the folk music festival that occurred annually in Royal Albert Hall. These included a mixed programme of folk music from the British Isles as well as traditions from across Europe:

> Traditions from Belgium, France, Denmark, Germany, Italy, Spain, Portugal, Macedonia, Russia and many others were all performed under the Royal Albert Hall's glass dome at the Folk Festival. For many members of the audience in the early years of the Festival, the international performers provided something of great excitement in an age before mass travel. The exotic dances were one of the closest experiences the British audience had of lands beyond the coast. (Baulcombe 2014)

Ron also references smaller venues which, in the 1950s and 1960s, were holding nightly events featuring world music traditions. Sometimes these venues were exclusively flamenco-oriented, such as at the Acapulco on Hanway Street. Other places, such as The Troubadour, marked spaces for collaboration between various music and dance traditions. Ron also mentions private house parties where he was invited to fuse flamenco with other instruments and genres. To contextualise this era in flamenco's history in the UK, for the most part up until World War II, it had primarily existed in this country as part of travelling theatre and ballet shows and were described as Spanish dance or ballet. In the interwar years, popular dance (especially from the UK and Latin America) began to evolve as pastimes (Abra 2012).[5] It is unclear if flamenco was included in these popular dance interests. Leisure activities, accessible to upper and middle classes since the Victorian years, became possible for a wider range of people after the war, as did an interest in foreign cultures. These factors, plus increased immigration and travelling artists[6] from Spain to escape the Franco regime, set the scene for an increase in flamenco participation in the UK.

It is significant to note, at this point, that based on Ron's evidence, flamenco was an activity often combined with something else—such as other Spanish folk, Indian ragas, and Peruvian music. It is unclear what the reason for this would have been, other than perhaps the presence of a condensation of cultures coming into contact that maybe had not been utilised as leisure activities previously. This is not to say that flamenco did not exist in the UK as a separate entity during the 1950s, just that the British enthusiast's engagement with it seems to have occurred in a fusion/ combination format.

Ron's story progresses to descriptions of flamenco experiences in London which are more exclusively devoted to the art form—such as Casa Pepe, where he performed with a mostly Spanish group. This was part of a professional flamenco world that existed alongside the amateur scene (inhabited by Ron and his classmates) from the late 1950s through the late 1980s (give or take a few years) (M. Basilisco, personal communication, Mar. 19, 2014). Several informants who were performing in that era cite an atmosphere in London where the intrepid performer could acquire gigs in two or three locations a night—especially around Tottenham Court Road at places like Sevilla Mia and Costa Dorada. A turning point in the London flamenco scene seems to have occurred

---

[5] See Allison Abra, 'The evolution of popular dancing in Britain in the 1920s', in *Leisure and Cultural Conflict in Twentieth-Century Britain*, ed. by Brett Bebber (Manchester: Manchester University Press, 2012), 41–62.

[6] Such as Antonio and Rosario, Carmen Amaya, and La Argentina.

when Ron began his 'Flamenco Place' evenings at Sultan Ahmet's, which brought together amateur, professional, and visiting Spanish flamencos from across London. Ron's evenings marked seemingly one of the first times that British hobbyists received the opportunity to interact in a *peña* format and hone their skills alongside Spanish professionals. Flamenco Place evolved into Peña Flamenca de Londres, which is London's biggest and longest running flamenco group, pulling together students and professionals from across the city.

The London flamenco scene has expanded to include dance studios in practically every neighbourhood in London (R. Ritchie, personal communication, May 27, 2015). Ron attributes this to students gradually splintering off to form their own studios. There are also an increased number of dance academies that facilitate workshops and shows (such as Flamenco Express and Escuela de Baile). Interestingly, although the number of students and institutions are at saturation level, the number of cafés and restaurants that regularly book flamenco evenings has declined to almost nothing, in comparison to post-war through 1990s London (Vivian, personal communication, May 2015). It is no longer possible to perform flamenco on a nightly basis in London—the storied venues have all stopped hiring. Peña Flamenca de Londres is widely considered to be the focal point of the London flamenco scene, but their performance options are limited to once every few months and are usually reserved for local stars and visiting artists. Flamenco Express and España On Fire host performances as well, but also are reserved for local stars and visiting professionals. There are, of course, Spanish flamencos who live in London, although they tend not to run sub-scenes, only act as performers and workshop technicians. Essentially the London flamenco scene has evolved from a scene almost entirely professional (pre-World War) to one that is mostly amateur, with the professionals predominantly teachers and visiting artists.

The British Hobbyists

Ron represents the history of flamenco in the UK as a leisure activity, having been one of the few on the scene since the beginnings of its existence as a leisure activity. He also exemplifies the typical flamenco hobbyist (albeit a very accomplished and dedicated one), as well as being an example of the quintessential British approach to leisure—as something to be cherry-picked and consumed. Ron became dedicated to learning flamenco, among several other types of dance as a leisure activity. He never considered it a profession, and, although sometimes paid for his performances, never considered himself a 'flamenco', just a guy who loved to dance in general and liked flamenco in particular. This is characteristic of 'local' music in the UK—the absence of a clear distinction between amateur and professional artists (Finnegan 2007, p. 15). In my interview with him, Ron was quick to point out that flamenco was just one aspect of his life; he could take it or leave it because he had so many other things to be interested in.

Ron's approach to flamenco is representative of how most British participants approach the art complex and is indicative of how the British approach leisure activities in general. Flamenco is something to be engaged with as an exotic social activity; one to be consumed and discarded at will. This attitude will be corroborated in the next case study by Rita's observations about her students. Finnegan also confirms my assessment of the British approach to leisure in her study of Milton Keynes' amateur music scene. She surmises that musical activities for the British are set within a wide range of other social activities (Finnegan 2007, p. 328). Paula, the cosmopolitan hub of Hebden Bridge Flamenco, notes that even in a small town, she often loses students to other activities such as yoga or trapeze classes. Cultural activities, such as flamenco, become one of any of several ways in which leisure time could be spent. Eduardo De la Fuente, in his article, 'Signs and Wonders', considers the trajectory of cultural consumption versus 'spiritual fulfilment':

> The 'infinite' and the 'unattainable' become questions of gratification, or what we moderns term 'consumption'. Culture becomes reduced to taste, or to lifestyle choices. (De la Fuente 2011, pp. 39–40)

What this suggests is that in 'modern' Western countries, culture and its consumption are reduced to activities, cherry-picked, and discarded at will. Pastimes, such as flamenco, are engaged with to a limited level— usually once a week in a dance or guitar class—as something to accompany the rest of 'life'.

Leisure consumption activities are likely the root of acceptance of foreign art complexes like flamenco and are common amongst privileged, high-income, and well-educated individuals (Aoyama 2007, p. 110). Miller (2013) observed that 'when music is consumed as a lifestyle choice there is no curiosity about a music's history, how it works or where it originated' (Miller 2013, p. 112). In the UK flamenco scene, I perceived a certain lack of interest about aspects of the art form outside of the dance or guitar. As has been mentioned previously, flamenco is an art complex that involves *cante*, *baile*, *toque*, *jaleo*, and *ritmo* in communication with each other via the *compás*. Its meaning is heavily linked with Andalucían culture and history of socio-political oppression. Therefore, it seems unfathomable that one aspect (i.e. dance or guitar) could be separated from any other part. However, flamenco is very much treated as a 'lifestyle choice' to be cherry-picked and consumed at will. While there are those, even amongst the hobbyists, that display an interest in learning a bit more than 'just the dance', it is rarely considered essential to flamenco education. Because of this, many UK flamenco students never grasp the entirety of flamenco culture; they are content to attend a once-a-week class, maybe perform in a few class performances, and otherwise focus on other aspects of their lives. For most, flamenco is a dance, not a culture. The most important feature of learning flamenco for most students seems to be a perceived presence of Spanishness in their dancing, a sense of empowerment, elements of physicality, and exoticness. This has bearings on how flamenco is taught, as will be demonstrated in the next ethnography.

The Hobbyist as a Cosmopolitan Human Hub

While Ron is in many ways represents the quintessential British hobbyist, he has been integral to the development of the London scene. He brought together students within the community first with his 'Flamenco Place' evenings and then with his involvement with Peña Flamenca de Londres. He facilitated transcultural interactions between visiting Spanish artists with the local UK scene through his parties and his outgoing, welcoming personality and vivacious dancing. He is perceived as an important hub within the London flamenco community. Across the city's scene, he is viewed as someone knowledgeable about the history of flamenco (especially as it relates to the London scene) and an accomplished dancer. Most importantly, Ron is viewed as a vital transcultural connection with Spain. Although most of these cross-cultural interactions have occurred on an individual level, they have had an impact on the scene. Within London, he is granted significant capital because of the many important artists who know him and visited his house. Amongst some facets of the professional flamenco community in Spain, Ron is considered a novelty—an Anglo-Chinese man, who understands flamenco. He is also someone that they are told to visit because of his welcoming attitude and parties. Overall, Ron's parties represent an occasion of transcultural interactions with Spain—ones where professional artists engage with local UK flamencos, instead of just teaching or performing for them.

Ron characterises a cosmopolitan hub in the UK flamenco scene. He is someone who has great knowledge of the local scene and connections with the Spanish one. He is a hobbyist, like most participants in the UK community. He has been instrumental in the London flamenco community's development because of these factors. Most importantly, Ron is someone who is known and respected by the London flamenco community and has served as a vital connection with Spain.

5.4   Rita: Oxfordshire Culture Broker

While Ron's status as a hobbyist is representative of a sizable proportion of the British flamenco experience, it is important to understand that there are those who endeavour to build a UK-based career—many of whom were once flamenco travellers in Spain. It is also crucial to grasp the differences between how flamenco is practiced in London versus the rest of the county. The scenes have some noticeable differences. Rita, the focus for this ethnography, was one of the more prominent flamenco teachers in the UK. She teaches numerous courses and sponsors many performances—both student and professional—throughout the year.[7]

---

[7] Based on queries in UK interviews.

Operating out of Oxfordshire now, Rita, during my research, was connected with most of the UK flamenco community through her Facebook persona of 'Camino del Flamenco'. She is significant for the purposes of this book because she was one of the cosmopolitan human hubs in Spain and now transmits the culture in the UK, while maintaining strong transnational connections with the Spanish scene.

Camino del Flamenco *Spanish Evening*

I walked along the darkening path beside Banbury's River Cherwell towards the Mill Arts Centre, formerly a working mill which still features the old water wheel. Now an arts and performance venue, it is home to Camino del Flamenco's Spanish Nights. I trekked down to Oxfordshire that evening to see the show and to meet Rita for the first time. At the suggestion of a mutual friend, Theresa from Liverpool, I contacted Rita via Facebook about coming to one of her events and conducting an interview. She agreed, so I went down for her February show.

Entering the building, I noticed a small café bar so went and bought a cup of tea. I sat at a table near some stairs that appeared to lead up to the theatre. After a few moments, the door from upstairs opened and a blond woman with her hair in an elaborate up-do and a red flower tucked behind her ear appeared. I recognised Rita from her Facebook photos and stood up to introduce myself. She embraced me and kissed me on both cheeks, saying she could not talk at the moment but was looking forward to our conversation after the show. I followed her upstairs to the theatre (another small attic room) and to a café table where she had a reserved a seat for me. Eventually three other strangers joined me for the performance.

The room was dimly lit and decorated with Spanish flag bunting. The café tables had red and yellow paper tablecloths to match. Each table had a candle and plastic plates of olives, pork scratchings, and *kikones*.[8] The room was set up with about fifteen tables surrounding twenty square feet of wooden floor space where the artists would perform. There were four chairs at the edge of the 'stage' designated for the *cuadro*. Behind the

---

[8] Salted fried corn kernels.

artists' seats was a long table with punch bowls of *sangria* (a glass of which was included in the ticket price). The café table had fliers for Rita's courses as well as the following month's Spanish Night.

The room began to fill and soon it was at capacity (70 guests). Some people were wearing flowers or flamenco-inspired attire. Soon the audience, who mostly were middle-aged and British, was seated with glasses of sangria and ready for the show to commence. Rita came onto the stage to introduce the *cuadro*—Roderigo on guitar, Javier Macías singing, Anita La Maltesa dancing, Antonio Romero playing cajón and darabuka, and Attab Haddad on the Iraqi oud. The first part of the show would be a fusion of Middle Eastern oud/darabuka and flamenco *cante*, *toque*, and *compás*. It would demonstrate the musical connections between the Iraqi and Spanish musical styles via historic Moorish influences in flamenco. 'But don't worry', Rita assured the audience, 'there will be plenty of dancing in the second half'.

As Rita left the stage, Javier, a tall Andalucían *cantaor* up from London, walked through the door and onto the makeshift stage. He began to sing a slow, soulful song, a *martinete*. This is a beautiful old *palo* which is unaccompanied and takes its rhythmic feel from the tempo of a blacksmith's hammer—harking back to the days of this being a typical *Gitano* profession. Javier lightly clapped *palmas* during the song. At the conclusion of the haunting *cante*, Roderigo, Attab, and Antonio came onstage. Before beginning the next piece, Roderigo gave some background on how the group came together. Already a prominent flamenco guitarist, South African-Spanish Roderigo met Iraqi Attab in London and they began experimenting with fusion. Now they work as a trio alongside Antonio. That evening, they included singing and dancing to more clearly demonstrate the Arabic links with flamenco.

For their second piece, Attab began a solo based on an Iraqi melody, which then led directly into a *bulerías* where he was joined by Roderigo and Antonio. Somehow the styles of the two musics seemed to meld together seamlessly. The remainder of the first half consisted of the instrumentalists plus Javier performing several Spanish folk songs and flamenco *palos*, often fusing the two together. The shared roots of the two styles were demonstrated to the audience by use of similar melismatic vocal and guitar techniques, as well as the use of the Spanish Phrygian mode. The first act ended with another energetic *bulerías*. Before leaving the stage to appreciative applause, Roderigo assured us that there would be dancing in the second half, almost as if he expected people to leave.

As the interval began, audience members arose to stretch their legs and get more sangria. I introduced myself to the people at my table, who were all former students of Rita's. They agreed that the show so far had been enjoyable, although they had expected more dancing. During the break, there was a raffle to raise money for Calvert Trust. All items were related to Spain or flamenco. I won a bottle of Tio Pepe Fino—what luck! Then the lights dimmed, and the audience took their seats for the second half.

First the musicians came back onstage with Javier and performed another solo *siguiriya*. The audience primarily watched without contributing *jaleo*. Following that, Attab performed a *tangos*-esque solo. After the applause at the end of that piece, Roderigo began to play the *salida* (opening improvisation) to an *alegrías*. Finally, Ana La Maltesa, adorned in a long red and white dress, entered the room. She was greeted with enthusiastic claps from the audience. She walked to the middle of the stage and danced a *llamada* which signalled to the rest of the ensemble to begin the next section of the piece. The audience participated a bit more in this piece and clearly had been anxiously anticipating the dancer. They shouted a few '*olés!*' and a few people even clapped *palmas*.

A highly structured *palo*, the *alegrías* typically ends with a modulation to a minor key into a *bulerías de Cádiz*. Ana La Maltesa danced a few *letra* of this and then invited Rita and her thirty-year old daughter, Madeleine, to begin the *fin de fiesta*—the improvised end to a flamenco show which is not often executed in UK shows. All three performed two *pataitas de bulerías* interspersed with cante before dancing out of the room to the audience's standing ovation and shouts of '*olé!*' The crowd immediately began filtering out of the venue, and I looked around for Rita to say good-bye, as I needed to run to catch the last train out of Banbury. She seemed pleased with the performance and the sold-out tickets. However, she commented that this was not the type of performance she normally presented, in that dance was not the focus and audiences generally associated dancing with flamenco.

I found the show to be representative, both from an audience and artistic standpoint, of a flamenco performance in the UK. The UK's municipal centres provide opportunity for transnational interactions—not only between British and Spanish but also between many other cultures. This performance represented a multicultural collaboration finding a common ground between flamenco and Iraqi music, whilst maintaining aspects of each individual genre. This type of fusion is an example of taking artistic risks and expanding the definition of flamenco. These collaborations are not the norm within the more purist Sevillano flamenco scene, nor are they part of the flamenco education offered there. It is not unusual in the UK. I suspect that it is in part something that occurs not only because of the large number of cultures that come into contact here, but also because the audience is more receptive to fusion and possess a more flexible concept of 'authenticity'. This expansion of flamenco's artistic parameters is typical of the broader UK scene (as will be discussed later). Also typical in this performance was the obvious preference for dance—the audience appreciated the instrumental/vocal performance but were most animated during the *alegrías*. Rita, as the event organiser, recognised this and felt the need to continually reassure the crowd that they would see dancing. Most attendees, even those who take classes, do not link it with an art form that encompasses song, music, rhythm, and *jaleo* as well. This will be explored later in this chapter.

Camino del Flamenco as a UK Cultural Hub

Later I would meet with Rita in The Jam Factory, a little café near Oxford rail station set in a former marmalade factory. Rita told me that 'somehow or other, I have been lucky enough to spend most of my adult life in flamenco' (Rita, personal communication, June 2, 2015). She did not intend to pursue it as a career, although she always loved dancing and is half-Andalucían. Rita did not begin flamenco until her late teens—and then only because some of her friends did it. After a few years, she went to Andalucía to study flamenco and before long found herself in a professional job on stage in one of the tablaos, even though she was still learning. Rita recounts that she had some lucky breaks in Spain and learned just as much performing as in class. At that point, all her friends in Spain were involved in flamenco. She spent several years learning and performing amongst some of the top tablao artists in Andalucía. Rita describes experiences dancing as part of the ensemble behind these top artists and how she, for several years, had to keep her blonde hair dyed black and her skin tanned to an orange-ish brown hue to meet expectations of the tourist audiences. She also describes instances of teachers taking advantage of foreign students. Amongst positive and negative experiences in the Sevilla scene, Rita gained important flamenco knowledge and contacts that would serve her well in developing a teaching and performance business in the UK.

After returning to London, she continued to perform. One evening, she and another dancer, Nuria García, were parked in a car outside a London tablao. Nuria turned to Rita and said, 'You know, I am thinking of starting a flamenco school in London, would you like to come in with me?' And so Escuela de Baile was born. Nuria did the teaching and Rita did the administration and marketing. Rita remembers that it was fun and successful for eleven years, but it stretched their friendship. At the same time, Rita's husband, who is from outside of London, wanted to leave the city. They moved to Oxfordshire (in 2003), leaving Escuela de Baile in Nuria's hands.

After a few months, Rita realised she would have to do something other than clean house all day and that the only thing she knew how to do was run a dance school. Applying the same techniques that had made Escuela de Baile a success, Rita opened Camino del Flamenco.

London Versus Outside: Adjusting the Business Plan

Rita quickly realised that Camino's outside-London location required a new marketing strategy for her classes. She noticed that students outside London oftentimes had different motives for pursuing flamenco than those in London. London has multiple performance venues, a strong Spanish community, and a large population which allows students to actually envision flamenco as a career path. Because of this, classes are geared towards a holistic approach to flamenco technique, with frequent performance opportunities, and a focus on constant improvement. Escuela de Baile even offers a Full Time Professional Dance Course

("Escuela de Baile", n.d.). Rita found this not to be the case in Oxfordshire. She observes:

> In London, they can start at the beginning in children's classes and can see themselves doing it professionally, teaching, maybe even dancing in Spain. Alicia is a good example of this. When students come to me that isn't even something that has ever entered their minds. They tend to be, in the adult classes, late twenties through early sixties. [...] These people already have a career, often a family. They have their life in place and are looking for an interesting hobby—something to do once a week where they will make friends, have one, do the occasional show. And that is IT. They aren't interested in anything beyond that. I don't think most of them realise you can become professional. (Rita, personal communication, June 2, 2015)

When she began her classes in Oxfordshire, one of the first things which shocked Rita was that most students did not speak a word of Spanish, had never visited Spain, and knew nothing about it or flamenco. This poses a stark contrast to the London scene which, as indicated by Ron's story, has long harboured a Spanish population and considerable cultural interactions. 'This was my new normal', she marvels; 'I wanted to say, "why are you here? If you know nothing, what are we going to do?"' Most of her former students tell Rita that they were looking for something to do on an evening, saw her advert and thought flamenco might be fun to try for a while.

In order to create a sustainable business, Rita had to ascertain what motivated her students to begin in the first place, if it was not for the same motivations that applied at Escuela de Baile. Her findings indicate that people generally start because they have something lacking in their lives and want to make new friends, start a hobby, and do something interesting and exotic. However, she realised that these adult students in Oxfordshire were really only interested in a once-a-week class commitment. They had no concrete end goal beyond attending a class and no long-term commitment to flamenco. The majority of Rita's clients come for a year or two and then move on to another activity. She remembers losing a student who had been with her for several courses:

Out of interest, I contacted her and asked why she wasn't coming back. She replied "well, I absolutely loved the courses, but I decided I am going to start pottery". That is so normal for students I lose. The majority come for one or two courses, love it, and then go flick the brochure to find something else that is interesting to do on a particular night; maybe yoga, knitting, or belly dancing. (Rita, personal communication, June 2, 2015)

This is representative of the British level of commitment to leisure activities and is echoed across the other groups I studied in the UK. Most Brits are interested in the exotic novelty value, but not in embracing the art form in its entirety, even amongst many London aficionados. As a result, Rita found that her courses must be very routine-focused. She found that she could not hammer technique-oriented classes and mostly had to teach dance routines that were straightforward and enjoyable. 'Listen, they're choosing between me, pottery, and yoga. Why would they want to stand in their own sweat and stamp?', she asks. Rita adjusted the Camino del Flamenco business plan to accommodate these motivations. She now structures her courses into five-week sessions, where a specific routine to a particular *palo* is taught during that time period. In a class of twenty people, she finds that usually half are completely new. In several locations throughout Oxfordshire Camino del Flamenco teaches about twenty-five kids, and between fifty and sixty adults. Most of these students are British, although she has seen an increase in Spanish clients over the last three years because the ongoing economic crisis in their home country, which sends them searching for work in the UK. In addition to the professional Spanish Nights, Rita also puts on a student show every June where those who are willing can perform. She employs a dressmaker specifically for this student event, as many can usually be persuaded to perform just because of the costume! Rita's business approach demonstrates the differences between flamenco in London and outside, as well as, in a broader sense, how an international music culture can be adapted to UK leisure consumption patterns.

A View of British Perceptions of Authenticity

Of course, Rita's business plan for Camino del Flamenco must constantly address the perceptions that British students have as to what it means to be authentically flamenco. In the case of students, this revolves around what they feel it means for them to be a flamenco dancer—even if for only once a week. In general, students want to feel more Spanish, usually by dressing up or dancing as well as they can in what they feel is a 'Spanish' style. In addition to having a dressmaker, Rita meets these expectations by utilising upbeat Spanish rumbas and *bulerías* for many of her choreographies; these are the sounds students most associate with flamenco—at least the tourist version. When Rita worked in London, she created a sort of depth chart which addressed the hierarchy of flamenco professionals, ranked in terms of how British consumers perceived their authenticity. In the first (and highest) tier are *Gitanos*, then Andalucíans, followed, by Spanish, Hispanics, non-Spanish who are married to a Spaniard, then Brits who have studied in Spain, anyone outside of London, and, finally, Brits who have not studied in Spain. This phenomenon of outward-looking authenticity will be discussed later, specifically with regards to how that affects cultural capital in the UK flamenco scene.

In terms of performances, Rita strives to create an atmosphere that audiences associate with Spain—for example the Spanish flag bunting, typical Andalucían bar snacks, and sangria. She also generally puts on performances that are dancer-focused (although the previous night's *espectáculo* was an exception). Naturally, these perceptions of authenticity are not usually equivalent to reciprocal concepts of flamenco culture in Sevilla. It is rare to see Spanish flags hanging in taverns—at least in part because of the regional and municipal identities which often outweigh the national. Furthermore, as noted earlier, local Andalucían performances are often more focused on *cante* or holistic flamenco group performances. Rita balances the perceptions of UK punters with her knowledge of 'the real thing', whilst also paying homage to artistic advances—fusions—that are faithful to flamenco's focus on individuality and history of globalisation. Rita recognises that the concept of 'authenticity' in flamenco is a loaded term:

> At the end of the day, if you get too caught up in 'authenticity' you are holding up the creative process. Then you just bring it back to some sort of folk art, some sort of anachronism and that's not the way flamenco is supposed to be. (Rita, personal communication, June 2, 2015)

Uniquely, the UK consumption of flamenco as a leisure activity relies on Andalucían performers for inspiration, as opposed to reaching inwards towards the many British aficionados. This phenomenon is in stark contrast to other foreign music/dance interest groups, such as salsa, which tend to look inwards towards local experts.

Post-Journey Perspectives of a Transcultural Broker

Rita occupies a unique vantage point from which to grasp the journey of the transient flamenco ex-pat between the UK and Spain, as well as the changes which occur within the art form as it travels from the 'local' to the 'glocal'. While this ethnography has not focused so much on her time in Spain, the practices that she utilises in her 'Camino del Flamenco' business plan, as well as the Spanish artists she chooses to engage for workshops and performances, are a product of her lengthy residency in Sevilla. The alterations Rita applies to the art complex's practice are in part a response to cultural norms, as well as incomplete perceptions of flamenco culture. These assumptions, in themselves, relate to the fact that dance (and to some extent guitar) are the most transferrable aspects of the art form. Unlike my younger ex-pat informants, Rita has completed the transnational circuit and returned to the UK as a cultural broker both 'inside' and 'outside' of London. Although she is obviously devoted to flamenco and wants other Brits to appreciate and understand it, Rita voices scepticism about the wisdom of them embarking on a similar transcultural journey to her own. She cites the difficulties of life in Andalucía as a flamenco student, paying for expensive classes and only befriending other ex-pat flamencos who, ultimately, are the competition. Rita also cites the prejudices that foreign performers often experience, especially (but not limited to) finding performances. She offers a cautionary tale for those that would try to assume this culture as their own:

> Why do they want to make a life in flamenco? Why do they want to go to Spain? "Well, it's deeply fulfilling and in life we never regret what we do but the things we don't do!" Blah, blah, blah. You can go to Spain, you can achieve real, viable flamenco, but by the time you are in your thirties it is

over. Whatcha gonna do? Go back to England and teach where you are 1-2-3-4-5-6 7th down the pecking order? [...] I have to say, starting anew with flamenco [as a foreigner], even if you're only 18, dreams of professionalism are an illusion. No pension, inconsistent and badly paid performances, and there are already a lot of flamenco teachers in the UK. You face your middle years with no transferrable skills. Oh. But you'll be able to judge people on whether they have *duende* or not. Yay! (Rita, personal communication, June 2, 2015)

Rita's viewpoint is an important one when considering how flamenco develops transnationally. It indicates the difficulties that individual culture brokers must overcome to learn their art in a foreign locale, as well as the challenges creating a career back in the UK. She has learned the adjustments to make in her business and performances to sustain client expectations and maintains a grip on reality when advising other foreigners to do the same. Rita's business plan strives to find a balance between presenting and teaching 'good' flamenco, whilst attracting British consumers to the art form. These are the decisions that individual cultural brokers must make when returning to their home countries.

Rita is a particularly influential flamenco cosmopolitan hub because of her extensive transnational connections and experience moving between Spain and the UK via flamenco. Her teachings at one of the biggest flamenco schools in the UK inspire would-be flamenco ex-pats to pursue greater knowledge. She also provides performance opportunities to transient flamencos of both British and Spanish nationality. Because of these factors, Rita is representative of the influence an individual cultural broker can have on developing a glocal scene after returning to their home country—one that makes compromises but still reaches towards the 'original culture' and transnational interactions for inspiration.

Rita Analysis: The Completed Journey

Rita's ethnography is a depiction of the completed journey. She travelled to Sevilla to pursue flamenco, worked and learnt there, then carried her knowledge back home to the UK to transmit and create a glocal culture. Her story represents several key facets of British flamenco culture: first, the differences between the scenes in London and the rest of the UK; second, perceptions of flamenco authenticity in the UK; and third, how these factors influence flamenco pedagogy. Rita is also a significant figure because of her status as a cosmopolitan hub and the transcultural interactions she facilitates. She creates and links flamenco scenes outside of London, as well as maintaining transnational connections with Andalucía. This is important because, as indicated by Rita's cynicism towards the expat experience, completing the flamenco journey rarely comes to fruition. Rita's ethnography, overall, offers insight into how and why flamenco changes when it moves to the UK. These alterations are, in part, a response to perceptions of authenticity amongst British audiences, as well as the aspirations of dance students. They manifest themselves, most often, in how flamenco is taught but also, as demonstrated by Rita's 'Spanish Evening' how the art form is presented to uninitiated British audiences.

London Versus 'Outside'

Rita is in the unique position of having experienced flamenco scene creation both inside and outside of London, as well as in Spain. While most of the group characteristics and structures described in the early part of this chapter apply to the London flamenco sub-scene, there are some differences that must be acknowledged. One does not have to live in the UK for very long to understand that London is different from the rest of the UK, not just in the 'big city' versus 'small city' mentality, but they view themselves as different and approach everything from leisure to 'the local' to travel differently. London is the flamenco epicentre of the UK; there are more teachers, more students, more shows, and more *peñas* than anywhere else. There is even a flamenco radio show—Flamenco Fix—run by Alicia Graham, a former British flamenco ex-pat. My observations have been based on direct and indirect (email exchanges and websites) contact with numerous people and organisations associated with the scene. This suggested a wide spectrum of singers, instrumentalists, dancers, and non-performing aficionados, both professional and amateur. Interestingly, while there is opportunity to adopt a more holistic approach to flamenco, most participants still only choose to interact with dance and guitar.

The reason for this larger flamenco scene is primarily attributable to an increased contact with Spanish culture, compared with the rest of the UK. While exact years and dates are difficult to come by, it is possible to discern a roughly traceable history. This began with visiting performers in the mid-1800s, a trend that has continued through today. This contact also came in the form of Spanish immigration; significant waves of which occurred to escape persecution under the Franco regime, as well as to avoid the current economic crisis. Currently there are 60,000 Spanish citizens living in London, out of the 131,000 in the UK (Office for National Statistics 2016). As has been demonstrated, not all Spaniards do flamenco. Regardless, immigration increased London's contact with Spanish and flamenco culture, as did touring artists such as La Argentina and Antonio and Rosario, which ultimately contributed to British interest in learning it.

As was recounted in Ron's ethnography, in the middle of the century until around the early 1990s (accounts vary) there were multiple venues with regular performance opportunities for both amateurs and professionals. London flamenco aficionados, especially those of the older generation, have a keen awareness of their flamenco heritage and reminisce of the days when they could perform in several venues each evening (Finnegan 2007, p. 59). There seems to be a view amongst this older generation of flamencos that the art complex in London is on the decline. My research indicates that while dedicated performance venues and regular opportunities are potentially harder to come by, the number of classes and students has most certainly risen. The presence of multiple generations of aficionados represents a continuity pathway which is not as certain or evident in other scenes in the UK (Finnegan 2007, p. 323).

Despite the doubts from the older generation, London still boasts a significant number of flamenco performances; however, many of them are only offered to the absolute best British dancers, as Spanish performers are often sought out first (as per Rita's 'Flamenco Hierarchy' chart). The most prominent flamenco event in London is its annual Flamenco Festival London, occurring at Sadler's Wells for two weeks in late February. In recent years the festival organisers have received criticism for essentially booking the same acts every year, which are always the highest echelon of flamenco performance in Andalucía. They have been known to largely ignore up-and-coming artists who are making a name for themselves within Spain, as well as any local British stars (Vivian, personal communication, May 2015). In addition to this yearly spectacle, London hosts a number of touring artists as they pass through the UK, such as Vicente Amigo and Paco Peña. However, the main perpetuators of flamenco events are a few of the larger flamenco schools that also function as production companies, such as Flamenco Express, Ilusión Flamenco, and España On Fire. These organisations, along with Peña Flamenca de Londres, host monthly performances that incorporate either up-and-coming Spanish artists who want to enhance their reputation abroad or professional London-based performers.

Because of the numerous performance options and schools, students join flamenco classes with the knowledge that it is possible to be professional in London. As mentioned in Rita's ethnography, the most obvious difference she finds between students in Oxfordshire versus London is that, since the latter have so much more exposure to the art complex, more of them have professional aspirations. There are many classes to choose from and, unlike other British locations, teachers do not have to spend time explaining what flamenco is (Rita, personal communication, June 2, 2015). Students in London often intend from the outset to attend as many classes and workshops as possible to quickly attain a professional level. Therefore, many classes in London's more prominent flamenco academies, especially at the higher levels, are composed of dedicated and competitive students (Rita, personal communication, June 2, 2015). This is also evidenced by larger schools, such as Escuela de Baile offer courses aimed directly at aspiring professionals.

The difference in access to flamenco culture in the UK's most populous city is not a new concept in music migration cities. Kiwan and Meinhof demonstrate that capital cities in the global 'north', such as London and Paris, offer endless opportunities for migrants and their music to merge and 'transform the cultural fabric of the cities they reside in' (Kiwan and Meinhof 2011, p. 87). London is renowned for its world openness, cultural dynamism, and, with 36.7% of its population foreign-born, considered one of the most culturally diverse cities in the world (Office for National Statistics 2014). However, despite the large population of migrant cultures (in this case flamenco) in global cities, migration scholars such as Kiwan and Michael Peter Smith advocate for considering the role of the individual paramount for cultural transmission because of their 'extensive connectivity' with sending countries and influence on global flows (Kiwan and Meinhof 2011, p. 88).

Perceptions of Authenticity

Rita's ethnography draws attention to certain perceptions of authenticity that the non-aficionado British, in general, have of flamenco. This typically entails to a great extent by the imagery that Franco created in the 1950s for his tourism campaign. The image, like those in 1950s travel posters, is one of a sensual dancer, with flowers and a red, frilly dress. She has brown skin, black hair, and black eyes. She is a *Gitano*, dancing with castanets to a fast upbeat rumba. This has bearings on what audiences and students expect when they attend events and classes. Quite often these expectations are different from the realities that scene creators learn from their transcultural interactions with Spanish aficionados. Therefore, how these cosmopolitan hubs reconcile British expectations with the Andalucían version is imperative to not only their success in scene maintenance but also to the development of flamenco in the global flow. This will be discussed further in Chap. 6.

Many people in the UK (at least those who are not directly involved with the art complex) know very little about flamenco outside of these touristic images. To them it is fancy cabaret turns, stamping, and swishing skirts. They think all Spanish people have black hair, brown skin, and wear red and black flouncy dresses (Rita, personal communication, June 2, 2015). Rita also recounted several instances of having people walk out of her classes and treat her with scepticism because she does not meet this description. She advises:

> If you want to teach Flamenco successfully in the UK (particularly outside of London), then you need to think carefully about the way that you present yourself to your students. You need to look like a Flamenco dancer, sound like a Flamenco dancer and make quite sure that your students are left in no doubt that you are going to take them into the Flamenco world.

> It ought to be enough just to be a really good teacher who knows Flamenco inside out, but sadly it isn't. (Rita, personal communication, June 2, 2015)

Other dancers I interviewed have encountered similar experiences. Nancy remembers a time when she performed in a working men's club in Derbyshire and, upon arriving with her guitarist, was asked by the male event organiser if the lads were allowed to touch. They had assumed that 'sexy' flamenco dancing was akin to 'exotic dancing'! (Nancy, personal communication, Oct. 14, 2013). Although it was more common in the early days of UK flamenco, some British teachers and professional dancers still change their names to sound more Spanish. This, in the mind of students and audiences alike, lends an air of authenticity to the class or performance. Rita's ethnography describes numerous instances of her efforts to find compromise between British stereotypes and her perception of 'real' flamenco.

Other ethnomusicologists who examine British music cultures have noticed similar trends in how the British consume foreign musics. Miller (2013), in her study of *charango* music in the UK, notes that there is a certain lack of inquisitiveness in the UK about foreign cultures, which she refers to as 'globalised incuriosity' (Miller 2013, p. 100). This term refers to her perception that the general British public suffers from a disinterest in understanding particular music cultures outside of media and tourism-led stereotypes. She finds that this 'globalised incuriosity' on behalf of promoters and audiences regarding authenticity adversely affects the creativity and how music is consumed and distributed in the UK (Miller 2013, p. 101). Reductively, in Cuban music, dark-skinned Latinness and masculinity sells. However, Miller feels it is within the capacity, and in fact the responsibility, of promoters and performers to alter the exoticised images and educate the public (Miller 2013). This, however, in the case of flamenco, must be balanced with audience and student expectations:

> [outside of UK *peñas*] you have to incorporate a certain amount of stamping and swishing and definitely wear a red dress—if you expected the audience to think that they'd seen something good and you wanted to be asked back. So basically, and sadly, any Flamencos performing in the UK quickly

learnt that unless you were prepared to prostitute your art in a major way, you just wouldn't get enough work to live on. Since the audience wanted the cabaret cliché, they had to be given it and so it perpetuated. (Rita, personal communication, June 2, 2015)

Rita and other successful British flamenco teachers have adjusted the way they teach flamenco. Most classes I encountered in the UK have been focused on learning a particularly routine to a specific *palo*, with some time at the beginning spent on technique. There is very little discussion regarding improvisation or how the dance fits with the music—much less understanding the surrounding culture. Most students do not realise flamenco's status as an art complex, in which the dance is of equal importance to the other elements. Concessions that British flamenco aficionados make to remain in-demand amongst students and audiences result in variations to how the art complex is transmitted. These variations contribute to my designation of the UK flamenco model as 'glocal', as will be discussed in Chap. 6.

Rita as a Cosmopolitan Hub

Rita, as alluded to, in her ethnography, is an influential cosmopolitan hub in the UK flamenco scene. She spent many years learning and performing in Andalucía. Subsequently, Rita returned to London and utilised her knowledge of both the UK and Andalucían flamenco to influence the scene first there and then in Oxfordshire. She has maintained transcultural links with flamenco through visits to Spain and contact with the Spanish flamenco community in London. She utilises these transcultural connections not only to keep her knowledge current, but also to find artists to perform in her shows and teach workshops. Rita, despite her remote Oxfordshire location, is first and foremost a cosmopolitan hub because almost everyone who has been on the UK flamenco scene for any length of time has heard of Camino del Flamenco. They may not have attended a performance or a course, but Rita has enacted an extensive online business promotion campaign via Facebook. Rita actively sought out and 'Friended' potential students and audience members, as well as members of the British ex-pat flamenco community in Spain whom she could use as visiting performers. Most importantly, Rita plays a significant role in shaping the UK flamenco scene. She makes decisions regarding how to present the art complex within the context of UK culture, which often includes compromises in terms of how and what is taught, music choice, and performance practices. Essentially, Rita utilises her cultural knowledge of Andalucían flamenco and reconciles her business model with UK behavioural norms and concepts of authenticity. These variations made by influential cosmopolitan hubs, such as Rita, influence what flamenco's model abroad is.

5.5   Peña Flamenco de Liverpool

Of the groups I interacted with, the one that best represents my research is Flamenco de Liverpool. Significantly, it is among the only one with a connection to Spanish flamenco in an official capacity whilst maintaining British roots amongst the majority of its participants. It is organised by Liverpool native Trish; however, Sevilla-based flamenco dancer and teacher Catalina acts as the group's president.

My first interactions with Flamenco de Liverpool came at an invitation from Claire of Deva Flamenco (Chester) to attend an event the two organisations were running together at the new studio in Wavertree. The Liverpool and Chester groups, along with Bristol Peña brought Flamenco Azabache over from Fuengirola to perform at a *peña* and run workshops in Liverpool and Bristol (this is one of the rare occasions when I observed cross-pollination of groups).

I arrived in Wavertree, a suburb of Liverpool, on a chilly January afternoon and lugged my cajón to the newly opened Estudio Flamenco de Liverpool, which is situated in a small business park. Even though I knew few people that would be present, I had high hopes of playing, as instrumentalists are often few and far between in the flamenco community. Entering the studio, I saw Claire, and sat down next to her. Many guests had yet to arrive, so we were able to find adjacent seats in the front. Others had already claimed the tables set up on either side of the 3 long rows and had brought along food and alcoholic beverages. The room was large, with a dance floor taking up all but a small section by the entrance. The studio was dimly lit (stage lighting only) but I could make out flamenco posters on the wall and a small stereo system in one corner. As more guests began to arrive, I recognised a handful of attendants from previous flamenco events I attended in Chester. I also noticed a tall dark-haired man and shorter black-haired woman dressed in elaborate flamenco costumes. This was, evidently, Juan and Maria of Flamenco Azabache. Claire and I were soon joined by Penny, who was Deva Flamenco's teacher. She was in her late 20s, from Liverpool and makes her career as a professional contemporary dancer.

Although the evening was meant as an opportunity for the local flamenco enthusiasts to watch Flamenco Azabache perform, it was structured as a *peña*, which on this evening had an abundance of dancers and instrumentalists eager to perform both in groups and in solo. I recognised a teenage guitarist, Louis, who got up and played a solo *tangos* that he wrote himself. I was asked to play cajón while Claire and Penny danced *bulerías*. Demonstrating the spirit of fusion that often accompanies localised music traditions, one of the Liverpool dancers took the spotlight and danced a *tangos* while juggling. All these dances were accompanied by crowd interaction. Interspersing the performances by locals were exhibitions by Flamenco Azabache.

Flamenco Azabache performed several exuberant dances in quite elaborate costumes. Juan especially, had such enthusiastic *zapateado* that he stomped a hole in the dance floor. Despite their presence as revered performers, they invited Penny, Trish, and several other advanced dancers up to perform with them, in addition to allowing several guitarists and myself (on cajón) to play for them. This is not something I have observed often of visiting artists at *peñas*. The evening concluded with dancers from several different groups dancing *sevillañas*, teaching the moves to anyone who wanted to learn. While not considered flamenco by some Spanish schools of thought, *sevillañas* is a Spanish country dance that shares many musical and stylistic similarities. In the UK it is usually one of the first dances that students learn. It is a *palo* with a standard routine adaptable to varying levels of experience and can be performed amongst people who do not usually dance together. Because *sevillañas* is typically danced in pairs, this was by far the most social and merry part of the evening.

The next afternoon, I returned to the studio and attended Juan Antonio's Beginner *tientos* class, along with fourteen other dancers from Liverpool, Chester, and Manchester. The class was accompanied by Louis and the husband of a dance teacher (Brenda) from Manchester. It was by far one of the most difficult beginners' workshops I have ever attended. Juan, adorned in leggings, a vest and a skirt, moved quickly between several styles of *tangos* and *tientos*. This is typical of flamenco classes in Andalucía—the level of flamenco is such that often an intermediate or advanced dancer from the UK will only be able to cope with a Beginner level course there (Paula—2011, Claire—2011, Trish—2012, personal communications). Juan allowed the workshop attendees to video his choreography at the end of the class. While I have found this a common occurrence amongst English workshops, many dance teachers in Spain are reluctant to allow video-taping, fearing that the choreography would be stolen or end up on YouTube against their wishes (Paula—2011, Claire—2011, Trish—2012, personal communications). I stayed to observe the advanced workshop, which was run in similar fashion to the beginners only at a more rapid pace. The highlight was decidedly when Juan, once again, broke the floor with his impassioned *zapateados*. After the course ended, I walked to the bus stop with one of the advanced dancers, who introduced herself as Lena. I soon realised that I had been told about this woman in previous interviews—a nurse from Chester who had taken a year off work to advance her flamenco skills. Lena travelled to Spain once or twice a year, with one visit usually coinciding with the El Festival de Jerez,[9] and brought back choreography to teach monthly workshops at a studio in Liverpool. We sat in a coffee shop awaiting our respective trains home, discussing flamenco and realising how many of the same people we knew. It was due to her upcoming trip to El Festival de Jerez that would cause Lena to miss the next event in Estudio Flamenco de Liverpool—a weekend workshop and performance by Catalina of Sevilla (Fig. 5.3).

---

[9] Jerez's annual flamenco festival, one of the largest and most famous in the world.

Fig. 5.3 Trish Anderton performing with Sevillano troupe in Liverpool

Catalina in Liverpool

I had first heard of Catalina the previous year when interviewing Claire about the beginnings of Deva Flamenco. In 2007, Deva received a lottery grant and they decided to ask Catalina, a talented and famous dancer from Sevilla, to fly in and give a weekend workshop. It was during this workshop that Trish first met her (Trish, personal communication, May 10, 2012). Trish had attended many workshops before, mostly with short men, tall and skinny women, or doll-like girls, all who danced in a way that she never felt would be right for her body type. Catalina had the same frame as Trish and, moreover, was and is a phenomenal teacher. After having a fantastic experience at the workshop, she decided to schedule a trip to Sevilla to take lessons with Catalina. After booking time off work and communicating details with Catalina, Trish was advised by a doctor to postpone her trip due to the necessity of immediate cancer treatment. Reluctantly she agreed, sending heartfelt regrets to Catalina. In 2008 Trish was well enough to travel to her studio for lessons (Trish, personal communication, May 10, 2012). She found Catalina so inspiring, both as a person and a flamenco dancer that she travelled to Spain at least once a year since then to train with her.

In 2011, when Trish decided to form her own organisation, Flamenco de Liverpool, she asked Catalina to be their president. The reasoning behind this was twofold: First, because Trish wanted to honour her for the inspiration she provided as a teacher and a friend. Furthermore, Trish wanted Catalina as president to represent a seal of approval from a respected Andalucían dancer to lend more authenticity to what she is attempting to create in Liverpool—a network of professional and amateur enthusiasts (both performers and non-performers) devoted to sharing their enjoyment of flamenco (Trish, personal communication, May 10, 2012).

I returned to Estudio Flamenco de Liverpool in late February to attend the first day of Catalina's two-day workshop and the performance in the evening—held at the Cornerstone Theatre in central Liverpool. Catalina was to teach two levels of workshop, accompanied by her guitarist Jaime, and another member of her advanced class in Spain, Nieves. Unlike many Andalucían flamenco professionals I have encountered, Catalina speaks perfect English—a byproduct of having lived in Winnipeg for twenty years (Catalina, personal communication, Mar. 11, 2012). I entered the studio, having taken the train from Leeds that morning, to a flurry of activity. In each corner of the small studio, different dancers were practicing various routines with coaching from Catalina and Nieves, in preparation for the evening's show. In addition to Catalina and her troupe performing, several dancers from Flamenco de Liverpool would also participate.

The beginners' workshop had eleven women participating, including myself, and once again I recognised individuals from Manchester, Chester, and Liverpool. Catalina, over the two-day course, would be teaching us a *bulerías*, which is quite a tall order for a novice class because of its rapidity and difficult *compás*. Unlike Juan, she kept the warm-up short in an effort to make the best use of a condensed amount of time. Most workshops that I have attended feature warm-up exercises and stretches, followed by at least a half-hour of technique practice, followed by choreography. Catalina, instead, incorporated the technique section with learning applicable sections of the choreography. For simplicity purposes, she taught the intricate footwork first, followed by *braceo*. Her pedagogical methods primarily involved teaching sections and having us repeat them whilst Jaime played a slower-than-normal rendition on his guitar and she walked around providing individual corrections. Not only did she comment on the physical aspects of the dance, but also on the nature of learning flamenco itself and the intricacies of the dance's structure.

The evening's performance was to take place in the Cornerstone Theatre at Liverpool Hope University. It would feature Catalina singing and dancing, Jaime on guitar, and Nieves, Trish, and her students dancing as well. I arrived early and managed to snag a seat in the front row, which was fortunate because by the time the show began the theatre was packed. The evening commenced with fourteen of Trish's students performing *sevillañas*. It is often difficult to convince students to perform and some clubs even report losing students in the face of upcoming optional performances (Paula and Claire, personal communication, 2011). Trish, on the other hand, confided that she had no problems convincing her students to perform; it was more a matter of telling them when it was time to stop. For the evening's event, a group of her students would be performing *sevillañas* and had needed no cajoling, just instructions on what to wear and when they could practice (Trish, personal communication, May 5, 2012).

Trish performed a lovely *solea* with *bata de cola*, a very difficult technique which involves rhythmically flipping the long train of a frilly dress to emphasise *compás*. She was followed by Catalina singing a *siguiriya*.[10] There are not many flamenco singers in the UK, due to both the difficulty of the style, and the highly personal nature of the Spanish lyrics. When she later got up to dance, I was completely spellbound. The evening concluded with Catalina, Nieves, Trish, and another student taking turns to perform a short *fin de fiesta* and then, in a marvellous mixing of cultures, dancing in pairs. As I wandered through the empty streets back to the train station, I speculated on how Liverpool had managed to form

---

[10] A *palo* of flamenco music, noted for its deep, expressive style.

closer ties with Spain than any other group I had encountered outside of London. A faction made up of individuals not linked to Andalucía through heritage, they have established ties and gained the beginnings of acceptance from members of the Andalucían scene.

Flamenco de Liverpool Analysis

Flamenco de Liverpool's ethnography describes a scene in the north of England created by a British cosmopolitan hub (Trish) after being drawn to flamenco in her 30s. She studied in Liverpool and attended workshops all over the UK and in Spain before setting up her own organisation to share her knowledge with others. The ethnography supports several key observations about British flamenco culture: first, the role of Spanish professionals in the UK scene; second, a description of the scene at a UK *peña*; and third, the role of Trish as a human hub, linking sub-scenes in northwest England with Catalina's studio. Overall, Flamenco de Liverpool's ethnography offers insight into the nature of the connections with Spain, variations made from the Andalucían version, and the influence a singular cultural broker can have in developing a transculturally connected flamenco scene abroad.

Spanish Presence in UK Flamenco

This book has yet to touch directly on the Spanish presence in the UK flamenco scene. While this may seem like an oversight, the reasoning is that the focus of this chapter is on various aspects of the UK scene, situated around the cosmopolitan hubs that create and maintain it. Even though British flamenco is a cultural manifestation of its Andalucían cousin, upon closer scrutiny Spanish participants, while present, are on the fringes of British groups. It is significant to note their location within the grand scheme of British flamenco. There are few Spanish participants outside of London. They are usually professional performers or teachers, often just visiting, and rarely the drivers of the local flamenco scene. On the whole, Spanish aficionados are not scene creators (with a few exceptions, such as Ana in Birmingham and Barbara in Sheffield). Spanish participants are primarily brought in by these British cosmopolitan hubs to enhance an existing scene. Flamenco Azabache and Catalina are typical examples of Spanish presence in UK flamenco. They are a part of the cosmopolitan hub's social capital, to some extent, providing cultural information and a link to Andalucía but not actually contributing to the scene's continuity. Spanish flamencos are considered experts on the scene, their nationality granting them considerable cultural capital. Because of this they are highly sought after as teachers and workshop technicians. Even on the London flamenco scene, Spanish performers do not usually join Peña Flamenco de Londres; they are usually the paid performers. Their presence is imperative because it provides British aficionados who cannot travel to Spain the opportunity to directly associate themselves with the original culture instead of an interpretation.

The scarcity of Spanish flamenco hubs is not necessarily for wont of trying. After all, they do possess enough cultural capital regarding flamenco to be scene creators. As Spain's economic crisis has worn on, more artists have attempted to come to the UK (and other foreign locations) to make a career of flamenco. Vivian, the primary organiser of Peña Flamenca de Londres, imparted that her organisation often gets contacted by Andalucían performers seeking gigs and teaching opportunities. They are usually unable to help because there are so many local London artists. I interviewed several, such as accomplished guitarists Samuel and Cafuco from Sevilla. They come over trying to work in flamenco (due to lack of professional opportunities in Spain) but do not necessarily understand the way to go about creating an artistic career in the UK, or how to market it to UK hobbyist students and audiences who want their stereotypes verified. Essentially, most Spanish performers who have come here specifically for flamenco, lack the social and UK-specific cultural capital to develop a sustainable career. A further discussion of this will occur in Chap. 6.

The UK *Peña*

Flamenco de Liverpool's ethnography demonstrates the atmosphere at a local UK-based *peña* and the variations and transcultural interactions that can occur there. These are important events both in Andalucía and UK flamenco scenes. The *peña* is a crossroads where the different categories of flamenco participants can meet: students, teachers, instrumentalists, audience; often providing a platform for non-local interaction. I have attended *peñas* organised by several different British groups—namely in London, Leeds, Birmingham, and Liverpool. Although they lack the *aire* of Sevilla they shared some similarities. Structurally, events in the UK and Sevilla both featured performances by professional troupes, followed by a *juerga* where anyone could perform and collaborate. Both locations boasted a predominant presence of attendees who knew enough about flamenco to participate.

The *peñas* I frequented in Sevilla had a higher skill level of participants and more audience knowledge, as evidenced by a greater number of audience members clapping *palmas* during the performance. The *juergas* after Sevilla *peña* performances tended to occur with more fluidity and a greater level of participation. The guitars basically never stopped while singers traded *letra* and periodically dancers stood up to participate. The process was not as spontaneous in Liverpool—performers were cajoled into getting up and improvising and had to sort out structures with the instrumentalists before commencing. Also, while the audience was willing to dance in Liverpool, many of them had to be shown the steps. However, this is to be expected because most of the Liverpudlian attendees were hobbyists, who did not regularly engage with flamenco outside of their once-a-week class. Furthermore, the juggler marks an interesting fusion of flamenco with other areas of leisure. Incorporating other aspects of individual identity is an important feature of the art complex. It would be unusual to incorporate these identity fusions in Andalucía's traditional *peñas*. In Sevilla, many of those present at the *peñas* lived flamenco and had grown up with it as their identity. Even the foreigners at Sevilla *peñas* had come to Sevilla specifically to learn flamenco and visited these events to improve their understanding and skills. Significantly, British *peña* affords UK hobbyists the opportunity for transcultural interactions with flamenco. Sometimes this is merely in the form of further contact with the art complex itself, as at the events actors can practice, perform, and experiment with it outside of a structured class setting. Most professionals agree that performing is as much a part of learning flamenco as it is an art form that requires non-vocal communications and dance footwork signals between performers, so this makes *peñas* a valuable transcultural experience. Beyond that, *peñas* often enable direct interactions with Spanish performers—both local and visiting—who usually would not be present in dance classes. A final crucial difference between Sevilla *peñas* and Flamenco de Liverpool's event (as well as most other in the UK) is that the former showcase aficionados across all flamenco elements, with a specific focus on *cante*. UK *peñas* and *juergas* are dominated by dancers. The dance-centric nature of Flamenca Britannica will be elaborated on later in this chapter.

Trish as a Human Hub

Trish, as demonstrated in the Flamenco de Liverpool ethnography, is an influential cosmopolitan hub, linking the Liverpool scene with Spain, as well as with other scenes in northwest England. Beginning flamenco as an adult, Trish gathered information through workshop attendance with Rita in London, as well as through various journeys to Andalucía to study with Catalina and other teachers. She then returned to England to set up her own group, pulling from transcultural knowledge and utilising social capital to connect Flamenco de Liverpool with Andalucían flamenco. Trish is a cosmopolitan hub because she is the sole organiser of flamenco in her city and she enables associations with the original culture through her knowledge and workshops. She also provides a link to the UK for the Spanish performers mentioned to international performance. Trish's role in shaping flamenco in her locality is imperative to its continuation, especially that she can facilitate direct interactions with the Andalucían scene, which otherwise her students would not experience.

5.6 Conclusion: The Grand Scheme of Flamenca Britannica

Overall, there are several primary issues to extract from this ethnography on British flamenco. First, the scene revolves around dancers and the dance class, which is dissimilar from Sevilla. Second, on the whole, the motivations of its participants differ from those in the Andalucían scene. Finally, since flamenco is not native to the UK's cultural framework, as it is in Andalucía, it must be created. This signifies the importance of the individual cosmopolitan hubs and their transcultural interactions in creating and maintaining a flamenco scene outside of Andalucía.

To develop an understanding of the broader UK scene it is important to grasp students' motivations for learning flamenco. As demonstrated in all three ethnographies in this chapter, most participants are not doing it to become flamenco stars or to pursue it as part of their cultural background, as they would in Spain. This sort of cultural adoption is especially interesting as it occurs in the presence of an existing music culture, rooted in the personal and national histories of most UK participants. So why do they take on such a demanding art complex?

In her book, *The Hidden Musicians,* Finnegan notes several prominent patterns regarding why people join UK amateur music and dance organisations. The two primary reasons she cites are sociability (a desire to spend time with other people outside of work) and empowerment (a path to a socially-recognised position and the opportunity to make an aesthetic contribution) (Finnegan 2007, p. 328). Eisentraut, in his study on samba groups in Wales, notes a similar pattern. His research reveals a group that is not motivated by any sort of ethnic background, but by a desire to create music in a group setting, or to just have a unique hobby (Eisentraut 2001, p. 89).

Finnegan and Eisentraut's observations are true of the UK flamenco scene as well. While there are a few people who decide to take on flamenco as an identity, the majority participate on a more superficial level—to enjoy the social context. They make friends through classes and group events, and are drawn to communing over a shared involvement in flamenco. Like other musical interest groups, it provides a collective aesthetic experience (Finnegan 2007, p. 329). It is a style of dance that does not require a partner, nor does one have to be young and thin to excel (Trish—2012, Claire—2011, personal communications). Another common motivation is for fitness reasons. Related to this is the desire to learn a new skill that would distract the mind from the stresses of everyday life. It is a complicated dance with rhythms that are uncommon in British and American music. Between the intricate body movements and the footwork which is often using contra-rhythms to the hands, it keeps the brain and body very active. A third explanation given by students regarding their interest in flamenco is that they had seen it performed, thought it looked intriguingly exotic, and decided to try it out. In the UK, there seems to be a part of society that loves the musical 'other', which is possibly attributable to a colonial past, which inspired the UK 'world beat' movement of the 1990s. Steven Feld (1994) attributes this phenomenon to:

> [...] a long history of essentializing and racializing other bodies as possessing a "natural" sense of rhythm, the invention of "world beat" reproduces a Western gaze towards the exotic and erotic, often darker-skinned, dancing body. (Feld 1994, p. 266)

Many of these 'world music' genres, including flamenco, have made recent appearances in popular culture on television shows such as 'Strictly Come Dancing' (Paula, personal communication, Mar. 27, 2011). In addition to glamorous dancing, women love the idea of wearing exotic clothes, specifically those that aren't skimpy. With Spain being a common UK tourist destination, people have been exposed to flamenco that way as well. The final reason for beginning flamenco, and in fact the most common, is via 'the road less travelled'—strange circumstances that for some reason resulted in joining a class. I found flamenco dancing because I was hired to play a percussion gig that required it. An engaged couple in my class had decided to make their first wedding dance a flamenco number to surprise the wife's Spanish family. Then there were several occasions where people had thought they were attending a different type of dancing class, such as Welsh national dancing (Holmes 2010).

These motivations are not necessarily enough to keep hobbyists occupied long-term. As Rita's ethnography demonstrates, most students only want a superficial engagement with flamenco, enough to learn a routine and attend a class for a couple of years. Finnegan explains this phenomenon by pointing out that music and dance are not the only activities that bring people together—other leisure pursuits can fulfil a similar role (although she views music's role of collectiveness as having wider societal implications) (Finnegan 2007, p. 329).

Of course, to some UK flamenco participants, such as the cosmopolitan hubs described above, the art complex becomes a new cultural identity—something maybe that did not exist in other aspects of their lives (Claire, personal communication, Apr. 14, 2011). These individuals opt to pursue flamenco beyond a classroom level and become obsessed with it. As described by several informants, flamenco has something to say to some people, which takes them back to its origins as an art complex that expresses intense, human emotions and moves them beyond ethnic boundaries (Vivian, personal communication, May 28, 2015). While its Andalucían history of shared suffering is not something that British participants can comprehend, they can relate to the need to express this concept on a personal level. For this small group of UK aficionados, flamenco physically and mentally is an area of liminality and a ritualised state of escaping the everyday.

Dance-Centricity

It will be noted that the bulk of this ethnography has focused on the dance element of flamenco in the UK. The reasoning for this is not an oversight, but simply because the UK flamenco scene, as mentioned earlier in this chapter, is focused around the dance class. Most participants in UK flamenco are dancers with the other elements (with the possible exception of guitar) falling by the wayside. The primary reason for this is that the *baile* is an element that requires very little pre-existing cultural or dance knowledge. The ability to speak Spanish is not required, nor are pre-existing instrumental skills. To simply attend a flamenco dance class in the UK requires only the ability to follow an instructor's movements and walk. Dancing requires less cultural context than the other elements and therefore easier to replicate at some level. Unfortunately, this focus on *baile* perpetuates the long-established stereotype that flamenco is a dance, as opposed to an entire culture, thus simplifying the art form as it globalises.

This dance-centricity is not unique to flamenco when it comes to holistic music cultures that are reinterpreted in the UK. Miller (2013) notes a certain disconnect between music and dance in the UK salsa scene, which has resulted in Latin music marketing focused on stereotypes and 'a clumsy understanding of ethnicity' (Miller 2013, p. 112). Urquía, similarly, observes that British participants in London's salsa scene emphasise 'ethnically neutral aspects' (Urquía 2005, p. 389). This shift focus away from features outside of their cultural comfort zone (particularly language and musical knowledge) and towards those that play towards skills they already possess, such as the ability to dance a routine (Urquía 2005, p. 389). He refers to it as 'de-ethnicization of salsa and integration into local sensibilities'; I will later describe it as 'glocalisation' (Urquía 2005, p. 391). Eisentraut also discusses samba's de-ethnicisation in Wales, pointing out that 'most samba played in the UK is percussion only', removing melody and words, the two most important elements of the Brazilian version (Eisentraut 2001, p. 97). Martin Stokes, in his article 'On Musical Cosmopolitanism', surmises that an ethnomusicologist can learn a lot about musical cosmopolitanism in the examination of dance. He sees dance as a cultural feature that circulates quickly and easily across borders where other elements are rebuffed (Stokes 2007, p. 14).

While Flamenca Britannica is dance-centric, with less focus on the other elements, I would not go so far as to suggest it is de-ethnicised. In the examples of samba and salsa, focus has been shifted to favour British participants as artistic authorities. The British flamenco scene values, above all, Andalucían flamenco knowledge and transcultural interactions between the two scenes. The emphasis on the dance is most likely a product of it being the easiest to access on a hobbyist level of participation, coupled with the fallacious stereotype that flamenco culture is only a dance.

Flamenco Britannica and Human Hubs

This chapter and its three ethnographies demonstrate the structure and development of flamenco in a UK context. I specifically have focused on the role of individual cosmopolitan hubs and their transcultural interactions in the creation and maintenance of the British flamenco scene. These cultural brokers are important because, unlike in Andalucía where flamenco is built into a subset of local culture, or Madrid where it has a deep commercial history, in the UK flamenco must be facilitated and created. The majority of local British groups are driven by dedicated aficionados who had discovered flamenco through means outside of cultural heritage. These individuals, with or without a committee and devoted students, are responsible for the continuance of flamenco in their locality and push the organisation forward. These individuals have significant influence regarding the shape of the UK flamenco model. As will be elaborated upon in the next chapter, instead of existing as a de-ethnicised cultural appropriation, like UK salsa, flamenco's aesthetic inspiration rests with Andalucía. This is at least in part due to British human hubs who reach towards the original culture and facilitate transcultural interactions in the UK. Paula (Hebden Bridge Flamenco) emphasises that, as a dancer and a teacher 'you have to keep one foot in Andalucía, in order to maintain a feel for the music and culture' (Paula, personal communication, Mar. 27, 2011).

The cultural capital of UK flamenco is also prompted by cosmopolitan hubs. This is, essentially, specific knowledge or characteristics necessary for acceptance into restricted groups without reference to economic capital. The required information includes behaviours, languages, education, and cultural history. In the case of British flamenco, the acceptance requirements are two-pronged: firstly, a desire to understand flamenco and secondly, the possession of Andalucían culturally specific experience. By those standards, individuals with the most cultural capital, and therefore the highest degree of respect, are the artists from Andalucía which, as mentioned above, usually hold loose associations with local groups. Significant authority is given to those who have first-hand knowledge of flamenco from study in Andalucía. Flamenco musicians are gauged as knowledgeable based on their familiarity with the typical *palos* and accompanying *compás*. Cultural capital is also manifested in dance class and workshop attendance, attire and execution of proper performance conventions.

Although the UK interpretation may appear to Andalucían aficionados as a watered-down departure from tradition, I maintain that it merely is a negotiation of transcultural boundaries that take the form of local (UK) cultural variations. This differs from the cultural appropriation that characterises UK salsa or diasporic formations such as bhangra. As described in the following chapter, these variations which occur in conjunction with the reverence for perceptions of the Andalucían version signify a glocal cultural model for UK flamenco.

References

Abra, A. (2012). The Evolution of Popular Dancing in Britain in the 1920s. In B. Bebber (Ed.), *Leisure and Cultural Conflict in Twentieth-Century Britain* (pp. 41–62). Manchester: Manchester University Press.

Aoyama, Y. (2007). The Role of Consumption and Globalisation in a Cultural Industry. *Geoforum, 38*, 103–113.

Baltanás, E. (2002). The Fatigue of the Nation: Flamenco as he Basis for Heretical Identities. In G. Steingress (Ed.), *Songs of the Minotaur: Hybridity and Popular Music in the Age of Globalization* (pp. 139–168). London: Transaction Publishers.

Baulcombe, H. (2014, January 13). *Folk Festivals at the Hall, 1927–1984.* Retrieved from http://www.royalalberthall.com/about-the-hall/news/2014/january/folk-festivals-at-the-hall-1927-1984/

Becker, H. (1984). *Art Worlds.* Berkeley: University of California Press.

Escuela de Baile. (n.d.). Retrieved from http://ledb.co.uk/about-us/

De la Fuente, E. (2011, June 2). Signs and Wonders. *Times Educational Supplement*, 39–40.

Eisentraut, J. (2001). Samba in Wales: Making Sense of Adopted Music. *British Forum for Ethnomusicology – Music and Meaning Special Issue, 10*(1), 85–105.

Feld, S. (1994). *Music Grooves: Essays and Dialogues.* Tucson: Fenestra.

Finnegan, R. (2007). *The Hidden Musicians.* Connecticut: Wesleyan University Press.

Holmes, A. (2010). *Spanish Steps* [Motion Picture]. Independent.

Kiwan, N., & Meinhof, U. (2011). *Cultural Globalization and Music: African Musicians in Transnational Networks.* Basingstoke: Palgrave Macmillan.

Miller, S. (2013). Perceptions of Authenticity in the Performance of Cuban Popular Music in the United Kingdom: 'Globalized Incuriosity' in the Promotion and Reception of UK-Based Charanga del Norte's Music since 1998. *Journal of European Popular Culture, 4*(1), 99–116.

Office for National Statistics. (2014). *Census Update.* Retrieved from http://data.london.gov.uk/dataset/population-country-birth

Office for National Statistics. (2016). *Underlying Datasheets for Population by Country of Birth and Nationality.* Retrieved from www.ons.gov.uk

Stokes, M. (2007). *On Musical Cosmopolitanism*. The Macalester International Roundtable 2007, Paper 3. Retrieved from http://digitalcommons.macalester.edu/intlrdtable/3

Troubadour London History. (n.d.). Retrieved from http://www.troubadour-london.com/history

UK Coffee Revolution, the Third Wave. (2013, April 1). Retrieved from http://lyndonscoffee.com/uk-coffee-revolution/

Urquía, N. (2005). The Re-Branding of Salsa in London's Dance Clubs: How an Ethnicised Form of Cultural Capital Was Institutionalised. *Leisure Studies, 24*(4), 385–397.

6

Connected by the *Compás*: An Analysis of Cultural Transmission and Links Between Spain and the UK

In this book, I have described the flamenco scenes that exist in Spain (specifically in Sevilla Madrid) and the UK. In Chap. 3, I provided a detailed ethnography of the Sevilla flamenco which describes the scene in Sevilla as it is experienced by locals. I pointed out that the extent to which Sevillanos identify with flamenco is minimal compared to that which is broadcast by various governmental and tourist agencies to foreigners. The latter part of Chap. 3 addressed the experiences of foreigners who come to Sevilla to experience flamenco. While many foreigners experience the art complex solely on a tourist level in the tablaos, I described the dynamic ex-pat scene, which is made up of foreign aficionados who travel to Sevilla, usually for short periods of time (one month to several years), for the sole purpose of learning and absorbing flamenco culture. In doing this, I presented the structure, cultural aspects, and competing notions of identity and authenticity. In doing so, I demonstrated how socio-political organisations and transcultural interactions inform the scene and contribute to the postnational social space (within Sevilla) which is then transported abroad by these foreign ex-pats.

Chapter 4, on the contrary, discussed the realities of the Madrid flamenco scene. The capital city is often overlooked by scholars and flamenco

T. Martin, *Transnational Flamenco*, Leisure Studies in a Global Era,
https://doi.org/10.1007/978-3-030-37199-9_6

tourists alike. It does, however, have a long history of a flamenco scene, although, unlike Sevilla's, it is almost entirely public-facing. This commercial scene, consisting of tablaos, smaller performance venues, theatres, and the famous *escuela de flamenco*, Amor de Dios, is a haven for professional performers. Since its beginnings in the mid-nineteenth century, professional flamencos of all levels have flocked to Madrid to further their careers. Nowadays, most major flamenco artists base themselves in the capital, where they perform and collaborate. Madrid is also where most significant record companies are based in Spain. This means the professional, more technical, and often more open-minded version of flamenco is the one that gets transported abroad. There are also significant numbers of foreign flamenco students, many studying at Amor de Dios with the flamenco stars who teach there. The scene in Madrid differs from Sevilla because of this outward-facing characteristic, but also because of its open-mindedness towards interpretation of the art complex. Creative interpretations involving fusion, props, lighting, and other factors are more accepted and encouraged on the scene. International performers also are more accepted here, although the competition for employment is fierce. This competition leads to a less cohesive ex-pat flamenco scene than in Sevilla, which also could relate to foreigners being accepted by the scene as a whole. International connections are significant here, because many of these collaborations are precursors to tours to major flamenco hubs abroad. Significantly, similar to Sevilla, there is a historic animosity and lack of respect towards flamenco by those who do not claim it as a part of their identity. All of these factors indicate that the Madrid flamenco experience is significant to the art complex's understanding abroad, but also, to the cosmopolitan hubs who experience it, represents a different experience that is carried home than that in Sevilla.

In Chap. 5, I resumed the journey of these ex-pats, using the UK as an example, when they return to reside in their home country. Specifically, I considered how they use their transcultural capital (regarding flamenco) to create a UK scene, which is composed of a number of loosely connected hobby-oriented groups. The chapter, through individual bio-ethnographies, demonstrates the functioning of the UK scene, particularly the structure, demographics, and cultural norms that determine how it is appropriated. This provided insight into how the British approach multiculturalism, which often influences how foreign music cultures are deciphered there. Most notably, through these bio-ethnographies, I established that individual human hubs are imperative to the maintenance of local UK flamenco communities. I examined the motivations and forces within the British culture that inspire these aficionados to assume flamenco as an identity. Significantly, these individual cosmopolitan hubs (and through them, the local British groups) persistently reach outwards towards Spanish scenes for cultural and aesthetic inspiration, as opposed to internally towards local British experts. However, due to significant differences in the broader national and regional cultures, the UK scene is a glocalised (as described in the introduction) version, adapted to UK societal norms and regional variations, but in the image of a British aficionado's perception of Andalucían flamenco.

So how do we make sense of the two flamenco cultures (Spain and the UK) that are in contrast but also in contact? Through my experiences interacting with flamenco in Spain and the UK, I have made several observations regarding the pathways which gave rise to flamenco globalisation. An example of this is 'scene creation' in the UK which involves a certain amount of cultural exchange with Spanish destinations, such as Sevilla and Madrid. This is a music culture that is assumed to be intrinsic to Spanish national identity and is promoted as such by various sociopolitical and tourist institutions. In reality it is rejected by the majority of Spanish society, as evidenced by my interviews and observations. There are groups of aficionados that exist in scattered enclaves, concentrated mainly in Andalucía, Extremadura, Murcia, and Madrid. I painted a paradoxical picture of Spanish cultural identity that on one hand largely rejects flamenco, whilst those select few who do embrace it treat foreign interest with scepticism. I observed that individuals in the UK who were not satisfied with the offerings at home come to Andalucía to learn more and holistically approach flamenco education. Once there, they can immerse themselves in all aspects of the culture (*baile*, *toque*, *cante*, *jaleo*, and *aire*). Most ex-pat aficionados must adjust their perceptions of what flamenco entails since the British version is mostly dance-centric. For a variety of reasons, many ex-pats opt to resume contact with the UK, on varying levels. Upon re-engagement with the UK flamenco scene, these transient flamencos often must create their own flamenco space in order to transmit their knowledge. Due to a lack of an existing original culture, this is often in the format of performance or teaching. This is a shift in roles from their position of 'student' and 'foreigner' in Spain. Due to differences in cultural norms, the parameters for what flamenco 'is' shifts and the individuals must adjust how they present the culture to fit in so to attract clients and audiences. As a result of these shifts, a glocal culture is created, which begs the question: how do we account for the changes that occur during flamenco's journey from its homeland? Or, more importantly, how do we account for what occurs on the journey between flamenco's homeland as it travels with these transient aficionados? And, how do the scenes in either locale affect what travels? Finally, how is it modified when it lands?

6.1   Frameworks

Several frameworks are useful in the development of a model that helps address the above questions. This chapter will address these frameworks and then construct a new model from them which suggests new ways in which flamenco cultures travel and adapt to new surroundings. First, I will discuss flamenco in the global flow, utilising a postnational viewpoint (advocated by Knudsen and Corona and Madrid) and explain how borders are obsolete when considering flamenco culture (Knudsen 2011; Corona and Madrid 2008). Applying Roberts' (1995) concept of glocalisation I will examine flamenco's status in the UK as an art complex that is continually mirroring perceptions of the Spanish scene whilst responding to regional British variations. Next, applying Kiwan and Meinhof's 'Human Hubs' concept (Kiwan and Meinhof 2011a, p. 6), which rests on network migration theories, I will examine the role of the individual in postnational cultural development and transmission, focusing on how they utilise transcultural capital and links to influence and create glocal flamenco culture in Spain and the UK. Finally, I will propose a new model that encapsulates the phenomenon of British nationals (as an example) becoming the culture brokers of an art form not associated with their national or ethnic identity. Ultimately, I will analyse how individual non-native human hubs, through transcultural interactions and networks, are influential in the creation and maintenance of a postnational, glocal flamenco culture.

6.2 Postnational Culture

While flamenco is assumed by outsiders to be intrinsic to Spain's grand, national rhetoric, upon closer inspection my research has demonstrated considerable detachment and even animosity on the part of Spanish nationals. Reasons for this, as outlined in the chapters on Sevilla and Madrid, include associations with Franco and *Gitanos*, identity associated with other folk musics, and preference for popular music. At the same time there is extensive foreign interest in flamenco which has in part emanated both from Spanish performances and from immigration abroad, as well as the extensive and ongoing tourist campaign using flamenco as the poster-child. This calls into question the correlations between ethno-national musical identities and globalisation processes. The dichotomy between lack of identity amongst the Spanish and foreign interest encourages new ways to look at this travelling cultural complex, which are possible from a postnational viewpoint.

'Postnationalism' refers to the process or trend by which nation-states and national identities lose their importance relative to supranational and global entities. Corona and Madrid in their book, *Postnational Musical Identities*, define 'postnationality' as the unsuitability of the nation-state as a basis for identity analysis which, therefore, replaces the nation as a 'frame for considering the relationship between identity and music' (Corona and Madrid 2008, p. 3). Because of this, they make a case for music's role in moulding social networks that go beyond ethno-nationalistic boundaries (Knudsen 2011, p. 78). What this suggests is that identity is no longer necessarily based on national and ethnic background. Jan Knudsen, in his article 'Music of the Multi-ethnic Minority: a Postnational Perspective', ascribes the rise of postnational music cultures to two factors: first to demographic changes resulting from increased immigrant groups which form social communities in their new country of residence; and more relevantly in this context, he attributes the rise of postnationalism to the emergence of cultural groups founded on transnational exchange which contravene ethnic and national identifiers as their defining feature (Knudsen 2011, p. 78). He stipulates that post-national thought provides a structure to examine ideas regarding how national identities lose their importance in comparison to transnational configurations, emphasising the importance of socio-cultural communities that ignore borders (Knudsen 2011, p. 79). Knudsen surmises that whilst national background cannot be discounted 'the focal point for understanding cultural dynamics is not the relationship to any situated "authentic sources", but rather the innumerable ways in which groups and individuals choose to build their own cultural worlds based on the sum of links to the network available to them' (Knudsen 2011, p. 81).

Flamenco, as a case study, connects conceptually to postnational thought, which is a useful mechanism for understanding some of the cultural phenomena described in this book. First, there is a certain lack of identity with flamenco amongst the Spanish. For one thing, it is an art form that has been propagandised as a symbol of Spain since the beginning of Franco's 1950s tourism campaign, but my research has indicated that this did little to endear it to the citizens. It imposed a nationalist culture upon a country that had previously been culturally and politically decentralised. Spain has typically been a country characterised by extensive regionalisation with many different music styles and dances that citizens feel are representative of their specific town or province. Flamenco within Spain, although possessing a following in Madrid, is primarily an art form that a minority of Andalucíans identify with. Therefore, other regions were having flamenco thrust upon them as their new national identity and felt some resentment. To add insult to injury, not long into his reign, Franco enacted strict censorship measures, enforced with a brutal secret police force. He viewed regionalisation as 'the enemy within', which included regional languages and culture (Barton 2009, p. 232). These policies strangled (oftentimes literally) any discordant words and images which included cultural dissent in the form of folk music (Washabaugh 1997). Regional music cultures, such as the Catalonian *sardana* were illegalised. Even flamenco was affected, as Franco suppressed its local and non-commercial variations because of its association with politic subversion and revolutionary protest. All the while he promoted a professional, sanitised version as a tourist attraction (Washabaugh 1997).

It was at this time that a concept of 'outside' and 'inside' flamenco began (as referred to in Chap. 2)—one version for the tourists, one for the aficionados (Malefyt 1998, p. 65). These official versions removed the regional emphasis and encapsulated more accessible versions of the art form (Heffner Hayes 2009, p. 125).

After Franco's death (1892–1975), when Spain's transition to democracy culminated with the ratification of their Constitution of 1978, there were strong movements towards decentralisation. This was encouraged by rules set out by the Constitution that allowed for territorial governments that could be autonomous from the national government. By 1983, all 17 regions had gained autonomy. This caused a wave of cultural decentralisation as well, which resulted in regions reinvigorating their particular cultures that had been quashed under Franco. Andalucía, in the previously described 2007 Statute of Autonomy, used flamenco as a marker of cultural distinctiveness. While this strengthened flamenco as a symbol of Andalucía for governmental organisations, non-aficionados, and foreigners, most Spaniards outside the region (and indeed inside) disassociated themselves from the art form. My interviews and research have corroborated this indifference. Many non-flamencos with whom I spoke decried flamenco as something they did not identify with. They cited reasons ranging from having a regional music of their own, negative associations with Franco or *Gitanos*, or simply preferring other types of popular music (L. Perez, personal communication, Aug. 1, 2015).

Somewhat ironically, it was the very same Franco-led tourism campaign that alienated other Spanish regions that attracted some foreigners to assume flamenco as an identity (albeit sometimes a skewed one). Foreign audiences are responsible for the maintenance of a flamenco performance industry in Spain. My informants have told me most Spaniards would not pay to see a performance—especially because if they were interested they could see a show for free on the streets or in a *peña* (Aurora, personal communication, Jan. 11, 2014). According to the *Guía de Flamenco* website, there are 133 official tablaos in operation across Spain and a number of flamenco schools which mostly cater to foreigners. Cristina Heeren, founder of the largest flamenco school in Sevilla, vouched that at least half of her students are foreign, stating that they had students from 28 countries (Neild 2015, Feb. 11). There are flamenco schools in practically every country on the planet and academic studies have been done on academies in the US and Japan.[1] During the course of my research, most of the Spanish flamenco performers who I interviewed were even hired to go to Japan to teach for three- to six-month stints (Aurora and Yolanda, personal communications, Feb. 2014). My fieldwork in the UK has corroborated this assertion of global flamenco, as I have demonstrated. There are performances in larger cities by touring artists on a semi-regular basis which are generally sold out. The more enthusiastic UK participants travel to Spain specifically for lessons. Most of the UK scene members are not of Spanish heritage. As indicated, the British flamenco groups are small and generally only maintaining a loose connection with one another yet link themselves with the Andalucían scene.

Postnational Flamenco: En la Casa del Herrero, Cuchillo de Palo

While there is a certain place association (Andalucía) with flamenco, the fact that most of the Spanish population does not associate itself with it and the significant influence of foreigners on local Andalucían scenes indicates that the nation-state is no longer suitable as a framework for identity analysis in flamenco. In accordance with Corona and Madrid's theoretical study, there is a case for examining flamenco as an art form that moulds socio-cultural networks in a postnational manner—as connections that are developed through the art form and its participants, rather than on an ethno-national level. The necessity for this postnational perspective can be summarised by two quotes from my interviews. The first is by renowned flamenco film star Merche Esmeralda in an interview imparted that she travels around the world giving performances and classes, as do many flamenco performers. She describes the dichotomy of flamenco's lack of respect inside of the country, whilst incredibly popular outside with the proverb '*En casa del herrero, cuchillo de palo*' (M. Esmeralda, personal communication, Feb. 17, 2014). This translates as 'In the

---

[1] While this may seem a sweeping claim, Google searches (as well as connections with other foreigners made in Spain) have revealed the existence of flamenco in some truly astonishing locations such as Iraq, Afghanistan, Democratic Republic of the Congo, Iran, Syria, and Cape Verde.

House of the blacksmith, knife of wood', which means that someone who is specialised in creating something particular does not appreciate it. In utilising this proverb, Merche is referencing how flamenco is not, on the whole, appreciated inside of Spain. She explained that when she grew up, even in Andalucía flamenco was considered vulgar and something only poor people engaged with. On the other hand, Merche's extensive experiences performing abroad have given her the impression that flamenco is respected and understood outside Spain's borders:

> Probably because flamenco is a very natural expression of being. When you are sad, your expression is in pain. When cheerful, your face lights up. And that happens to everyone. Then there is the attraction that the dancer has a percussive movement, expression, arm movement, character ... may things come together because the simple dance is a complete spectacle that leaves no one indifferent or passive, and it is contagious. Flamenco has something contagious that 'takes' people. (M. Esmeralda, personal communication, Feb. 17, 2014)

These quotes from Merche are relevant because they demonstrate evidence given by a prominent and well-travelled dancer noting the lack of respect towards flamenco in Spain. The quotes also indicate Merche's feeling that foreigners understand, even if they do not understand the language. The final quote, in particular, suggests this understanding extends a line of communication between the performer and foreign audience which is not widely accepted in Spain.

The second quote is mentioned earlier in this paper by British dancer Alicia, while we attended a *peña* in Sevilla: 'Can't you see this is my culture too?' We were standing in a dingy, low-ceilinged room after the performance had finished while an impromptu *juerga* had begun. Surrounded by local Sevillano aficionados improvising *baile* and *cante*, Alicia clapped *palmas*, shouted *jaleo*, and even danced. Through her actions and her words, Alicia reveals the connection, both perceived and actual, that foreigners can feel flamenco. She understands the cultural conventions and feels that she shares flamenco with the Andalucíans. These quotes by Merche and Alicia epitomise the complex postnational boundaries that characterise global flamenco culture. They represent, most importantly, the concept that flamenco is an art complex shared by informed individuals who are not necessarily of the same ethno-national background.

6.3 A Glocal Cultural Model

When considering a travelling culture in a postnational light, it is imperative to assess how that manner of culture is being created at various points on the global network. Obviously a culture will possess a particular place of origin, but what is necessary is to assess the nature of those flamenco cultures that exist outside the parameters of the sending region and the reciprocal effects and developments on the culture in the place of origin (Aoyama 2007, p. 106). This designation is important because of globalisation critics who maintain that music traditions are diluted and homogenised when they travel. Scholars such as Hamelink have insisted: 'the impressive variety of the world's cultural systems is waning due to a process of "cultural synchronization" that is without historical precedent' (Hamelink 1983, p. 3). The general fear is that the 'global' is overriding the 'local', thus homogenising cultures across the world (Robertson 1995, p. 25). As an initial outsider to both cultures, the interactions and compensations granted between two cultures as different as British and Andalucían were intriguing. This 'predicament of culture' (after James Clifford) is a byproduct of the twentieth century's unparalleled overlapping of traditions, where Western products, power, and popular culture can be experienced at the ends of the earth and, yet, a foreign culture can be experienced in the next neighbourhood (Clifford 1988, p. 14). This creates a constant negotiation between two 'metanarratives': homogenisations and cultural loss versus emergence and invention (Clifford 1988, p. 16). Naturally, all cultures do not interact at the same rate, even within the borders of the UK. The salsa and Neo-Balkan genres value a mere perception (Baudrillard's simulacra) of their original culture to the extent that they are almost a different music style, albeit a talented one, as evidenced by groups such as Alejandro Toledo and the Magic Tombolinos. Baudrillard's theory of simulacra postulates that postmodern societies (including politics, social life, and culture) are based on simulation, whereby identities are created by image appropriation and simulated models determine how individuals perceive themselves in relation to other ('Jean Baudrillard' 2007). He also stipulates that postmodern identities are characterised by the implosion of distinctions (i.e., between genders, societies, and cultures), meaning that such divergent entities such as politics and culture begin to converge and affect one another. Connected to these is Baudrillard's concept of hyperreality, which holds that in the postmodern world, entertainment, information, and communication impart experiences more intense and engaging than real life, spurring individuals to seek out spectacle instead of actual meaning ('Jean Baudrillard' 2007). The simulacrum is not a copy of the real, but a truth in its own right, often bearing no similarity to any reality. One might propose the notion that Baudrillard's simulacra theory is accurately represented in the worlds of salsa and Neo-Balkan in the UK, as they merely imitate a stereotype of Cuban and Romani music, to the extent that those within these scenes believe them to be 'the real thing'. As will be demonstrated later, this is not entirely the case with flamenco.

Sociologist Roland Robertson (among others) has refuted this viewpoint of the 'global' in constant conflict with the 'local', instead maintaining that globalisation actually entails the 'incorporation of locality' (Robertson 1995, p. 40). In the context of my research, this suggests that musics engage in a sort of cultural exchange, rather than a hostile takeover, when they encounter cultures from outside their historic ethno-national borders.

Proposing a Glocal Cultural Model

Flamenco in the UK, despite its differences, is reliant on the Andalucían version for inspiration and grants it the utmost aesthetic authority. Based on this reference to the original culture by 'outsiders', I maintain that flamenco is actually an example of a glocal culture.

Glocalisation, a term popularised by Roland Robertson, involves 'the simultaneity and the interpenetration of what are conventionally called the global and the local [...]—the universal and the particular' (Robertson 1995, p. 28). He observed a tendency for some scholars to imagine globalisation as a macro-phenomenon but felt this was part of a 'mythology of globalization', as per Ferguson (1992). This mythology references developments that eliminate locality through the 'triumph of culturally homogenizing forces over all others' (Robertson 1995, p. 25). He criticises Giddens' view that globalisation should be understood as expressing time-space distanciation and the intersection of social events 'at distance' with local cultures' (Giddens 1991, pp. 21–22).[2] Robertson does not feel this viewpoint fully accounts for global-local complexities and maintains that sociologists need to surpass arguments which pit homogenisation against heterogenisation since globalisation is not either of these (Robertson 1995, p. 27). However, unlike homogenisation scholars Hamelink and Barber, Robertson did not see the global as necessarily detrimental to the local; instead he viewed globalisation as the 'compression of the world as a whole, involve[ing] the linking of localities [...and] the invention of locality' (Robertson 1995, p. 35). Robertson, instead, stipulated that the universal and the particular should be synthesised, which led to the development of his theory of 'Glocalisation'. Glocalisation is akin to micro-marketing in that it implies the adaptation of global cultures on a local scale (Robertson 1995, p. 28). An example of this is McDonald's regionalising their menus—such as using beefless burgers in India (Prakash and Singh 2011, p. 19). This also occurs at a cultural level, for example, the combination of Catholic saints and African Deities is Afro-Caribbean religious life (Herskovits 1937, p. 635). Robertson introduced this term at a time (the mid-1990s) when most globalisation discussions assumed that the global subverted the local. He felt this ignored several key eventualities, including how the 'local' is created on a 'trans'-local level (Robertson 1995, p. 26). Robertson asserts that there is a tendency to assume there is a conflict between local cultures and globalising forces which involves a clear-cut polarity, however in many ways they define each other. It does not make sense to assume the global omits the local; it is composed of local, diversifying aspects (Robertson 1995, p. 29). Glocalisation falls in line with speculations by Hannerz which describe two possible outcomes of long-term transnational flows:

---

[2] Giddens in later writings defines globalisation as 'the reason for the revival of local cultural identities in different parts of the world' (2000, 31); however, this was not one of the inspirations for Robertson's glocalisation theory.

saturation and maturation. The former suggests the preponderance of homogeneity. The latter, which Hannerz views as the most likely, rests on the possibility that eventually imported cultures which were originally unaltered, would come to evolve in a manner more aligned with a fundamentally local disposition (Hannerz 1999, p. 74).[3] Basically, globalisation increasingly entails creating and incorporating locality, in a mutually beneficial relationship. The concept of glocalisation addresses how local cultures travel and is adapted to other localities. Glocalisation suggests an element of 'selective incorporation', which addresses a nation-state's propensity to mimic aspects of cultural practices from other societies, and incorporating a range of foreign ideas into their own culture (Hannerz 1999, p. 41). The model of the 'glocal', combining the 'global' and the 'local', both at a linguistic and cultural level, transcends the propensity to assume a constant global-local conflict. 'Local' refers to cultural aspects that are supposedly divorced from globalising influences. Globalisation inevitably involves the creating or amalgamating of locality (Hannerz 1999, p. 40).

Ethnomusicologists have adopted the term 'glocalisation' into music globalisation studies to refer to the 'appropriation of globally available music styles and products and their reterritorialization and redefinition in local communities around the globe' (Knudsen 2011, p. 88).[4] At a musicological level, this concept describes both the differences that occur when music travels and the locally specific adaptations that are made. This has been utilised to examine various popular music subcultures, such as the Mitchell's relocation of rap music and St. John's Global-Local Psytrance scene. The latter, in particular, exemplifies how glocalisation operates in that it details the interconnectedness of the various Psytrance scenes around the world which are linked by referring back to the 'original' culture in Goa whilst applying variations specific to their local cultures (St John 2010, p. 50). The focus on glocal variations in relocated music serves to reduce focus on nationality and ethnicity (Knudsen 2011, p. 81).

---

[3] Hannerz (1999), p. 74.

[4] See also Tony Mitchell *Global Noise: Rap and Hip Hop Outside the USA* (Connecticut: Wesleyan University Press, 2001).

There are assumptions amongst Sevilla aficionados which fall along the lines of pessimistic globalisation theories. This line of reasoning maintains that the 'global' will override and dilute the local. The UK flamenco does anything but dilute flamenco culture. Similar to St. John's Psytrance study, flamenco is epitomised by a glocal cultural model. It is inspired by a rich, place-based culture (Andalucía and Madrid) and strives to emulate the original whilst enacting local variations in response to local (in this case, British) culture. The UK flamenco scene can be classified as a glocal model because it is set up primarily by outward-looking British aficionados and created as hybrid versions of a local phenomenon. This differs from concepts of cultural appropriation because the participants are actually looking outwards instead of assuming it as their own private property. Glocalisation explains the phenomenon of cultural similarities between, for example, flamenco groups which exist halfway around the world from each other. They may all know how to interpret a certain *palo* through dance but will often put regional variations that refer to their home country or individual backgrounds—such as combining flamenco with circus skills or bellydancing choreography. Glocalisation also explains how those who choose to fully engage with the culture can have a similar understanding of its intricacies, even when they are from different cultural backgrounds. These variations are enacted by the foreign aficionados who run the specific local scene and their experiences. Finally, glocalisation demonstrates how someone from Andalucía, flamenco's ancestral homeland, can have less of a connection with it than someone from the UK or Japan.

There are several reasons that explain why flamenco in the UK is representative of a glocal culture, as opposed to a simulacrum, appropriation, or diaspora. The first of these is the concept of looking to Andalucía as an authority on the art form. This demonstrates that cultural capital lies with the Andalucían scene, those of that ethnicity, or foreigners who have participated in it. Rita's description earlier of the hierarchy in the London flamenco scene is indicative of the preference for Spanish connections. As demonstrated by my ethnography on the UK, each sub-scene is limited to one or two individual drivers, which grants significant authority to those present. Supporting the theory that cultural capital rests with Andalucían flamenco is the fact that most of the small UK sub-scenes physically reach towards Spain. For example, my research revealed that aficionados in Northern England were more likely to fly to Malaga for a flamenco course than take the train to London or Birmingham. There are plenty of flamenco experts of Spanish background in London, but even in London people are more likely to look south. Most of the UK flamenco groups I encountered with had particular Spanish flamenco dancers that they brought over to their town once or twice a year. Barring this, they all had annual or bi-annual workshops scheduled where a new teacher from Spain would visit each year. An example of this is Deva Flamenco (Chester) who hired Maria del Mar (from Malaga) or Flamenco de Liverpool who hired Catalina. This travel pattern suggests that sites within the UK flamenco scene are more connected with Andalucía than other flamenco groups in their own country. The location of cultural capital is significant in designating flamenco as a glocal culture. It indicates that UK flamenco is not attempting to appropriate the scene—only to adapt it to fit with local circumstances. This is contrary to other global music scenes in the UK, for example the salsa dance scene in London. Urquía, in his article 'The Re-Branding of Salsa in London's Dance Clubs', discusses how UK salsa dancing has actually been appropriated and excludes most of the Latino community (Urquía 2005, p. 395).

Variations

Additional support for considering flamenco as a glocal culture emanates from the British variations to the Andalucían version. Whilst the trajectory of Flamenca Britannica is towards emulating Andalucían cultures, alterations occur in response to local norms. These cultural alterations are due in part to decisions made by individual cultural brokers who facilitate the sub-scenes and are primarily aimed at attracting audiences and students. A key example of this is the lack of crowd participation. In Andalucía, *jaleo* is an important part of the performance. In the UK, audiences, on the whole, are not comfortable with the thought of shouting out or clapping during a piece. Therefore, some of the *aire* is altered and visiting performers must adjust to not hearing this additional element. Another significant change is the focus on dancing and guitar—most UK participants only engage with flamenco on this level, with only a handful of singers and percussionists across the country. The reasoning for this is that the dancing and guitar elements are the most accessible to those without detailed cultural knowledge. These components are considered to be the most quintessentially 'Spanish' to the uninitiated—a notion that is incorrect, as in Andalucía *cante* is probably the most respected and utilised. The singing requires knowledge of Andalucían dialect and specific techniques that are unfamiliar to UK vocal practice. The percussion entails very specific and syncopated rhythmic patterns which fit in a particular way with the music and dancing, which are unfamiliar to UK ears, but present even in non-flamenco Spanish music. To some extent this removes an ethnic element, although it makes flamenco more accessible to UK practitioners, who still value the *cante* and *compás* even if they do not personally practice it.

Another variation is the increased presence of fusion in UK flamenco. This was demonstrated in the ethnography about Camino del Flamenco's night—where Iraqi music and flamenco were fused. The definition of flamenco is also extended in classes that teach *Sevillañas* and rumbas, which are not considered flamenco in Andalucía, but folk music. This expansion of flamenco is used to make it accessible to a wider audience. A final variation to consider is the differing roles that flamenco plays in each location (Andalucía and the UK). In the UK, flamenco serves as an exotic pastime or performance to view for most who engage at all with it. Most, as noted previously, participate on a superficial level that involves a dance or guitar class once a week. In Sevilla, flamenco (although not liked by all) is representative of a subculture. Those that participate are familiar with all elements and it is, to some extent, influential on regional culture (such as Semana Santa and annual *ferias*) and popular music. The variations exemplified demonstrate flamenco as a glocal culture in accordance with Robertson's definition which specifies that the original culture is maintained but is influenced by globalised Western (in this case the UK) culture.

Glocality in Sevilla

Of course, as per Robertson's stipulations, glocalisation is not a one-way street. Despite being part of 'the original', the Sevilla flamenco scene could also be considered 'glocal', as it too represents a local scene influenced by the global. Whilst the 'global' is considered a homogenising threat, in reality it has created a cultural industry. Aoyama, in her article 'Artists, Tourists, and the State', stipulated that in 2004 flamenco tourists accounted for 3.8% of Andalucía's €54 million tourist revenue (Aoyama 2009, p. 95). The foreign interest in flamenco is almost entirely responsible for its presence as an industry (Aoyama 2009, p. 96). There is a certain paradox in this because of the feeling amongst some Andalucían flamencos that the art needs to be protected from foreign dilution but the foreign interest generates significant income for performers and teachers, not to mention landlords, restaurants, and other service providers. Merche Esmeralda, in an interview, informed me that actually:

> It is we [the Spanish performers] who are doing the diluting. Not because we live outside the country, but because we are doing terrifying fusions and aberrations. [...] I teach the traditional flamenco because, although the artist needs innovation, it must be from the roots. (M. Esmeralda, personal communication, Feb. 17, 2014)

This quote indicates that foreign dilution can be prevented with proper teaching of techniques.

Anthropologist Ulf Hannerz accounts for the dynamics between the UK and Sevilla and Madrid scenes in his chapter 'Cosmopolitans and Locals in World Culture' in a discussion regarding local-cosmopolitan distinction. He stipulates that, on a local level, diversity is the determinant that allows 'locals' to stay within their particular cultures, whilst cosmopolitans depend on 'the other' creating 'special niches' for their cultures: 'Cosmopolitans cannot exist without locals' (Hannerz 1990, p. 250). This outlines the mutual reliance that Andalucía and the UK have upon each other in the maintenance of a flamenco scene. To put it another way, Andalucía possesses the cultural capital that the UK relies upon for its glocal scene, whilst the UK (and other glocal flamenco locales) provides the economic capital that enables the Sevilla scene to flourish.

In summation, global and Andalucían flamenco combine to create a glocal flamenco culture. This exists on a postnational level because of flamenco's broad rejection in Spain and its assumption as identity by small groups in varying locales around the world. There is not an exact copy of the hallowed 'original' in any one place due to variations in local norms. Global and Andalucían flamenco are mutually dependent upon each other, with the 'global' receiving cultural capital from Andalucía, and Andalucía receiving economic capital. These glocal cultures exist on a network linked by a mutual passion for flamenco, as opposed to particular ethno-national associations. Deleuze and Guattari, in their work *A Thousand Plateaus*, discuss this phenomenon under the premise of Rhizome Theory, which is an allegory for a vibrant cultural complex comprised of decentralised, yet connected, nodes with no references to a tangible origin.[5] Mitchell, in his discussion of glocal rap surmises that rhizomatic tendencies result in the formation of a plethora of 'syncretic "glocal" subcultures, involving local indigenization of [a] global music idiom' (Mitchell 2001, p. 108). This rhizomatic pull is evident in flamenco as well. My research suggests multiple glocal scenes, decentralised, but loosely connected nodes which are glocal versions of a global music. Robertson implies that the process of intertwining localities and 'inventing' a new local is, in fact the process of glocalisation (Robertson 1995, p. 35). The interweaving rhizomes accurately describe the shape of glocal flamenco, but the final question is to assess the rhizomatic pull of cultural information in the art complex.

6.4   Hub Theory and the Role of the Individual

Although Deleuze and Guattari's Rhizome Theory suggests a macro shape for flamenco's glocal scenes, in order to understand how particular local scenes manifest, it is important to understand how cultural capital travels and re-forms into its glocal format. This links with discussions of 'network migration theory' which examines factors that encourage migration temporally and spatially, with a focus on interpersonal connections between migrants and non-migrants (Kurekova 2011, p. 10). A branch of

---

[5] See Deleuze and Guattari, *A Thousand Plateaus* (1993).

network theory that is particularly relevant is Transnational Migration theory, which hypothesises about social spaces which exist on a transnational level. This theory focuses on migrants who stay connected with and participate in the culture in both sending and receiving countries (Kurekova 2011, p. 11). These concepts of network migration begin to make sense of how flamenco moves between global locations. The primary carriers are foreigners who, living in their home country, maintain a link with the Andalucían scene.

Human Hubs: Individuals in Global Cultural Transmission

Recent tropes in ethnomusicological scholarship and migration studies portray individuals as crucial catalysts for the creation of glocal communities and flows between network nodes. Migration is viewed as an agent for development, marked by transnationalisation, with mobile individuals transpiring as central to social transformation (Glick Schiller and Faist 2010, p. 14). Global networks, such as that described above, are composed of a series of linkages between individual actors who facilitate 'multi-connected forms of social interconnection' (Holton 2008, p. 1). While the concepts of 'culture' and 'society' are macro constructs which involve vast numbers of people, Tim Rice points out that it is the distinctions between individual participants that are imperative to the creation and shaping of a music culture (Rice and Ruskin 2012, p. 307). Rice also argues that culture cannot be situated in a spatial field any longer, both 'culture' and 'field' are more accurately considered as 'constituted in and through the relationship of individuals' (Rice and Ruskin 2012, p. 317). Transnational individuals, as well as transported culture, have also taken responsibility in re-creating it abroad. This marks a power relations shift in the politics of globalisation, in that individuals are seen to have the ability to engage with globalising forces, which have previously been thought to exist outside of their sphere of influence (Kiwan and Meinhof 2011a, p. 9).

Kiwan and Meinhof, as mentioned previously in this book, created a theoretical model inspired by Transnational Network Migration theory, which addresses this phenomenon of individual influence on cultural migration. Their concept of human hubs addresses the phenomenon of individual influence on globalisation due to its emphasis on specific artists as culture brokers (Kiwan and Meinhof 2011b, p. 3). Kiwan and Meinhof, utilising African musicians in London and Paris, created this network model to exemplify the transnational connections which link migrant musicians with their sending and receiving countries, and examine how migrants self-perceive and execute their global movements (Kiwan and Meinhof 2011b, p. 6). These human hubs, in their case study, are African migrants who are 'significant individuals' (musicians, cultural organisers, etc.) within the musical community, the 'main focus of the network [...] known by everyone in the network although not all the members of the network know each other' (Kiwan and Meinhof 2011b, p. 6). These individuals are significant because they transcend and link far-flung geographic and social spaces from sending to receiving country (Kiwan and Meinhof 2011b, p. 34). In many cases, the music scenes they create in their country of settlement would not exist if they were not present. Through the activities of these human hubs, translocal and transnational link music cultures in both sending and receiving countries and create sending/receiving circuits for migrant musicians (Kiwan and Meinhof 2011b, p. 4).

Transcultural Capital

The information and connections that result from interactions with the sending and receiving countries, the knowledge from both spaces that enables the creation of culture abroad, and the economic and social benefits that return to the hub's country of origin is known as 'transcultural capital'. Transcultural Capital theory, expounded by Meinhof and Triandafyllidou, integrates Bourdieu's 'capital' with Levitt's 'social remittances' and encapsulates their interactions in the lives of transnational artists (Kiwan and Meinhof 2011b, p. 8). It is a heuristic approach which enables the researcher to analyse resources of transnational migrants who maintain links with their home country, activate cultural interdependencies in cycles of migration (Kiwan and Meinhof 2011b, p. 9). Kiwan and

Meinhof's migrant musicians utilise their substantial transcultural capital (acquired in their country of origin) to validate and develop their art, supporting its commercial viability to new audiences. This imported capital demonstrates how migrant musicians retain connections with the home culture and how these links inform their creativity, thus pointing to a cyclical dimension between sending and receiving country (Kiwan and Meinhof 2011b, p. 9).

Flamenco Transmission and Cultural Creation: The Role of Cosmopolitan Hubs

As emphasised extensively in this book, individuals are largely responsible for the transmission of flamenco and creation of glocal scenes. Individuals inform how cultural identity is formed and maintained outside of flamenco's traditional national and regional identity. The concept of the 'individual' holds a unique place in this study, representing several different strands. In a methodological sense, it represents my approach to presenting a picture of the UK and Sevilla flamenco scene—from the eyes and experiences of the informants who live it. In an artistic sense, it represents how aficionados experience flamenco—it is an art complex that relies on the expression of deep, personal emotions which are accessible to all humans, regardless of ethno-national background. Structurally, it is a music that is made up of independent elements (*cante, baile, toque, jaleo, percusión*) which are linked by the *compás*, something that each performer will know, even if they have never met each other before. Metaphorically, this applies to the final theoretical aspect of this book. Glocal flamenco scenes, as described above, are independent aspects that are linked on a network by individuals who, similar to the *compás*' transportation of rhythmic information, transmit flamenco culture between nodes, creating glocal versions of the culture. These individuals fall into the category of Kiwan/Meinhof's human hubs because they connect with Andalucía to gain social and cultural capital, transmit or facilitate the transmission of culture outside of Andalucía, and, utilising their significant transcultural capital, become the centre of a local flamenco scene, which would oftentimes cease to exist without their influence. They differ from Kiwan and Meinhof's 'human hubs' because they are non-native culture brokers.

The concept of cosmopolitanism is one that has gradually edged its way into scholarly rhetoric surrounding globalisation, glocalisation, and transnationalism. Sociologist Ulf Hannerz defines cosmopolitanism as 'an intellectual and aesthetic stance of openness towards divergent cultural experiences', where particular individuals have the ability to access a variety of cultural competencies and interact within 'new meaning systems' (Hannerz 1990, p. 239). He outlines two types of cosmopolitanism: cultural and political. 'Cultural' cosmopolitanism refers to consumption of foreign cultures, while 'political' deals with 'global government and governance' (Hannerz 2005, p. 8). I will focus on the former category as that is most applicable to my research. Hannerz goes on to specify that these individuals endeavour to immerse themselves in foreign cultures, participating in them on a holistic level. This is in contrast to foreign tourists, who are attracted to specific qualities in a holiday destination (such as beaches and sunshine), and otherwise want them to be similar to their home environs (Hannerz 2005, p. 6). Hannerz is quick to point out that in both cases, the 'surrender to otherness' is generally a personal choice and does not require a definitive commitment to any particular culture, pointing out that 'one always knows where the exit is' (Hannerz 2005, p. 6). This implies that cosmopolitanism is always a personal choice. While this may be the case for citizens of the Western world, others, such as those in post-colonial countries, have also had to learn to handle cultures other than their own—and not by choice (Hannerz 2005, p. 16).

Building on Hannerz earlier definitions of cosmopolitanism, Szerszynski and Urry examine 'cultures of cosmopolitanism that transpire from various global processes'. Through research in the northwest of England, they examine whether globalisation is causing cosmopolitanism (Szerszynski and Urry 2002, p. 464). They define cosmopolitanism as 'a cultural disposition involving an intellectual and aesthetic stance of "openness" towards peoples, places and experiences from different cultures' (Szerszynski and Urry 2002, p. 448). It entails an appreciation for the differences between societies, as opposed to a desire to dominate. They identify a series of issues with previous definitions of cosmopolitanism, which indicate cultural receptivity is primarily a trait of affluent travellers from the Western world and occurs at the expense of local peoples. Szerszynski and Urry then suggest a general model for cosmopolitanism which avoids pitfalls of previous scholars (Szerszynski and Urry 2002, p. 469). This model focuses on several main traits of cosmopolites:

1. 'extensive mobility'—where people have the right and the means to travel;
2. 'capacity to consume many places en route';
3. cultural curiosity;
4. willing to risk encounters with the 'other'; and
5. ability to situate one's own culture on a historical and cultural map. (Szerszynski and Urry 2002, p. 470)

This builds on Tomlinson's expansion into 'glocalised cosmopolitanism', which focuses on an individual's ability to live in both the global and local, since cosmopolites regularly experience these 'other' cultures while residing in their own localities (Tomlinson 2003, p. 198).

These concepts of cosmopolitanism can shed light on certain aspects of musical globalisation. In 'On Musical Cosmopolitanism', Martin Stokes observes that 'supercultural, subcultural and intercultural music practices […] are now in close and unpredictable contact' (Stokes 2007, p. 4). He draws specific attention to the globalisation issue of musical encounters happening outside of their borders which challenges the logic of traditional 'bounded culture' (Stokes 2007, p. 4). Stokes proposes an approach which makes sense of globalisation not as a singular, holistic entity, but as a conglomeration of many cells, with 'cultural and institutional specificity' which approach the global as an operation zone in from diverse angles. This leads him to cosmopolitanism as it applies to music. Stokes believes cosmopolitanism inspires thoughts about how people embrace the music of the 'other' and how this embracement enables music to circulate globally, which inserts human agency back into globalisation analysis (Stokes 2007, p. 6). He asserts utilising cosmopolitanism as a tool for understanding music globalisation signifies conscious musical exchanges and hybridisation. However, 'cosmopolitanism' (as alluded to above) is a complicated term that also incites images of local music cultures fighting for prestige and cultural authenticity (Stokes 2007, p. 10). Stokes, warns that cosmopolitanism is no longer a benign concept, as it is now linked with 'acts of acquisitive consumption, and the control of others' (Stokes 2007, p. 10). Nonetheless, Stokes perceives music cosmopolitans as creating new musical worlds within specific circulation systems. These systems dictate what is available and how the music culture moves (Stokes 2007, p. 15).

In my research, I utilise the term 'cosmopolitan' to apply to the human hubs who transmit flamenco in between Spain and the UK. As these individuals are largely British transporting a local Andalucían art form, the term applies. However, it is important to consider Hannerz's words regarding the situational state of cosmopolitan consumption, for this points to how, quite often, aspects of flamenco change during the journey because, for whatever reason, they do not fit with British consumer or audience specifications. This refers to Stokes' statement regarding music cosmopolitans moving within specific circulation systems. As will be demonstrated throughout this thesis, flamenco's specific circulation system seems to be via cosmopolitan hubs that transport the music within the cultural norms of their home country.

As noted previously, most of the UK flamenco scenes documented in this book share the common characteristic of having the presence of a 'driver'. In larger cities, such as Birmingham, Bristol, and London, there is usually more than one of these individuals who create sub-scenes within the overarching scenario. These are individuals who, with or without a committee and devoted students, are responsible for the continuation of flamenco in their locality and truly push the local scene forward. These individuals are not always the teacher in the locale, nor are many of them Spanish, but they are the ones who facilitate the locality's interactions with flamenco. This can include activities such as classes, performances, film nights, lectures, and facilitating interactions with visiting Spanish performers. These cosmopolitan hubs are the focus of local scenes. They provide a link to their perception of the original Andalucían culture, not only through their pre-existing knowledge but through trips to Andalucía for lessons in addition to organising performances and workshops with visiting Spanish artists. Most importantly, they anchor their glocal scenes with considerable transcultural capital acquired through interactions with the Spanish side of the story. They create cultural exchange by rooting themselves in a British locale, while maintaining one foot in Andalucía in order to continue gaining cultural knowledge to transmit back home. The nature of these cross-cultural communications can range from extensive time spent studying in Andalucía (several years) to spending a couple weeks a year taking a course with a favourite teacher. It can also include facilitating activities or interactions with visiting Andalucían professionals to continue gaining cultural capital which can be applied to their local scenes.

Two examples of these hubs are Paula from Hebden Bridge (a small town in Yorkshire) and Claire in Chester. Paula teaches a group of 10–15 students who engage with flamenco once a week, but annually visits Andalucía to study with Chiqui de Jerez to top up her skills, maintain an emotional connection with the culture, and learn new routines to adapt for her teaching and personal performance. Claire makes an annual pilgrimage to the 10-day flamenco extravaganza of Festival de Jerez to take classes with various teachers, as well as visiting Malaga for lessons several other times a year. She also brings over Maria del Mar, a flamenco performer from Malaga, to teach workshops once a year, which are often attended by students from all over the Northwest of England. Both ladies, now in their 60s, picked up flamenco on a whim about twenty years ago and quit respectable university jobs to dedicate their lives to the art form.

In the case of both Claire and Paula, they are the sole facilitators of flamenco in their locale. While they consistently have a steady flow of students, they all fall into the category of 'hobbyists'. If Paula and Claire ceased to push flamenco as an activity, the scene would die out and their students would turn to belly dancing or trapeze class. Rita's ethnography also validates this point—specifically when she notes that most of her students only stick around for a few short courses or a couple years before moving on to some other activity to occupy their Tuesday nights. Another example of this point is Flamenco de Liverpool. The Liverpool flamenco community, run by Trish, was a vibrant one which facilitated connections with internationally performing dancer and teacher, Catalina from Sevilla. The scene began to taper off when Trish became terminally ill with cancer and upon her death most students moved on to other activities (although a few attended classes in Manchester). This demonstrates also the precariousness of a scene run by singular drivers.

Obviously, the London flamenco community is slightly different than the rest of the country, due to the large, multicultural population. However, attributable to the tendency of Londoners to stay within their own neighbourhoods, the theory of the individual hub there applies for each region of the city. Ron Hitchens characterises a variation on the hub for London's flamenco community. He connects local Londoners with visiting artists from Spain through his parties. He is a highly respected member of the London flamenco community, across several different sub-scenes. He is also known in Spain by artists who have visited, as well as their families and colleagues who have heard tales of the marvellous parties and dancing of 'El Chino'.

Alicia and Yazmin, of Dot-Dot-Dot flamenco are also examples of cosmopolitan hubs, even though they no longer live in the UK. They both believe that staying in Sevilla enables the most complete connection with the art complex. However, Yazmin explained:

> I think we created Dot-Dot-Dot from a real place of feeling British because we ARE British. I think all 3 of us as dancers. … Well I'll speak for myself. As a black woman there is not part of me that can pretend to be anything. I am not going to pretend to be Gypsy. I am not going to dye my hair so that I look like them. It has always been about being who I am and expressing myself from that perspective. So, I think a relationship with Britain has been very important because that is a part of who we are. And part of our experience as well, because before we came to flamenco, those were our references. I think it is wanting to embrace that. (Yazmin, personal communication, Nov. 4, 2015)

She and Alicia have expressed desires to communicate their practice in different ways, such as in community engagement (e.g., through SCOPE for adults with learning disabilities), in the form of fusion which connects with their cultural backgrounds (Yazmin is Afro-British and Alicia is Sephardi Jewish), or in workshops with school children. For example, while disabled people are more in the community in Andalucía, they are not often afforded the opportunity to learn to dance (Rita, Personal communication, Jun. 2, 2015).

Whilst the context is different from in Andalucía, the inspiration and information communicated still resides with the 'original culture'. These types of activities are not the norm in Andalucía, both for reasons involving concepts of 'authenticity' and for financial concerns. They approach flamenco in the UK as an opportunity not only to expand to whom flamenco is communicated but also to introduce context to the dance- and guitar-centric British flamenco world. This is accomplished through both their performances with Dot-Dot-Dot and the workshops they conduct on their annual UK tours.

Individual Roles in Spain

One of the reasons that Yazmin and Alicia cite for wanting to maintain contact with the UK involves the differing roles that cosmopolitan hubs (in the flamenco world) play between their home and receiving countries. In Sevilla, they are students and foreigners. The focus is on what they are doing wrong, what is missing from their flamenco education, and how they can prove themselves so as to acquire performance and teaching employment. There is also an emphasis on acquiring contacts (social capital) both in Sevilla and in the UK in order to achieve employment. Hubs such as Alicia and Yazmin, who have lived in Sevilla for an extended amount of time, also take on the additional role within that local scene as a human hub within the ex-pat flamenco community. They are known by everyone within the community and are considered experts in how to navigate the scene; this includes what teachers to use, what classes to take, which events to attend, where to look for work, and how to acquire housing and rehearsal space. In The UK, transient aficionados, such as Alicia and Yazmin, gain an opportunity to utilise their skills. Because of the transcultural capital that they convey from Sevilla, they are granted considerable respect within the UK scene, which increases their capacity to get performance and workshop dates. This sort of role is assumed by other cosmopolitan hubs such as Paula and Claire as well. Significantly, the role of the transient (or semi-transient) human hub in the UK is that of 'primary authority' within the flamenco community, since most of that group are casual hobbyists.

Drawbacks of Having a Singular Cultural Broker

The 'primary authority' position held by these individual scene drivers with their localities creates a certain conundrum with regards to what is transmitted, and continuity of the scene should they no longer facilitate. Cosmopolitan hubs, such as Paula and Claire, create local scenes and serve as an important link for their students to the original flamenco culture. Flamenco scenes in the UK would not exist without scene drivers like them; however, there are positives and negatives with having an individual act as the singular cultural broker. Many of the flamenco cosmopolitan hubs I have interviewed have reported that their students usually come into classes without knowing anything about flamenco other than castanets and polka dots, and many have never even been to Spain. The hubs, as a result, create the perception of what flamenco is and is not for the students. This is a complex question to answer even in Spain. Suffice it to say, this designation is much contested and combines multiple historically complex identities and opinions. What is certain is that flamenco can be described as a combination of dance, music, guitar, audience participation, and the surrounding culture. If it is presented as a dance-centric art form, dependent on a prescribed routine and only utilising the *cantes chicos*—characterised by lighter, upbeat, and generally more easily accessible flamenco *palos*, this is what the local UK flamenco community will believe is the REAL thing.

Despite the best intentions of these cosmopolitan hubs, they are also limited by the UK's approach to leisure—as something to be tried, cherry-picked, and consumed before usually moving on to some other exciting activity. Unless they become one of the few that truly embraces the art complex, they are generally disinterested in the broader cultural landscape, including how the routines they learn fit into it. Thus, drivers and teachers must present flamenco in a manner that keeps students' interest—a routine that they can see through to completion, with only brief flirtations with technique, *compás*, and the surrounding culture. Reciprocally, these created assumptions will determine what these students expect when they visit Spain and attend classes or shows, which will inevitably have a knock-on effect for how flamenco is performed, taught, and presented in Spain. This indicates that the cosmopolitan hubs play an important role in maintaining and influencing perceptions of the 'original culture' not only at home but potentially within Spanish scenes as well.

Transcultural Capital of Glocal Flamenco

The decisions that cosmopolitan hubs make with regards to what is presented to foreigners as 'flamenco' can be thought of in terms of Robertson's concept of 'selective incorporation'. Specifically, Robertson refers to the propensity for nations to 'copy' practices and beliefs from other nation-states, incorporating a conglomeration of 'foreign' concepts into their culture (Robertson 1995, p. 41). On a micro level, this applies to how flamenco's cosmopolitan hubs utilise their knowledge of Andalucían flamenco to create scenes in their home countries. This is part of the transcultural capital that they utilise to navigate the Sevilla and UK environs. Transcultural capital, in the case of glocal flamenco, combines social and cultural capital from Spain with economic capital from the UK. Cultural capital comes in the form of knowledge gained from the flamenco scene in Spain—through classes, performing, and cultural participation there, and interactions with visiting Spanish artists in London. Social capital comes in the form of Spanish artists and teachers that the hubs connect with and utilise in workshops, performances, and general information acquisition. They simultaneously contribute social remittances to the Andalucían scene through paying for lessons and performances (not to mention paying for meals and accommodation while there). Additional social remittances are provided when cosmopolitan hubs provide information and social connections with the British scene to Andalucían performers which will enable them to gain economic capital in the UK. Cosmopolitan hubs create and influence their local British scenes utilising transcultural capital. It manifests itself in routines learnt abroad, artists met, and cultural information acquired.

Most importantly, transcultural capital is used by individuals to create a glocal scene in the UK, which results in economic capital. It manifests itself by combining information and connections from Spain, with non-flamenco cultural knowledge in the UK. In order to succeed in doing this, cosmopolitan hubs must understand how flamenco is perceived and used in the UK, as well as general cultural norms regarding how British people typically consume culture and performance practices. These cultural consolations transpire primarily in the form of variations which fall in line with the greater non-flamenco cultural landscape of the UK. In the UK, flamenco is perceived as an upbeat, flashy, and Gypsy dance with castanets. Cosmopolitan hubs who want to teach must recognise that, for the most part, UK flamenco consumers only want to focus on the dance or the guitar aspects and even then, only on a casual, hobbyist level. They are generally not interested in understanding much of the culture; they just want to show up to class once a week, wear a pretty dress or play a *falseta*, and learn a prescribed routine, as evidenced by Rita's ethnography. They are usually not comfortable with improvising in the form of a *fin de fiesta*, most are not that receptive to having technique drilled into them, and many are not that interested in performing. The average British flamenco student's interest in flamenco is as an exotic hobby, which can easily be replaced with some other interesting activity. Cosmopolitan hubs, such as Rita, compensate for these expectations by running routine-based short courses which allow students to attain quick, tangible accomplishments.

In a performance sense, as noted earlier, cosmopolitan hubs must consider British audience norms. Most are not comfortable with the concept of *jaleo* and are accustomed to remaining silently respectful during a performance, so performers cannot force the issue. Furthermore, hubs must understand what the British audience's perception of flamenco entails, which is very different from what they will have experienced in Sevilla or Madrid. The UK understanding of flamenco is informed by mass media and tourist organisations, and involves upbeat flashy dancing, footwork, bright dresses, castanets, and Spanish flag bunting. It does not necessarily involve seriously emotional styles (*cante jondo*) and audience participation (*jaleo*). The cosmopolitan hub must decide how to balance their knowledge of 'the real thing' with audience expectations so as to inform without putting off their patrons.

Transcultural capital is the primary force that influences how flamenco travels and is transmitted abroad, as well as the lives of the artists in Spain. It is the information that flows between the two locations, carried by transient foreign aficionados. Most importantly, it informs the variations made by cosmopolitan hubs which result in the creation of a glocal scene. In flamenco, the cosmopolitan hubs make decisions about 'what will fly' within UK cultural norms, whilst still reaching towards the original Andalucían scene for inspiration.

6.5   Cosmopolitan Hubs: A New Model

Although Kiwan and Meinhof's 'human hubs' framework does, to some extent, encapsulate how a glocal flamenco scene is created, it falls short of a perfect match. This is because their theory is based on the premise that these culture brokers are from the same country as the music culture they are transporting. However, with the emergence of extensive transnational networks that are developing and thriving, especially in global cities such as London, the ethno-national dialogue of cultural homogeneity is challenged (Meinhof and Triandafyllidou 2006, p. 13). Anthony Cohen, in his 1964 book *Self-Consciousness: An Alternative Anthropology of Identity*, puts it best in his discussion of the virtues and flaws of Interpretivism:

> Societies do *not* determine the selves of their members. They may construct models of personhood, they may [...] *attempt* to reconcile selfhood to personhood. But they have no absolute powers in this regard, and almost certainly have an exaggerated view of the extent to which they can clone their members. (Cohen 1994, p. 71)

This suggests that individuals in our transnational world do not necessarily have their identity chosen for them by ethno-national associations.

Based on the concept of transnational identities, I propose a new model for cultural migration, building on the solid foundation of Kiwan/Meinhof's 'hub' theory. This model focuses on individual cosmopolitan hubs that move cultural information between the sending country and receiving country. This new type of human hub is not ethnically or nationally connected with the cultural capital they are transmitting and are characterised by having gained an interest in the art form in their home country. For this reason, I refer to them as 'cosmopolitan hubs'. This 'hub' designation incorporates the globalisation of 'cosmopolitanism', which refers to 'an intellectual and aesthetic stance of openness towards divergent cultural experiences' (Hannerz 1990, p. 239). A 'Cosmopolitan' is someone who immerses themselves in other cultures, displaying the ability to accept them and handles themselves in this culture. Beck furthers this designation by describing 'cosmopolitanisation' as the situation where people within the same national boundaries 'can inhabit markedly different "life-worlds" and be closer to or farther from people who live outside the borders of the state they live in' (Beck 2002, p. 17). My new model marks a significant departure from Kiwan/Meinhof's theory in that the primary actors that are transmitting culture are actually foreigners. Also significant to note is that the two aspects of this model that are moving in tandem are technically travelling in opposite directions to one another, with the culture moving from its sending country to a receiving country and the cosmopolitan hubs travelling from their sending country to a receiving country then back to the sending country carrying cultural information. This applies to the global flow of flamenco. Using the UK as an example, cosmopolitan hubs from the UK study flamenco in their home country, travel to Andalucía to gain social and cultural capital, and then return to the UK to act as a cosmopolitan hub for the glocal flamenco community there. This differs from Kiwan/Meinhof's human hubs who are Moroccan and who travel to and from Morocco with Moroccan transcultural capital. Similarly, though, both types of human hubs serve to create a glocal culture in the art form's receiving country (the UK) and have an economic effect on culture in its sending country (in this case, Spain).

There is certainly a case to be made for this model to be unique for flamenco; however, I suspect that due to increased global interconnectedness its applicability will be broader. For one thing flamenco is a very place-oriented art form. It also is largely rejected as an identity within Spain, with the exception of a comparative few enclaves. Spain is also a popular tourist destination, with flamenco as one of the primary cultural attractions. However, with cultures coming into increased contact and foreign music cultures increasingly accessible, it is conceivable, in fact, likely that this type of cultural migration model—one that operates through individuals that are foreign to the culture they are transmitting—is applicable to other migrating art forms as well (Argentinian tango and salsa come to mind).

Within this model, the individual maintains contact with the sending country, through transnational interactions such as visits/residency or relationships with particular artists who they bring to the UK for performances or workshops. The individual (British) cosmopolitan hub, who has transcultural knowledge of both the sending and receiving culture, must make decisions that balance economic and cultural capital. These decisions are aimed at attracting British leisure and entertainment consumers to the art form, either as students or as audience members. In doing this, these individual cosmopolitan hubs are utilising their transcultural capital to create a glocal version of flamenco culture. In the case of flamenco, while sometimes criticised by purists as cultural dilution, this advances the art form by creating significant economic benefits in Spain, which manifests in the form of a cultural industry.

Flamenco is an intriguing case in that despite its place-based identity and historical context, it has a larger following outside of Spain than within. It is primarily transported outside the country by foreigners. Inside of Spain, flamenco is marketed to foreigners—as audience members and students—as opposed to other Spanish people. In Spain, natives really only attend a show if they are actually aficionados, not those from outside the flamenco world—and even they would not pay the expensive admission price for a tablao show. While my foreign focus in this book is on the UK, I conducted formal interviews and informal chats with aficionados from the US, Mexico, Taiwan, Canada, and Japan. They confirmed my observations regarding cosmopolitan hubs being the primary cultural brokers and scene maintainers. It seems to be the norm for flamenco scenes to be driven by members of the home country, although they preserve a connection with the Andalucían version. Spanish artists were brought in as visiting performers and workshop technicians, but in general, were not a constant presence. Foreigners are the main carriers

and creators of flamencos scenes abroad. Therefore, I maintain that flamenco culture itself is global—with its cultural capital resting firmly in
Andalucía and its economic capital in the hands of intrigued foreigners
some of whom combine these to utilise transcultural capital and single-
handedly create glocal scenes in their home countries.

In this context, we see the emergence of extended social and cultural
capital, which contributes to the cosmopolitan hub's transcultural capital. This extended social and cultural capital exists due to pre-existing
capital in their home country. This greatly enhances the individual's
capacity to facilitate economic capital and create a glocal 'scene'. This is
information that Spanish artists generally do not possess which is a possible reason why they are not generally culture brokers and hubs in these
foreign locales. They nonetheless benefit in the form of social remittances
realised in Spain and stints as visiting teachers and performers. These
cosmopolitan hubs enact variations which comply with UK cultural
norms, expanding the ability for them to create economic capital. Alicia
explains her use of transcultural capital when performing in the UK as
understanding what it means to be British:

> They treat it as a concert. They don't know about *jaleos* and won't make a
> noise. They feel like they're ignorant if you egg them on too much. I'm
> English, so I understand English people. [...] Little by little I let them in.
> I get them to laugh, to warm up and feel more comfortable. Then they
> enjoy it more if they are comfortable and relax, and really experience fla-
> menco. It is just a different culture, a different way of communicating, but
> we are communicating. The only way an artist would understand how to
> communicate with an English audience is coming from that culture.
> (N. Luz, personal communication, Jan. 7, 2014)

This quote represents the glocal variations that inform how flamenco
travels abroad, largely communicated by individual cosmopolitan hubs,
who also nurture the Spanish scene through the economic sector whilst
receiving cultural and social capital from Andalucía. On a local level, they
single-handedly create a glocal culture in an unfamiliar environment
through transcultural capital and connections with perceptions and realities of the original culture.

6.6 Postnational, Glocal, Network, and a New Hubs Theory

Flamenco presents a unique challenge in understanding its status in a globalised music environment. On one hand, it is an incredibly place-based phenomenon, with roots firmly planted in the small taverns and plazas of Andalucía. Aficionados there are extremely protective of the culture and insistent on maintaining its purity. However, when the researcher gazes beyond the government and tourist propaganda, ignoring the assumptions made by those external to the scene, the picture is a bit more convoluted. It is a subculture shunned by most Spaniards, claimed as an identity by a comparative few. It is, however, embraced by small groups of foreigners hailing from practically every country in the world. This makes it necessary to consider flamenco in a postnational light. Given that flamenco cannot be an exact replica outside of its home environs, foreign versions manifest in the form of glocal variations. These are inspired by the Andalucían scene, but with alterations to ensure they are palatable to the new locale. Flamenco is transmitted primarily by foreign individuals (cosmopolitan hubs) who possess transcultural capital encompassing social and cultural capital from the Andalucían or Madrileño flamenco community, as well as from their home country, which are utilised to create economic capital in the UK. Overall this research suggests an alternative, postnational, model (cosmopolitan hubs) which describes how global music cultures travel and glocalise in a world that is becoming increasingly less focused on ethnicity or nationality for the formation of individual identities.

6.7 . Conclusions

Through a detailed cross-cultural qualitative study, this book has explored flamenco's place in the global flow. It has proposed modes of thought which allow us to make sense of how local flamenco culture has travelled and been reinterpreted outside of its historic Andalucían borders. Furthermore, it has provided an opportunity to problematise notions of identity and how some travelling music cultures, such as flamenco, under the right socio-political conditions, can erode fixed geo-political boundaries to create a postnational artistic conglomerate. It is an art complex that historically has been assigned as a marker of identity to those within Spain and Andalucía by national and regional governments. This has created false assumptions amongst those outside of the immediate flamenco scene (both at home in Spain and abroad). Nonetheless, a steady stream of foreigners from across the world has embraced flamenco and travel to Spain to gain an understanding of the art complex in its original context. Hence, labelling it as 'postnational' allows the researcher to designate it as a culture which, while rooted in a particular location, is one whose devotees are no longer limited by borders. However, when flamenco moves to these new localities, the rules under which it was initially established no longer apply. New cultural and historical truths must be negotiated, and decisions made by those establishing the culture in a foreign clime. British aficionados who strive to emulate their perception of the Spanish version must make decisions based on their knowledge of UK cultural norms and expectations. This results in variations localised to the UK, but which still reach towards Andalucían flamenco for inspiration, thus necessitating a glocal cultural model. Significantly, UK scenes are predominantly created by native British individuals who discover an affinity to the art complex, form transcultural connections with the Andalucían scene, and are almost entirely responsible for the maintenance of a flamenco community in their home country. Building upon Kiwan and Meinhof's musical migration theory of hubs, I refer to these individuals as cosmopolitan hubs.

This book has discussed the effects of globalisation on the scene in Andalucía and the influence of the individual in transmitting and creating the culture outside of Spain. What it has avoided is any sort of value judgement involving the foreigner's ability to grasp flamenco and re-create it 'authentically'. Yet, this is a question I wrestled with throughout the duration of this research. As alluded to earlier, globalisation theorists also grapple with the quandary of music globalisation, homogenisation, and authenticity. Perceptions of authenticity shadow the foreign flamenco performer, both in Spain and when they return home. Pohren, in his flamenco ethnography in the 1950s, observed that regardless of the non-Spaniard's flamenco adeptness, they will always be referred to as 'that fellow who performs well [...] considering he is a foreigner' (Pohren 1962, p. 78).

To answer criticisms regarding globalisation and homogenisation, it is necessary first to ask: what is authentic flamenco? This is a difficult question to address; even amongst Andalucían aficionados, finding a definitive consensus would be unlikely. One person's ideal of excellence is their friend's idea of a soulless artistic tragedy. The dividing lines are ambiguous: sometimes they are based on ethnicity, other times the discord occurs between specific regions or villages. Still others prefer the more traditional interpretations to the fusions or themed stage shows which have become common in the bigger festivals (although these tend to be marketed to foreign aficionados). *Gitanos* think *payos* do not express the music properly, whilst the latter believes that when the former shows up at a *juergas*, they ruin the *compás* (J. Martín—2014, L. Perez—2015, personal communications). Aficionados from East Andalucía sometimes believe those from the west do not understand particular *palos*, whilst some from Jerez harbour the opinion that Sevillano flamenco does not 'swing' enough. Most from Andalucía believe flamenco from Madrid is technically brilliant but lacks the soul that can only be learnt while immersed in its homeland (Machin-Autenrieth 2015, p. 16). This ethnic essentialism and regionalism as applied to flamenco is well depicted in Elizabeth Kinder's 2013 BBC programme 'Flamenco: Gypsy Soul' (Whalley 2013). Whilst the documentary itself contains numerous factual inaccuracies, simplifications, and omissions, the interviews she conducts with famous artists across Andalucía are indicative of a lack of cohesiveness when it comes to aesthetics: no matter which city or town Kinder is in, the performers tell her that it is flamenco's birthplace and they are the only ones who correctly perform *real* flamenco (Whalley 2013). Prominent tablao singer Aurora imparted:

> I have my own authenticity and you have yours, my brother, a guitar player, has his It is very difficult to know the quality of each one. The definition of *pureza* is not established. *Pureza* for me can be Israel [Galvan] and for you, Eva Yerbabuena, Camarón, or Mayte Martín, it is very subjective. Thirty-nine years of singing and I don't know what *pureza* is. (Aurora, personal communication, Jan. 11, 2014)

The reasons for these discrepancies are purely speculative. Flamenco, until the latter part of the twentieth century, has existed primarily as an oral tradition and, indeed, is still usually taught that way in Andalucía and Madrid. It is a compilation of many different *palos* which originated from different ethnic groups and locations. Flamenco has continued to evolve as it encounters different music cultures and foreign audiences. Beyond this, it is an art complex whose general aesthetics and emotional feel is based on individual expression. Whilst numerous flamencologists, *concursos*, the Andalucían government, and UNESCO have attempted to place flamenco into a musical museum, it remains artistically subjective. The most cohesive, inarguable definition I have gathered breaks down to flamenco's basic components: 'authentic' flamenco is *baile, cante, toque, percusión*, and *jaleo* based on various aspects of Andalucían culture. It is composed of several *palos* which, in themselves, are defined by distinctive artistic specifications and a rhythmic backbone—the *compás*. Beyond these basics, flamenco becomes incredibly subjective. Along this line of reasoning, Aurora commented:

> For me, all these things we are speaking of, authenticity, *pureza*, they do not exist. If I am sitting in a theatre and you are singing, and I am feeling something. That is it. It is difficult to define a good artist and bad artist. Flamenco is a very strange culture because it is difficult to define something authentic. *Pureza* is *duende*. (Aurora, personal communication, Jan. 11, 2014)

Duende is a difficult concept to define or quantify, especially in an academic context, but it is also what most will agree is the definition of an 'authentic' flamenco performer—the ability to find and communicate *duende*. It is, in a way, a spirit of evocation which emanates a physical or emotional response and is embodied in the performer's ability to communicate their feelings through flamenco. The poet Federico García Lorca defines *duende* as:

> [...] a power, not a work. It is a struggle, not a thought. I have heard an old maestro of the guitar say, 'The duende is not in the throat; the duende climbs up inside you, from the soles of the feet.' Meaning this: it is not a

question of ability, but of true, living style, of blood, of the most ancient culture, of spontaneous creation. He suggests, 'everything that has black sounds in it, has duende. [i.e. emotional "darkness"]' [...]. This 'mysterious power which everyone senses and no philosopher explains' is, in sum, the spirit of the earth. [...] The duende's arrival always means a radical change in forms. It brings to old planes unknown feelings of freshness, with the quality of something newly created, like a miracle, and it produces an almost religious enthusiasm. (García Lorca 1998)

The vagueness of this concept is difficult to reconcile, however similar definitions have been echoed by numerous informants. Aurora described it as a 'magical, existential moment' that she has felt many times during her singing career and as an audience member. She explains 'I don't know the reason why, but in a moment you don't see the public; I close my eyes and I see colours, hear the claps, the guitar, and just sing' (Aurora, personal communication, Jan. 11, 2014). For me, *duende* is the performer's ability to access and communicate their emotions through flamenco and, reciprocally, the individual audience member's openness to connect and understand them.

6.8 'Authenticity' and the Foreign Aficionado

The ambiguity and subjectivity of flamenco within Spain makes classifying 'authenticity' problematic (as is the case with many other music cultures). However, these discrepancies lend credence to the capacity for the foreigner to grasp flamenco to the same level as the Andalucían. The only aspects flamenco aficionados agree on is an understanding of the culture, the technique, and, above all, the ability to access and communicate deep emotions on an existential level. In terms of what this says about 'authentic flamenco', I understand it as performing truthfully to one's self and bringing receptive audience members into those magic moments.

Miller discusses concepts of musical 'authenticity' and finds that the term can refer to the performer's ethnicity or the 'execution of the music [style]' (Miller 2013, p. 102). She purports that it should be feasible and acceptable to engage with music styles not from one's home country and 'we must therefore embrace the fact that as music travels, it undergoes modification wherever it settles due to the creativity and curiosity of human beings' (Miller 2013, p. 102). I speculate that this is true of flamenco. In order for one to be good at it, the first step is to learn the tools with which to express it—the elements, how these interact with each other, and the Andalucían culture. However, the second and arguably more important step is to find *duende*. This is the ability to send and receive authentic emotions to one's fellow performers and audience.

Duende, with its direct link with human emotions, like grief, love, ecstasy, and anger, transcends issues such as ethnicity and nationality. Good flamencos bring the audience in by not only physical skills but the innate ability to communicate authentic emotions. Ultimately, each artist brings not only this knowledge, but also their own individual emotions, personal cultural background, and past joys and sorrows to the table. It is the ability to truthfully express these very human emotions within a flamenco context, which is perfectly engineered for such heartfelt renderings, that separates good from the bad flamenco practitioners. A would-be flamenco (of any ethnicity) could have perfect *compás* and technique, but an inability to apply their own feelings to the performance would leave a knowledgeable audience dissatisfied.

In interviews, I often asked flamenco aficionados (foreign and Spanish) how they could tell if a student 'got' flamenco? Was it different teaching and performing in Spain versus in the UK? These sorts of questions were usually met with some degree of pensive uncertainty. Usually, the answer had to do with whether the student was comfortable enough with the styles to improvise and move with the music instead of always having to count *compás* beats, but more importantly is whether they understood *duende*. For as much as someone can transmit 'authentic' techniques to students, *duende* cannot be taught, it must be discovered. Familiarity with the techniques is necessary but not sufficient to achieving *duende* and flamenco excellence. On a personal note, I first experienced *duende* after I had been studying flamenco for four years. I was visiting Andalucía on a research trip shortly after the death of my father and desperately trying to come to grips with my research again. I decided to take a brief detour on my journey from Malaga to Córdoba and attend a flamenco festival in the quiet town of Linares. Arriving on a blisteringly hot summer afternoon, I walked straight to the theatre and bought a ticket for the *Concurso de Cante Libre* that evening (€10 for a second-row seat). I, at that point, was not a fan of *cante*, but the headline act was the legendary Carmen Linares (who happened to be from that town). That evening, sitting amongst local aficionados, and listening to Carmen's haunting voice, I discovered *duende*. I did not understand most of her words, but the *cante* cut straight to core emotions of love and grief, and I cried. It was the first time I really felt I came to terms both with death and with flamenco and reminded me that my heart was broken, but I was still there, clapping *palmas* with this amazing *cantaora*. Flamenco may be foreign to many who love and practise it, but the emotions being expressed are not.

Flamenco is something that can be understood by foreigners who find *duende* and understand how to utilise flamenco to express it. Whether or not foreign involvement dilutes the art complex is reflected in how it is taught to the cosmopolitan hubs who will carry it back home. Flamenco is about communicating aspects of the human condition in response to the surrounding culture, so as long as foreign aficionados stay true to that concept in combination with the *compás*, the danger of dilution seems minimal. There is a global paradox in cultural industries, where on one side a need is felt to maintain its 'place-based identity', and the other suggests the necessity for regional cultures to establish export markets in order to survive (Aoyama 2007, p. 103). Flamenco might not have survived the Franco regime if not for corresponding attempts to develop it as a sort of 'staged authenticity' by businesses, artists, and the nation-state (Aoyama 2009, p. 98). One might argue that this peril lies more in the hands of Spain, than the foreign aficionados. They are the gatekeepers who determine what is experienced by foreign audiences. Aoyama surmises that in the era of globalisation (which we are now in) cultural survival is a carefully orchestrated act which involves 'artists, businesses, and the state offering services and venues for efficient consumption' (Aoyama 2009, p. 99).

In many ways, flamenco is reliant on external interest for its survival, at least as an industry. As Tomlinson emphasises, cultures did not exist in a vacuum prior to our current era and cultural identity is more of a product of globalisation than its victim (Tomlinson 2003, p. 269). Flamenco culture is no exception. It has been continuously reinterpreted with varying elements emphasised or de-emphasised depending on contexts, such as its usage for Spanish national unity, as an Andalucían marker of identity, as a *Gitano* art form representing subcultural elements, or as a resistance to authority. Most significantly are the many multicultural influences which have assigned multiple meanings to its representation across its history, including a certain susceptibility to consumer manipulation (Aoyama 2007, p. 105). Because of this, decisions made by cosmopolitan hubs and those who convey flamenco to them in Spain affect whether or not flamenco is diluted, but at least in the case of the UK scene, it has evolved in the image of Robertson's glocal model. These human transcultural contact points enable occasions for exchange, transmission, and variation. Flamenco's evolution into a glocal art complex has transpired as a result of cultures in contact, so to put it in a museum because of fears of dilution would serve to incarcerate the quality that most defines it: the ability to respond to external factors and express individual emotions.

Although my concept of cosmopolitan hubs rested primarily on flamenco research in Spain and the UK, I believe that these instances of foreigners actually becoming the culture bearers of a foreign culture in a foreign country will only become more prevalent. As easy access to foreign cultures via travel and the internet persist, individuals will become increasingly interested in cultures that are not their own to the extent that they will travel to the music's origin country and bring it back to their own to transmit. An example of this already exists in the form of Leeds' vibrant salsa music community. There are eight salsa groups (and numerous unaffiliated singers and musicians) made up primarily of British (or at least non-Cuban) members.

The concept of 'cosmopolitan hubs' opens up an important area for further research—not only on the practices of these cultural brokers themselves but also regarding the effects of transcultural exchange on the Andalucían scene. Furthermore, research on the effects of commercialisation and tourism on the propensity of individual Andalucíans adopting flamenco as an identity and on the artistic decisions they make in response to foreign expectations. This would shed light on whether flamenco relies on foreign interest for survival. Expanding the area of study to include Madrid would provide another interesting angle on flamenco globalisation as it is acknowledged within the Spanish flamenco community as the most important locale for professionalisation. Work is currently in progress on this topic, but it was beyond the scope of this book to incorporate it.

Overall, this research signifies advancement in flamenco and cultural migration scholarship. With regards to existing flamencology research, it is often informed by a stationary depiction of the art complex, one that does not account for local variations and transcultural influences. These are glaring omissions in a world that will only become increasingly interconnected. Because of its postnational status, flamenco can also no longer be essentialised along ethnic or regional parameters. It must be considered as a culture which spans borders and is established glocally. My research marks an advancement in cultural migration literature in that it accounts for the individual's role in creating music scenes, and, more importantly, the phenomenon of foreign cultural brokers facilitating music cultural travels and subsequent scene creation. In order to accomplish this, I expanded Kiwan and Meinhof's 'hub' network migration model to include 'cosmopolitan hubs'.

Cosmopolitan hubs and their transcultural connections need to recognise that, despite multifarious concepts of 'authenticity', glocal variations and transcultural connections must account for the basic elements which inform flamenco's identity as an art complex: the *duende* which characterises individual emotional expression and the *compás* which grounds this mystical force into the material world and must remain ever-present not only on flamenco's world tour, but also on the individual flamenco journey.

References

Aoyama, Y. (2007). The Role of Consumption and Globalisation in a Cultural Industry. *Geoforum, 38*, 103–113.

Aoyama, Y. (2009). Artists, Tourists, and the State: Cultural Tourism and the Flamenco Industry in Andalusia, Spain. *International Journal of Urban and Regional Research, 33*(1), 80–104.

Barton, S. (2009). *A History of Spain*. London: Palgrave Macmillan.

Beck, U. (2002). The Cosmopolitan Society and its Enemies. *Theory, Culture and Society, 19*(1–2), 17–44.

Clifford, J. (1988). *The Predicament of Culture: Twentieth-Century Ethnography, Literature, and Art*. Cambridge/London: Harvard University Press.

Cohen, A. (1994). *Self-Consciousness: An Alternative Anthropology of Identity*. London: Routledge. 71.

Corona, I., & Madrid, A. (2008). *Postnational Music Identities: Cultural Production, Distribution, and Consumption in a Globalized Scenario*. Plymouth: Lexington Books.

Deleuze, G., & Guattari, F. (1993). *A Thousand Plateaus*. Minneapolis: University of Minnesota Press.

Ferguson, M. (1992). The Mythology About Globalization. *European Journal of Communication, 7*, 69–93.

García Lorca, F. (1998). Teoría y juego del duende. In C. Maurer (Ed.), *In Search of Duende* (pp. 48–62). New York: New Directions.

Giddens, A. (1991). *Modernity and Self-Identity: Self and Society in the Late Modern Age*. Cambridge: Polity Press.

Giddens, A. (2000). *The Third Way and Its Critics*. Cambridge: Polity Press.

Glick Schiller, N., & Faist, T. (Eds.). (2010). *Migration, Development, and Transnationalization: A Critical Stance*. Oxford: Berghahn Books.

Hamelink, C. T. (1983). *Cultural Autonomy in Global Communications*. New York: Longman.

Hannerz, U. (1990). Cosmopolitans and Locals in World Culture. *Theory, Culture and Society, 7*, 237–251.

Hannerz, U. (1999). Notes on a Global Ecumene. *Public Culture, 1*(2), 66–75.

Hannerz, U. (2005). *The Two Faces of Cosmopolitanism: Culture and Politics* (pp. 5–29). Barcelona: CIDOB Ediciones.

Heffner Hayes, M. (2009). *Flamenco: Conflicting Histories of the Dance*. Jefferson: McFarland & Company, Inc.

Herskovits, M. J. (1937). *African Gods* and *Catholic Saints* in New World Negro Belief. *American Anthropologist, 39*(4), 635–643.

Holton, R. J. (2008). *Global Networks*. London: Palgrave Macmillan.

'Jean Baudrillard'. (2007). *Stanford Encyclopedia of Philosophy*. Retrieved from http://plato.stanford.edu/entries/baudrillard/

Kiwan, N., & Meinhof, U. (2011a). Music and Migration: A Transnational Approach. *Music and Arts in Action, 3*(3), 3–20.

Kiwan, N., & Meinhof, U. (2011b). *Cultural Globalization and Music: African Musicians in Transnational Networks*. Basingstoke: Palgrave Macmillan.

Knudsen, J. (2011). Music of the Multiethnic Minority: A Postnational Perspective. *Music and Arts in Action, 3*(3), 77–91.

Kurekova, L. (2011, April). *Theories of Migration: Conceptual Review and Empirical Testing in the Context of the EU East-West Flows.* Paper Presented at Interdisciplinary Conference on Migration. Economic Change, Social Challenge, University College London.

Machin-Autenrieth, M. (2015). Flamenco ¿Algo Nuestro? (¿Something of Ours?): Music, Regionalism and Political Geography in Andalusia, Spain. *Ethnomusicology Forum, 24*(1), 4–27.

Malefyt, T. D. (1998). "Inside" and "Outside" Spanish Flamenco: Gender Constructions in Andalusian Concepts of Flamenco Tradition. *Anthropological Quarterly, 71*(2), 63–73.

Meinhof, U., & Triandafyllidou, A. (2006). *Transcultural Europe: Cultural Policy in a Changing Europe.* Basingstoke: Palgrave Macmillan.

Miller, S. (2013). Perceptions of Authenticity in the Performance of Cuban Popular Music in the United Kingdom: 'Globalized Incuriosity' in the Promotion and Reception of UK-Based Charanga del Norte's Music since 1998. *Journal of European Popular Culture, 4*(1), 99–116.

Mitchell, T. (2001). *Global Noise: Rap and Hip Hop Outside the USA.* Connecticut: Wesleyan University Press.

Neild, B. (2015, February 11). *Wall of Sound: Spain's Next Flamenco Stars.* Retrieved from http://edition.cnn.com/2015/02/11/travel/seville-flamenco-cnngo/

Pohren, D. E. (1962). *The Art of Flamenco.* Jerez de la Frontera: Editorial Jerez Industrial.

Prakash, A., & Singh, V. B. (2011). Glocalization in Food Business: Strategies of Adaptation to Local Needs and Demands. *Asian Journal of Technology and Management Research, 1*(1), 1–21.

Rice, T., & Ruskin, J. D. (2012). The Individual in Musical Ethnography. *Ethnomusicology, 56*(2), 299–327.

Robertson, R. (1995). Glocalization: Time-Space, and Homogeneity-Heterogeneity. In M. Featherstone, S. Lash, & R. Robertson (Eds.), *Global Modernities* (pp. 24–44). London: Sage.

St. John, G. (2010). *Local Scenes and Global Culture of Psytrance.* London: Routledge.

Stokes, M. (2007). *On Musical Cosmopolitanism.* The Macalester International Roundtable 2007, Paper 3. Retrieved from http://digitalcommons.macalester.edu/intlrdtable/3

Szerszynski, B., & Urry, J. (2002). Cultures of Cosmopolitanism. *The Sociological Review, 50*(4), 462–481.

Tomlinson, J. (2003). Globalisation and Cultural Identity. In D. Held & A. McGraw (Eds.), *The Global Transformations Reader* (2nd ed., pp. 269–277). Cambridge: Blackwell Publishing.

Urquía, N. (2005). The Re-Branding of Salsa in London's Dance Clubs: How an Ethnicised Form of Cultural Capital Was Institutionalised. *Leisure Studies, 24*(4), 385–397.

Washabaugh, W. (1997). Flamenco Documentaries of the Franco Era. *The Journal of Flamenco Artistry, 3*(2). Retrieved from https://pantherfile.uwm.edu/wash/www/francojfa.htm

Whalley, B. (2013). *Flamenco: Gypsy Soul* [Motion Picture]. BBC Four.

Appendix A: Glossary of Spanish Terms

Aficionado:	Flamenco enthusiast who may or may not perform, but has a passion for it that borders on obsession
Aire:	Ambience
Alegrías	originating in Cadíz, is a jovial song and dance which has a *compás* consisting of 12 beats.
Bata de cola:	A flamenco dress with a long train
Braceo:	Flamenco arm and wrist work
Baile:	Flamenco dance
Bailaor/a:	Flamenco dancer
Bulerías	is rapid and spirited, although oftentimes grave, and characterised by a 12-beat *compás* and impulsively placed *coplas*
Cajón:	A wooden box drum
Cante:	Flamenco song, lyrics often written by the *cantaor* reflecting personal experience, with themes like love, death, fate, and social-political commentary
Cantaor/a:	Flamenco singer
Cierre:	Footwork or guitar pattern signalling the end of a flamenco piece
Compás:	Flamenco beat

T. Martin, *Transnational Flamenco*, Leisure Studies in a Global Era,
https://doi.org/10.1007/978-3-030-37199-9

Concurso/s:	Competitions
Coplas:	Short verses, like stanzas
Cuadro:	Flamenco performing group usually consisting of a dancer, singer, guitarist, and percussion
Cuña de flamenco:	A city considered a birthplace of flamenco
Duende:	Literally, 'spirit' of 'demon'; suggesting possession
Espectáculo:	A flamenco performance
Farruca:	A flamenco *palo* typically danced by males with no lyrics
Falseta:	A melody played on the flamenco guitar, sometimes as an introduction or bridge
Fandango:	is a version of a seventeenth-century Spanish folk dance with roots as far back as the Arab invasion. It features the use of castanets and a six-beat *compás*
Feria:	A local Spanish street festival
Fin de fiesta:	'End of the Party'; the end of a flamenco shows where dancers or singers from the audience can come on stage and improvise
Flamenco Puro:	Pure flamenco, the most traditional variety
Flamenca Britannica:	My term for the British interpretation of flamenco
Gitano/a:	Andalucían Gypsy
Guiri:	A foreign flamenco student or performer
Hermanidades:	Brotherhoods
Jaleo:	'Hell-raising', audience participation at flamenco performances
Juerga:	A type of flamenco party or jam session
Llamada:	A dance movement signalling a change of end of section
Letra:	Flamenco lyrics
Mantones:	Traditional Andalucían scarves
Nivel:	Level
Palmas:	Rhythmic hand-clapping used to accompany flamenco song and dance
Palmera:	One who performs *palmas*
Pataitas:	Short sections of footwork, usually the length of a few *coplas*
Palo:	General term for a flamenco genre
Payo:	A non-*Gitano* Andalucían

Peña:	A type of flamenco club or performance
Saeta:	A flamenco *palo* originating from Jewish religious songs
Sardana:	Folk dance from Cataluña
Sevillanas:	A Spanish country dance, not considered flamenco in Spain
Siguiriya:	A type of *palo*
Soleá:	A flamenco *palo*. Consists of 12 beats with accents on the 3rd, 6th, 8th, 10th, and 12th
Tablao:	A Spanish cabaret-like performance venue
Taverna:	A small Spanish café or bar
Tientos:	A type of *palo*
Tocacor/a:	Flamenco guitarist
Toque:	The guitar element of flamenco
Traje de flamenco:	Flamenco clothes
Zapateado:	Flamenco footwork

Appendix B: Cast of Characters

Aurora:	Sevillana flamenco tablao singer
Cafuco:	Flamenco guitarist from Málaga; met in the UK trying to find flamenco work there
Catalina:	Internationally performing flamenco dancer from Castilleja de la Cuesta (Sevilla); president of Flamenco de Liverpool
Chian:	Taiwanese flamenco dancer studying in Sevilla
Claire:	Head of Deva Flamenco in Chester
Elizabeth:	Leeds flamenco scene driver
Louis:	French-British flamenco guitarist living in Sevilla; *tocaor* for Dot-Dot-Dot flamenco
Manuela:	French-Spanish flamenco dancer living in Sevilla
Maru:	Sevillana friend who does not like flamenco
Lena:	Finnish flamenco dancer in Liverpool
Nancy:	Flamenco teacher in Matlock Bath (UK)
Alicia:	British flamenco dancer living in Sevilla; member of Dot-Dot-Dot Flamenco
Patricio:	Sevillano flamenco aficionado and civil servant
Paula:	*Bailora* and Head of Hebden Bridge Flamenco
Pepa:	Amateur cajón player in Sevilla, formerly lived in Newcastle

T. Martin, *Transnational Flamenco*, Leisure Studies in a Global Era,
https://doi.org/10.1007/978-3-030-37199-9

Roderigo:	Spanish-South African guitarist, formerly in Sevilla, now living and performing in London
Ron Hitchens:	Nonagenarian Chinese-British stalwart of the London flamenco scene
Rita:	*Bailora* and Head of Camino del Flamenco in Oxford
Samuel:	Young Sevillano guitarist who moved to England in an attempt to find flamenco work
Tino van der Sman:	Dutch guitarist who has created a professional career in Sevilla
Trish:	British Head of Peña Flamenca de Liverpool
Vivian:	Former journalist; head and founding member of Peña Flamenca de Londres
Yazmin:	Afro-British flamenco dancer living in Sevilla; part of Dot-Dot-Dot flamenco

Bibliography

Abra, A. (2012). The Evolution of Popular Dancing in Britain in the 1920s. In B. Bebber (Ed.), *Leisure and Cultural Conflict in Twentieth-Century Britain* (pp. 41–62). Manchester: Manchester University Press.

Actividades. (n.d.). *La Federación Provincial de Sevilla de Entidades Flamencas.* Retrieved from https://www.sevillafederacionflamenca.com/

Adler, P. (1977). Beyond Cultural Identity: Reflections on Cultural and Multicultural Man. In R. W. Brislni (Ed.), *Culture Learning: Concepts, Applications and Research* (pp. 24–41). Hawaii: East-West Center Press.

Afinoguénova, E. (2010). "Unity, Stability, Continuity": Heritage and the Renovation of Franco's Dictatorship in Spain 1957–1969. *International Journal of Heritage Studies, 16*(1), 417–433.

Afinoguénova, E., & Martí-Olivella, J. (2008). *Spain Is (Still) Different: Tourism and Discourse in Spanish Identity.* Plymouth: Lexington Books.

Álvarez, S. (2007). *Tauromachie et Flamenco: Polémiques et clichés, Espagne, fin XXIXe-début XXe.* Paris: L'Harmattan.

Álvarez Junco, J. (2000). *Spanish History Since 1808.* London: Bloomsbury.

Aoyama, Y. (2007). The Role of Consumption and Globalisation in a Cultural Industry. *Geoforum, 38*, 103–113.

T. Martin, *Transnational Flamenco*, Leisure Studies in a Global Era,
https://doi.org/10.1007/978-3-030-37199-9

Aoyama, Y. (2009). Artists, Tourists, and the State: Cultural Tourism and the Flamenco Industry in Andalusia, Spain. *International Journal of Urban and Regional Research, 33*(1), 80–104.

Appadurai, A. (1990). Disjuncture and Difference in the Global Cultural Economy. *Theory, Culture and Society, 7*, 295–310.

Baliñas, M. (2002). Cuplé. In E. Casares Rodiciao (Ed.), *Diccionario de la Música Española e Hispanoamericana* (pp. 317–325). Madrid: Sociedad General de Autores y Editores.

Baltanás, E. (2002). The Fatigue of the Nation: Flamenco as he basis for heretical identities. In G. Steingress (Ed.), *Songs of the Minotaur: Hybridity and Popular Music in the Age of Globalization* (pp. 139–168). London: Transaction Publishers.

Barbaret, R., & García-España, E. (1997). Minorities, Crime, and Criminal Justice in Spain. In I. H. Marshall (Ed.), *Minorities, Migrants, and Crime: Diversity and Similarity Across Europe and the United States* (pp. 175–197). California: Sage Publications.

Bartal, Y. (2014). *Flamenco's Repression and Resistance in Southern Spain*. Retrieved from http://www.truth-out.org/news/item/27946-flamenco-under-attack

Barth, F. (1969). *Ethnic Groups and Boundaries: The Social Organization of Cultural Difference*. Boston: Little Brown Books.

Barton, S. (2009). *A History of Spain*. London: Palgrave Macmillan.

Barz, G., & Cooley, T. J. (1997). *Shadows in the Field: New Perspectives for Fieldwork in Ethnomusicology* (2nd ed.). New York/Oxford: Oxford University Press.

Baudrillard, J. (1994). *Simulacra and Simulation*. Ann Arbor: University of Michigan Press.

Baulcombe, H. (2014, January 13). *Folk Festivals at the Hall, 1927–1984*. Retrieved from http://www.royalalberthall.com/about-the-hall/news/2014/january/folk-festivals-at-the-hall-1927-1984/

Beck, U. (2002). The Cosmopolitan Society and Its Enemies. *Theory, Culture and Society, 19*(1–2), 17–44.

Becker, H. (1984). *Art Worlds*. Berkeley: University of California Press.

Belarde, F., & Navarro, J. G. (1985). *Sociedad y Cante Flamenco: El Cante de Las Minas*. Murcia: Editora Regional de Murcia.

Bennett, A. (2002). Researching Youth Culture and Popular Music: A Methodological Critique. *British Journal of Sociology, 53*(3), 451–466.

Bennett, A. (2004). Consolidating the Music Scenes Perspective. *Poetics, 32*, 223–234.

Bethnecourt Llobet, F. J. (2011). *Rethinking Tradition: Towards an Ethnomusicology of Contemporary Flamenco Guitar* (Unpublished Doctoral Thesis). Newcastle: Newcastle University.

Blacking, J. (1995). *Music, Culture and Experience: Selected Papers of John Blacking*. Chicago: University of Chicago Press.

Blas Vega, J. (1990). *Vida y cante de Don Antonio Chacón: La Edad de Oro del flamenco (1869–1929)*. Madrid: Cinterco.

Blas Vega, J. (2006a). *Flamenco en Madrid*. Córdoba: Editorial Almuzara.

Blas Vega, J. (2006b). *Los Cafes Cantantes de Madrid (1846–1936)*. Madrid: Ediciones Guillermo Blázquez.

Blas Vega, J., & Ríos Ruiz, M. (1988). *Diccionario enciclopédico ilustrado del flamenco (2 vols.)*. Madrid: Ed. Cintero.

Bloor, M., & Wood, F. (2006). *Keywords in Qualitative Methods: A Vocabulary of Research Concepts*. London: Sage Publications.

Borja Carballo, R. P., & Vicente, F. (2008). *El ensanche de Madrid: Historia de una capital*. Madrid: Editorio Compultense.

Bourdieu, P. (1985). The Social Space and the Genesis of Groups. *Theory and Society, 14*(6), 723–744.

Bourdieu, P. (1997). The Forms of Capital. In A. Halsey, H. Lauder, P. Brown, & A. Stuart Wells (Eds.), *Education: Culture, Economy and Society* (pp. 45–86). Oxford: Oxford University Press.

Brown, I. H. (1929). *Deep Song: Adventures with Gypsy Songs and Singers in Andalusia and Other Lands*. New York/London: Harper & Brothers.

Burkhalter, T. (2013). *Local Music Scenes and Globalization: Transnational Platforms in Beirut*. Oxford: Routledge.

Chuse, L. (1993). *The Cantaoras: Music, Gender and Identity in Flamenco Song*. New York: Routledge.

Clifford, J. (1988). *The Predicament of Culture: Twentieth-Century Ethnography, Literature, and Art*. Cambridge, MA/London: Harvard University Press.

Cohen, A. (1994). *Self-Consciousness: An Alternative Anthropology of Identity*. London: Routledge.

Comaroff, J., & Comaroff, J. (2003). Ethnography on an Awkward Scale: Postcolonial Anthropology and the Violence of Abstraction. *Ethnography, 4*(2), 291–324.

Cooper, D., & Dawe, K. (Eds.). (2005). *The Mediterranean in Music: Critical Perspectives, Common Concerns, Cultural Differences.* Lanham: Scarecrow Press.

Corona, I., & Madrid, A. (2008). *Postnational Music Identities: Cultural Production, Distribution, and Consumption in a Globalized Scenario.* Plymouth: Lexington Books.

Cristina Heeren Foundation. 2014. Retrieved from http://www.flamenco-heeren.com/en/

Cruces Roldán, C. (2002). *Más allá de la música: Antropología y flamenco (I): Sociabilidad, transmisón y patrimonio.* Seville: Signatura.

Cruces Roldán, C. (2003). *Más allá de la Música: Antropología y flamenco (II): Identidad, género y trabajo.* Seville: Signatura.

de Falla, M. (1950/1972). El Cante Jondo (Canto Primitivo Andaluz). (in the Apéndice). In *Escritos sobre música y músicos* (pp. 137–162). Madrid: Espasa-Calpe.

De la Fuente, E. (2011, June 2). Signs and Wonders. *Times Educational Supplement,* pp. 39–40.

Deleuze, G., & Guattari, F. (1993). *A Thousand Plateaus.* Minneapolis: University of Minnesota.

Diéguez, F. (2008). *Historia de un tablao: Las Brujas. Sus gentes, susartistas y su época.* Cádiz: Ed. Absalon.

Diversions publicas. (1922, August 8). *La Época.*

Eisentraut, J. (2001). Samba in Wales: Making Sense of Adopted Music. *British Forum for Ethnomusicology, 10*(1), 85–105. *Music and Meaning.*

Escribano, A. (1990). *Y Madrid se hizo flamenco.* Madrid: Al Avapiés.

Escuela de Baile. (n.d.). Retrieved from http://ledb.co.uk/about-us/

Feld, S. (1994). *Music Grooves: Essays and Dialogues.* Tucson: Fenestra.

Ferguson, M. (1992). The Mythology About Globalization. *European Journal of Communication, 7,* 69–93.

Fernandez, L. (2005). *Flamenco Music Theory: Rhythm, Harmony, Melody, Form.* London: Mel Bay Publications.

Finnegan, R. (2007). *The Hidden Musicians.* Middletown: Wesleyan University Press.

FlamencoTickets.com (2019). Retrieved from https://www.flamencotickets.com/madrid-flamenco-shows

Floyd, L. G., & Quintana, B. B. (1971). *!Qué Gitano!: Gypsies of Southern Spain.* New York: Hold, Rinehart and Winston.

Frutos de la Restauración. (1888, July 8). *El Motín.*

Geertz, C. (2000). *The Interpretation of Cultures: Selected Essays*. New York: Basic Books.

Giddens, A. (1991). *Modernity and Self-Identity: Self and Society in the Late Modern Age*. Cambridge: Polity Press.

Giddens, A. (2000). *The Third Way and Its Critics*. Cambridge: Polity.

Glick Schiller, N., & Faist, T. (Eds.). (2010). *Migration Development, and Transnationalization: A Critical Stance*. Oxford: Berghahn Books.

Gramsci, A. (2003). *Selections from the Prison Notebooks*. London: Lawrence and Wishart.

Grimaldo, A. (2010). *Historia social del flamenco*. Barcelona: Ed. Península.

Hamelink, C. T. (1983). *Cultural Autonomy in Global Communications*. New York: Longman.

Hannerz, U. (1990). Cosmopolitans and Locals in World Culture. *Theory, Culture and Society, 7*, 237–251.

Hannerz, U. (1999). Notes on a Global Ecumene. *Public Culture, 1*(2), 66–75.

Hannerz, U. (2005). *The Two Faces of Cosmopolitanism: Culture and Politics* (pp. 5–29). Barcelona: CIDOB edicions.

Harney, L. D. (2009). Controlling Resistance, Resisting Control: The "Género Chico" and the Dynamics of Mass Entertainment in Late Nineteenth-Century Spain. *Arizona Journal of Hispanic Cultural Studies, 10*, 151–167.

Heffner Hayes, M. (2009). *Flamenco: Conflicting Histories of the Dance*. Jefferson: McFarland & Company, Inc.

Hernandez Girbal, F. (1933). *Salvador Sánchez "Frascuelo": Una vida popular: biografía novelesca*. Madrid: Sociedad General Española de Liberaría.

Herskovits, M. J. (1937). *African Gods* and *Catholic Saints* in New World Negro Belief. *American Anthropologist, 39*(4), 635–643.

Holmes, A. (2010). *Spanish Steps* [Motion Picture]. UK: Independent.

Holton, K. D. (1998). Like Blood in Your Mouth: Topographies of Flamenco Voice and Pedagogy in Diaspora. *Text and Performance Quarterly, 18*, 300–318.

Holton, R. J. (2008). *Global Networks*. London: Palgrave Macmillan.

Hoy. (2006, June 8). Extremadura critica que Andalucía quiera la exclusividad del flamenco.

Ingelmo, L., & Smith, M. (2012). *Cantes Flamencos: The Deep Songs of Spain*. Bristol: Shearsman Books.

Jean Baudrillard. (2007). *Stanford Encyclopedia of Philosophy*. Retrieved from http://plato.stanford.edu/entries/baudrillard/

Katz, I. J. (1974). The Traditional Folk Music of Spain: Explorations and Perspectives. *Yearbook of the International Folk Music Council, 6*, 64–85.

Keating, M., & Wilson, A. (2009). Renegotiating the State of Autonomies: Statute Reform and Multi-Level Politics in Spain. *West European Politics, 32*(3), 536–558.

Kiwan, N., & Meinhof, U. (2011a). Music and Migration: A Transnational Approach. *Music and Arts in Action, 3*(3), 3–20.

Kiwan, N., & Meinhof, U. (2011b). *Cultural Globalization and Music: African Musicians in Transnational Networks.* Basingstoke: Palgrave Macmillan.

Knudsen, J. (2011). Music of the Multiethnic Minority: A Postnational Perspective. *Music and Arts in Action, 3*(3), 77–91.

Kurekova, L. (2011, April). *Theories of Migration: Conceptual Review and Empirical Testing in the Context of the EU East-West Flows.* Paper Presented at Interdisciplinary Conference on Migration. Economic Change, Social Challenge, University College London.

La Plaga Flamenca. (1888, July 9). *La Época.*

Lavaur, L. (1976). *Teoría romántica del cante flamenco.* Madrid: Editorial Nacional.

Leake, J. (2008). Flamenco Compás for Alegrias: Analysis of the 12-Pulse *Palmas* (Clapping) Rhythm and Its Relationship to the Standard African Bell Pattern. *Percussive Notes, 46*(2), 44–49.

Levitt, P. (1998). Social Remittances: Migration Driven Local-Level Forms of Cultural Diffusion. *International Migration Review, 32*(4), 926–948.

Llano, S. (2018). *Discordant Notes: Marginality and Social Control in Madrid, 1850–1930.* New York: Oxford University Press.

Lortat-Jacobs, B. (1995). *Sardinian Chronicles.* Chicago: University of Chicago Press.

Machin-Autenrieth, M. (2013). *Andalucía Flamenca: Music, Regionalism and Identity in Southern Spain* (Unpublished Doctoral Thesis). Wales: University of Cardiff.

Machin-Autenrieth, M. (2015). Flamenco ¿Algo Nuestro? (Something of Ours?): Music, Regionalism and Political Geography in Andalusia, Spain. *Ethnomusicology Forum, 24*(1), 4–27.

Machin-Autenrieth, M. (2017). *Flamenco, Regionalism and Musical Heritage in Southern Spain* (p. 2017). New York: Routledge.

Malefyt, T. D. (1998). "Inside" and "Outside" Spanish Flamenco: Gender Constructions in Andalusian Concepts of Flamenco Tradition. *Anthropological Quarterly, 71*(2), 63–73.

Malinowski, B. (1922). *Argonauts of the Western Pacific: An Account of Native Enterprise and Adventure in the Archipelagoes of Melanesian New Guinea.* London: G. Routledge & Sons.

Manuel, P. (1989). Andalusian, Gypsy, and Class Identity in the Contemporary Flamenco Context. *Ethnomusicology, 33*(1), 47–65.

Manuel, P. (2002). From Scarlatti to "Guantanamera": Dual Tonicity in Spanish and Latin American Musics. *Journal of the American Musicological Society, 55*(2), 311–336.

Manuel, P. (2006). Flamenco in Focus. In M. Tenzer (Ed.), *Analytical Studies in World Music* (pp. 92–119). Oxford: Oxford University Press.

Marotta, V. (2014). The Multicultural, Intercultural and the Transcultural Subject. In F. Mansouri & B. E. de B'béri (Eds.), *Global Perspectives on the Politics of Multiculturalism in the 21st Century: A Case Study Analysis* (pp. 90–102). London: Routledge.

Martí, J. (1997). Folk Music Studies and Ethnomusicology in Spain. *Yearbook for Traditional Music, 29*, 107–140.

Martínez, E. (2003). *Flamenco…All You Wanted to Know*. London: Mel Bay Publications Inc.

McRobbie, A. (1994). *Postmodernism and Popular Culture*. London: Routledge.

Meinhof, U., & Triandafyllidou, A. (2006). *Transcultural Europe: Cultural Policy in a Changing Europe*. Basingstoke: Palgrave Macmillan.

Miller, S. (2013). Perceptions of Authenticity in the Performance of Cuban Popular Music in the United Kingdom: 'Globalized Incuriosity' in the Promotion and Reception of UK-Based Charanga del Norte's Music Since 1998. *Journal of European Popular Culture, 4*(1), 99–116.

Mitchell, T. (1994). *Flamenco Deep Song*. New Haven: Yale University Press.

Mitchell, T. (2001). *Global Noise: Rap and Hip Hop Outside the USA*. Middletown: Wesleyan University Press.

Molina, R. (1967). *Misterios del Arte Flamenco*. Barcelona: Sagitario.

Mora, K. (2008). *Las raíces del "duende": lo trágico y lo sublime en el cante jondo* (Unpublished Doctoral Thesis). Columbus: The Ohio State University.

Mora Guarnido, J. (1922, July 11). El Cante Jondo. *La Voz*.

Morca, T. (1990). *'Becoming the Dance': Flamenco Spirit*. Dubuque: Kendall/Hunt Pub. Co.

Murillo Saborido, E. (2017). *Los Tablaos Flamencos En Madrid Entre 1954–1973: Una Aproximación Académia a su Escena Musical* (Unpublished Masters' Thesis). Madrid: Universidad Complutense de Madrid.

Neild, B. (2015, February 11). *Wall of Sound: Spain's Next Flamenco Stars*. Retrieved from http://edition.cnn.com/2015/02/11/travel/seville-flamenco-cnngo/

O'Reilly, K. (2009). *Key Concepts in Ethnography*. London: Sage Publications.

O'Reilly, K. (2012). *Ethnographic Methods* (2nd ed.). Abingdon: Routledge.

Office for National Statistics. (2014). *Census Update*. Retrieved from http://data.london.gov.uk/dataset/population-country-birth

Office for National Statistics. (2016). *Underlying Datasheets for Population by Country of Birth and Nationality*. Retrieved from www.ons.gov.uk

Orellana, R. P. (2005). *Bailes de Andalucía en Londres y París (1830–1850)*. Spain: Arambel Editores.

Ortiz Nuevo, J. L. (1975). *Pepe el de la Matrona: Recuerdos de un Cantaor Sevillano*. Madrid: Ediciones Demófilo.

Ortiz Nuevo, J. L. (1985). *Pensamiento político en el cante flamenco: Antología de textos desde los orígenes a 1936*. Barcelona: Editoriales Andaluzas Unidas.

Pack, S. (2006). *Tourism and Dictatorship: Europe's Peaceful Invasion of Franco's Spain*. London: Palgrave Macmillan.

Paco de Lucía. (2011). *All About Jazz*. Retrieved from http://www.allaboutjazz.com/php/musician.php?id=6218

Papapavlou, M. (2003). The City as a Stage: Flamenco in Andalusian Culture. *Journal of the Society for the Anthropology of Europe, 3*(2), 14–24.

Payne, S. G. (2000). *The Franco Regime, 1936–1975*. London: Phoenix.

Pohren, D. E. (1962). *The Art of Flamenco*. Jerez de la Frontera: Editorial Jerez Industrial.

Prakash, A., & Singh, V. B. (2011). Glocalization in Food Business: Strategies of Adaptation to Local Needs and Demands. *Asian Journal of Technology and Management Research, 1*(1), 1–21.

Rice, T. (1994). *May It Fill Your Soul: Experiencing Bulgarian Music*. Chicago: University of Chicago Press.

Rice, T. (2003). Time, Place, and Metaphor in Musical Experience and Ethnography. *Ethnomusicology, 47*(2), 151–179.

Rice, T., & Ruskin, J. D. (2012). The Individual in Musical Ethnography. *Ethnomusicology, 56*(2), 299–327.

Rito y Geografía del Cante (1971–1973). Televisíon Española.

Robertson, R. (1995). Glocalization: Time-Space, and Homogeneity-Heterogeneity. In M. Featherstone, S. Lash, & R. Robertson (Eds.), *Global Modernities* (pp. 24–44). London: Sage Publications.

Robertson, R. (1997). Comments on the 'Global Triad' and 'Glocalization. In I. Nobutaka (Ed.), *Globalization and Indigenous Culture* (pp. 217–225). Tokyo: Institute for Japanese Culture and Classics.

Roudometof, V. (2005). Transnationalism, Cosmopolitanism and Glocalization. *Current Sociology, 53*(1), 113–135.

Schippers, H. (2006). Tradition, Authenticity, and Context: The Case for a Dynamic Approach. *British Journal of Music Education, 23*(3), 333–349.

Schreiner, C. (Ed.). (1990). *Flamenco: Gypsy Dance and Music from Andalusia.* Portland: Amadeus Press.

St. John, G. (2010). *Local Scenes and Global Culture of Psytrance.* London: Routledge.

Starkie, W. (1935). Gypsy Folk Lore and Music. *Journal of English Folk Dance and Song Society, 2*, 83–91. International Festival Number.

Steingress, G., & Baltanás, E. (2002). El Flamenco como Patrimonio Cultural o una Construcción Artificial más de la Identidad Andaluza. *Revista Andaluza de Ciencias Sociales, 1*, 43–64.

Stock, J. P. J. (2001). Toward an Ethnomusicology of the Individual or Biographical Writing in Ethnomusicology. *The World of Music, 43*(1), 5–19.

Stokes, M. (2007). On Musical Cosmopolitanism. *The Macalester International Roundtable 2007*, Paper 3. Retrieved from http://digitalcommons.macalester.edu/intlrdtable/3

Stone, R. M. (2008). *Theory for Ethnomusicology.* Upper Saddle River: Pearson Prentice Hall.

Storm, E. (2013). Un España más Española: La influencia del turismo en el imagen nacional. In L. J. Moreno & S. X. M. Nuñez (Eds.), *Ser españoles: imaginarios nacionalistas en el siglo XX* (pp. 530–560). Barcelona: RBA.

Straw, W. (1991). Systems of Articulation, Logics of Change: Scenes and Communities in Popular Music. *Cultural Studies, 5*(3), 361–375.

SUMA Flamenca. (2019). Retrieved from http://www.madrid.org/sumaflamenca/2019/entradas.html

Szerszynski, B., & Urry, J. (2002). Cultures of Cosmopolitanism. *The Sociological Review, 50*(4), 462–481.

Thiel-Cramér, B. (1991). *Flamenco: The Art of Flamenco, Its History and Development Until Our Days.* Lidngo: REMARK.

Thomas, K. (2002). Flamenco and Spanish Dance. *Dance Research Journal, 34*(1), 98–102.

Tomlinson, J. (2003). Globalisation and Cultural Identity. In D. Held & A. McGraw (Eds.), *The Global Transformations Reader* (2nd ed., pp. 269–277). Cambridge: Blackwell Publishing.

Torres, N. (2005). *Historia de la guitarra flamenco: El surco, el ritmo y el compás.* Córdoba: Ed. Almuzara.

Tremlett, G. (2012). *Ghosts of Spain: Travels Through a Country's Hidden Past.* London: Faber & Faber.

Troubadour London History. (n.d.). Retrieved from http://www.troubadour-london.com/history

Turino, T. (1993). *Moving Away from Silence: Music of the Peruvian Altiplano and the Experience of Urban Migration.* Chicago: University of Chicago Press.

UK Coffee Revolution, the Third Wave. (2013, April 1). Retrieved from http://lyndonscoffee.com/uk-coffee-revolution/

Urbano, M. (1995). *La hondura de un antiflamenco: Eugenio Noel.* Córdoba: Ayuntamiento de Córdoba.

Urquía, N. (2005). The Re-Branding of Salsa in London's Dance Clubs: How an Ethnicised form of Cultural Capital was Institutionalised. *Leisure Studies, 24*(4), 385–397.

Vetrovec, S. (1999). Three Meanings of 'Diaspora', Exemplified Among South Asian Religions. *Diaspora, 7,* 2.

Washabaugh, W. (1996). *Flamenco: Passion, Politics and Popular Culture.* Oxford: BERG.

Washabaugh, W. (1997a). Flamenco Music and Documentary. *Ethnomusicology, 41*(1), 51–67.

Washabaugh, W. (1997b). Flamenco Documentaries of the Franco Era. *The Journal of Flamenco Artistry, 3,* 2. Retrieved from https://pantherfile.uwm.edu/wash/www/francojfa.htm.

Washabaugh, W. (1998). *The Passion of Music and Dance: Body, Gender and Sexuality.* Oxford: Berg.

Washabaugh, W. (2012). *Flamenco Music and National Identity in Spain.* Surrey: Ashgate Publishing.

Webster, J. (2003). *Duende: A Journey in Search of Flamenco.* London: Doubleday.

Young, J. O. (2010). *Cultural Appropriation and the Arts.* Chichester: Wiley-Blackwell.

Index[1]

[1] Note: Page numbers followed by 'n' refer to notes.

9783030372019